RECORDS and DATABASE MANAGEMENT

COLLEGE SERIES

FOURTH EDITION

JEFFREY R. STEWART, Jr., Ed.D.

Professor of Business Education
Virginia Polytechnic Institute and State University
Blacksburg, Virginia

JUDITH SCHARLE GREENE

Instructor
Maury High School
Norfolk, Virginia

JUDITH A. HICKEY, Ed.D.

Professor, Division of Business
Thomas Nelson Community College
Hampton, Virginia

Gregg Division
McGRAW-HILL PUBLISHING COMPANY

New York   Atlanta   Dallas   St. Louis   San Francisco
Auckland   Bogotá   Caracas   Hamburg   Lisbon
London   Madrid   Mexico   Milan   Montreal   New Delhi
Paris   San Juan   São Paulo   Singapore
Sydney   Tokyo   Toronto

Sponsoring Editor: John King
Editing Supervisor: Melonie Parnes
Design and Art Supervisor: Janice Noto
Production Supervisor: Catherine Bokman

Text Designer: Levavi & Levavi
Cover Designer: Nicholas Krenitsky

Library of Congress Cataloging-in-Publication Data

Stewart, Jeffrey Robert, date
Records and database management.

(College series)
Rev. ed. of: Filing systems and records management /
Jeffrey R. Stewart, Jr. . . . [et al.]. 3rd ed. ©1981.
Includes index.
1. Filing systems. 2. Business records—Management—
Data processing. 3. Information resources management.
I. Greene, Judith Scharle, date. II. Hickey,
Judith A. III. Filing systems and records management.
IV. Title
HF5736.S815 1989   651.5   88-31510
ISBN 0-07-061474-1

Color insert photos (in order of appearance): © Jules Allen Photography;
© Acme Visible Records, Crozet, Virginia; © Kardex; © Color Micro-
imaging Corp.

RECORDS AND DATABASE MANAGEMENT,
Fourth Edition

  2 3 4 5 6 7 8 9 0   DOCDOC   9 6 5 4 3 2 1 0

ISBN 0-07-061474-1

CONTENTS

PREFACE

Not too long ago, all files were on paper. Then along came microfilm and microfiche, opening up a new world of records management. Now the personal computer is adding another dimension—the computer database.

The fourth edition of *Records and Database Management* will help you manage paper, film, and computer records. You will learn how to solve records and database management problems faced by employees in a variety of office occupations: administrative support, junior management, accounting, data processing, word processing, stenography, and records management.

Indexing Rules

Indexing procedures have changed since our third edition, *Filing Systems and Records Management*. Here again the computer database has had an influence. The Association of Records Managers and Administrators (ARMA) developed new rules so that you can apply standard indexing procedures when working with computer or paper files. All the indexing rules in this edition are compatible with the ARMA standards.

Computer Databases and Other Technologies

Chapter 4 shows you the special indexing techniques that apply to computer databases, while Chapter 6 teaches you how to manage records using an electronic database system. There is a chapter on setting up your electronic workstation, and our coverage of equipment includes supplies for electronic filing. Throughout the book you will find information that applies to the use of computer databases.

The chapter on equipment also lets you see how modern technology is making it easier to work with paper files and to develop film records. In addition, there is a full chapter on micrographics and advanced systems so that you will know your way around microfilm and microfiche records and equipment.

Records Management

Basic filing skill is essential to any type of effective records management. Chapters 7, 8, and 9 cover the essential topics of numeric, subject, and geographic filing. In Chapter 8, you'll also see how you can manage personal records, so you can be as efficient at home as you are in the office. The final chapter shows you how to analyze and design records management systems.

Practice Sets

Building good skills in records management requires lots of practice with records. There are two practice sets related to this text. One trains you in the use of manual systems. The other lets you manipulate and create records using a personal computer and Lotus or dBase III software.

Conclusion

Records and Database Management, Fourth Edition, prepares you for all of today's records management environments. If you work diligently through this text and the practice materials, you should acquire strong skills in basic filing procedures and develop competence in managing computer records. These abilities will impress many potential employers.

Jeffrey R. Stewart, Jr.
Judith Scharle Greene
Judith A. Hickey

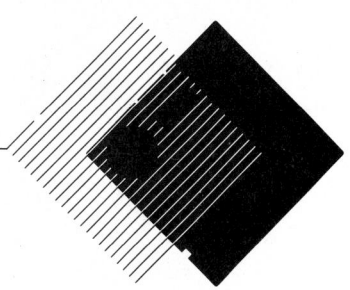

1

INTRODUCTION TO RECORDS AND DATABASE MANAGEMENT

COMPETENCIES

When you have completed this chapter, you will be able to:

1. State why filing and records and database management are important to you.
2. Define the terms *record, database management,* and *filing.*
3. State why records are necessary and give examples of records needed by businesses and individuals.
4. Name the two basic methods of storing and maintaining records.
5. Define the terms *correspondence, filing system, system, procedure, method, caption, database, backup, input/output, data, field,* and *file.*
6. List the four classifications businesses use to value their records and give examples of each classification.
7. List and describe the stages in the life cycle of a business record.
8. Compare the Freedom of Information Act with the Privacy Act and state why each is important in records and database management.
9. State why the *need to know* is important to the file worker.

10. State why office employees need to have a knowledge of records and database management.
11. Name five job titles in records and database management and list two duties of each.

There was a time when records management meant simply *filing,* or the storage, retrieval, and protection of business papers. It later included the creation, control, use, and disposition of records. With the advent of microcomputers, such as the personal or home computer, records management and filing have taken on new meaning and new procedures in business.

Responsibilities regarding records and database management are not delegated to one person within a firm. They are the responsibilities of everyone who handles business records. All office workers need to be aware of the importance of correct creation, storage, protection, control, use, and disposition of records.

For this reason, it is important that you study carefully the information presented in this textbook. It will help you handle your responsibilities on the job. Failure to classify, store, and retrieve records accurately and efficiently can result in records lost forever. This can be a serious loss to an organization.

RECORDS ARE NECESSARY

Without records, a business cannot function. They contain all the information vital to the day-to-day operation of the business or organization. Numerous studies have shown that businesses that lose their records through fire, disaster, or negligence cease to operate. When government agencies lose records, it often creates a hardship for private individuals who may need these records to prove date of birth, date of military discharge, or ownership of property. Medical records may be essential years later for reference or for identification purposes. An individual may want to return a defective piece of merchandise. Without the original sales slip to prove the price paid and the date of the purchase, this may not be possible.

Individuals who lose certain records may experience merely an annoyance. However, when a business cannot find records, it costs money and often goodwill. Businesses, as well as individuals, need to keep complete, accurate records for tax purposes. Failure to comply with the tax laws may result in fines or, in extreme cases, prison sentences. Accurate records of earnings, expenses, and deductions can result in substantial savings by avoiding the overpayment of taxes.

METHODS OF MAINTAINING RECORDS

Manual. You are probably familiar with some methods of maintaining and storing records. Each time you look for a number in the telephone directory, you use alphabetic filing because names are arranged alphabetically. Your knowledge of the alphabet helps you to find the name you want. When you look for an auto repair shop in the classified section of the phone book, you use the subject method of filing. If you have a checking account, you are probably aware of the fact that the bank uses a numeric method of filing. Your car insurance policy has a number which is used by the insurance company to store your records. These are all methods for the manual filing of records. They have been used for years, and most people are accustomed to them.

In a manual system, the information that business needs to carry on vital activities is contained in various business *records* which are stored in *filing systems*. *Records* refers to all the information that is kept by an organization. It may be in the form of correspondence, cards, tapes, or microforms. *Correspondence* refers to any written communication that has not been designed to be placed in a card or forms file.

A *system* is a series of related steps followed in accomplishing a major office activity. A *manual filing system* is an arrangement of equipment and supplies to permit the storage of records according to a definite plan. A *procedure* is a series of related substeps performed to carry out part of the system. A *method* is the breakdown of a procedure into the steps by which the procedure is accomplished.

A *caption* is a name or number used to identify records for filing purposes. For example, if a letter is to be kept in the Brian Electronics Company file, the name of the business is the caption. A caption is typed on a folder label.

An alphabetic filing system uses business and special organization names (such as names of hotels, hospitals, educational institutions) and/or individual names as captions. Examples of alphabetic captions are *Bradley; Bradley, Edward C.;* and *Bradley Medical Supplies.*

A subject filing system uses the names of items or objects as captions. For example, subject captions might be *Automobile; Repair: Automobile;* and *Sales: Automobile.*

A numeric system assigns numbers to the business or special names and individual names. For example, Edward C. Bradley might be assigned *File No. 9706; Bradley Medical Supplies, File No. 9765.* Because these captions do not readily reveal the contents of the folder, an alphabetic card index is usually part of the numeric filing system.

A geographic system uses the names of places or locations (such as cities, towns, counties, states, or countries) as captions. Such captions might include *Richmond, Virginia: Bradley Medical Supplies; Winchester, Virginia: Aleck Motors.*

Computer. Both at home and in businesses and organizations, computers have become the rule rather than the exception when it comes to managing records. A software application assigned specifically for managing records is called *database* software. The task of maintaining these files in order to obtain, or retrieve, the data from them, requires a *database management* system.

Through the database management system, the computer user can retrieve information alphabetically, numerically, by subject, or geographically.

The data entered into the computer for it to process is called *input*. The input might be numbers or characters. Input is usually received through a keyboard or from a storage device such as a floppy disk.

The *output* is the information that the computer generates as a result of its calculations. Output may be printed on paper, displayed on a terminal, or stored on magnetic disks.

Database management is the action of storing and retrieving data. There are three aspects of database management: entering data, modifying or updating data, and presenting output reports. Database applications include maintaining employee lists and preparing payrolls, maintaining parts order lists and keeping track of inventories, maintaining customer lists and preparing bills for credit customers, and keeping track of the students at a school.

Information is usually stored in several different *files*. For instance, a business will often have a file of regular customers and a file of employees. Each file consists of a series of *records*, and each record contains information on an individual situation, such as one employee or one customer. Each record consists of several *fields* containing an individual item. For example, in an employee file, there is one record for each employee including a field for the person's name, a field for the address, a field for the Social Security number, and so forth.

A database management system must provide for the addition and deletion of records. For instance, a new employee may be hired and a new record generated, or an employee might retire or be fired and the record would need to be deleted. Provision must be made for updating or modifying records as well. If an existing employee moves, for example, the address would need to be changed in the record.

The main purpose of either a manual system *or* a database management system, of course, is to make it possible to retrieve meaningful and useful information from it.

CLASSIFICATION OF RECORDS

To determine the value of records and how long each should be kept, many businesses analyze and classify them as follows:

Vital Records. These records include legal papers of incorporation, titles to ownership, deeds, major contracts, property plans, reports to stockholders, minutes of directors' meetings, and insurance policies. They should never be destroyed because they are essential to the existence of the organization and are often irreplaceable.

Important Records. These include invoices, accounts receivable, sales records, quotations, financial statements, tax records, and certain correspondence.

They facilitate the routine of the business and are replaceable only at great cost and with much delay. If they are not being used, they may be transferred to inactive storage space. In a manual system, they are placed in containers that will keep them in good condition. In a computer system, a *backup* disk is made and stored away from the working disks. Microcomputers with hard disks generally use flopppy disks for storage of this type. A *hard disk* is a storage medium using rigid aluminum disks coated with iron oxide; hard disks have a much greater storage capacity than floppy disks. A *floppy disk* is a computer storage medium made of plastic covered with a magnetic coating.

Useful Records. These records include some general correspondence, memorandums, and bank statements. They are temporarily helpful and are replaceable at slight cost. They are often destroyed from a few weeks to a year after they are received. Birthday Cards, First Day at school Paper - Personnal Items

Nonessential Papers. These include routine inquiries, announcements, and acknowledgments. They should never be filed with more important records, and they may be destroyed after temporary use.

LIFE CYCLE OF A BUSINESS RECORD

A knowledgeable businessperson is not only concerned with how records make it possible to run a business at a profit but is also aware of the complete life cycle of each record and knows that some provision must be made for the eventual transfer and disposition of records.

LIFE CYCLE OF A BUSINESS RECORD

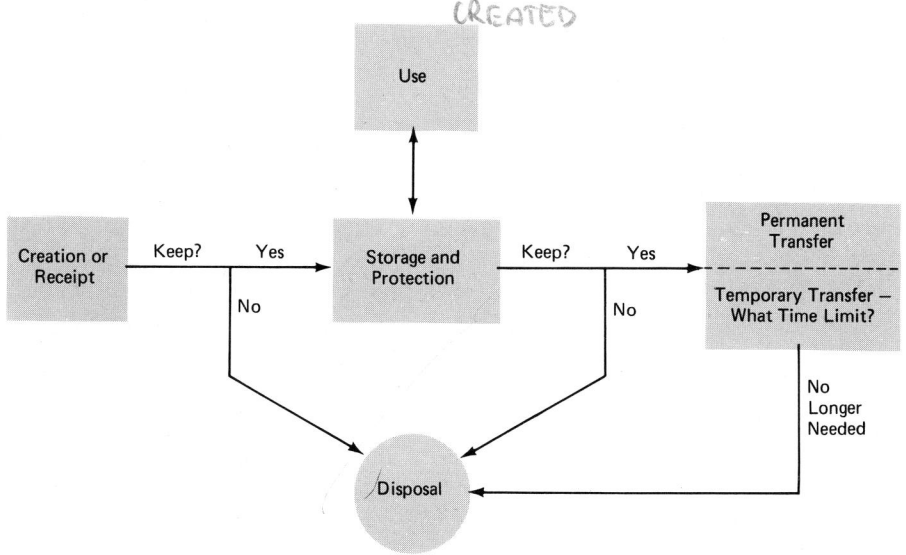

The life cycle of a business record has five stages: (1) creation or receipt; (2) storage, protection, and retrieval; (3) use; (4) transfer; and (5) disposal.

Creation or Receipt. A typical organization handles a staggering number of records daily. A large discount store, for example, will create hundreds of records every day—letters, advertising copy, accounting statements, purchase orders, sales slips, checks, receiving tickets, and so forth. That same store will also receive hundreds, if not thousands, of pieces of correspondence daily. These may be applications for credit, invoices, order letters, credit reports, price lists, catalogs, and so on. Workers spend hundreds of hours daily handling these records. Without the records, the business simply could not operate. Most records eventually find their way into one type of file or another, either a manual system or the database of a computer, so that they may be referred to when needed as a basis for important managerial decisions and action.

Storage, Protection, and Retrieval. When the decision is made to retain business papers, provision must be made for storing and protecting them during their useful lifetime. Some of these will go in filing cabinets and others will be maintained by computer. Size and shape, as well as use, will have a bearing as to how these records are maintained. For example, large blueprints in an architect's office will require equipment specially made for storing them. Papers such as legal documents are generally stored in insulated cabinets capable of withstanding extreme heat in case of fire. Any record worth retaining should be properly housed so that it can be located rapidly when needed and so that it is always adequately protected.

Use. Records are stored for one principal reason: use. Only records that will be needed for later reference are worth the time required to store them. Office space and filing equipment are too expensive to be used to "hide" papers that no one will ever use. Knowing which records will—and which will *not*—be used again requires knowledge about the business and a fair amount of judgment.

Transfer. As paper records become *inactive*—referred to only infrequently— they should be pulled from the files to make room for active records. Occupying valuable office space and equipment, inactive records get in the way of the efficient use of active ones. Periodically, then, inactive or infrequently used paper files should be removed from the main files and placed in *transfer files*. These files look somewhat like regular files, except that the containers are less expensive (usually pressboard containers), and they are kept in less accessible locations, such as the basement, where floor space is less expensive than in the main office.

Computer records which become inactive are often stored in what is called *archival storage*. This data will seldom be used but must be kept for a long time. Archival storage is usually in the form of floppy disks or magnetic tape. Neither of these take up much space.

Disposal. The last stage in the records management cycle is the disposal of records. Of course, all records that no longer serve a useful purpose should be destroyed. The decision as to when records are to be destroyed is usually made by management. The policy is determined by legal considerations and by the special needs of the business. At any rate some definite plan should be set up by management for the periodic destruction of records that are no longer of value to the organization.

THE FREEDOM OF INFORMATION ACT AND THE PRIVACY ACT

A great deal of concern has been generated about the use of computers to process and store information, much of which is confidential in nature. There is concern that information may be released to individuals or firms and used for reasons other than those for which it was originally intended. Because the information that is maintained by computers is entered by humans, the capacity for human error exists. If the information is incorrect, the problem can be compounded. For example, if a bank record contains inaccurate information regarding an individual, the individual's ability to obtain credit elsewhere could be hindered if the information containing the error were released. It's possible that the error could even cause a collection agency to locate the individual's place of employment and have the person's wages garnisheed for a debt that doesn't exist.

As a result of errors of this kind, in the fall of 1974, the U.S. Congress passed two laws to protect the individual against misuse of information on file. These laws affect the work done by the records and database manager, as well as the file worker, in some situations. One of these laws is called the Freedom of Information Act. This law affects individuals and gives them the right to ask for information that pertains to them.

Records such as those kept by doctors' offices, hospitals, dental clinics, psychiatric offices, and educational institutions can be requested by an individual. Those records kept by lawyers, government agencies, counselors, priests and lending institutions and employment application files are available to you to read when you obtain permission from the organization maintaining those records.

At the same time, another law was passed called the Privacy Act. This law controls information which is readily available to the public. It serves to safeguard individual privacy. Your permission is necessary for someone to see your records.

As a result, we can say that the Freedom of Information Act allows you to see records about yourself. The Privacy Act limits those people who are allowed to see information contained in files about you.

What does this mean to a file worker? A records or database manager? It's highly possible that any one of these workers may be responsible for files that are covered by these acts. People who request access to files need to be screened. If you held one of these positions, you might be in charge of checking permission granted to people who wish to use the files. It might also be your job to see to it that persons requesting various files sign a logbook before they are allowed to see the files. You might have the authority to refuse access to certain records and documents. Because of these responsibilities, you might have to qualify for a security classification in order to work for a government agency.

In addition to the laws which control access to the files, some businesses have files which they have determined contain confidential or secret information. These files are to be read and used only by those employees who have the "need to know" because their duties require working with this information. Charge-out systems for these files are strict and rigidly enforced. In most cases the files cannot be removed beyond a specified area after being checked out, and no copies may be made of the contents. The employee requesting the confidential or secret file must present proper identification or authorization to the file worker, or the worker must deny access.

EMPLOYMENT IN RECORDS AND DATABASE MANAGEMENT

The activities of every employee are influenced, in some way, by the records of an organization. That fact alone should stress the importance of records.

No matter what kind of office job you hold, you will have to work with records.
© Richard Hackett

Those who work in the office are especially concerned with records—creating or receiving them and later finding and using them.

For most office workers, handling records is one of a number of job responsibilities. The secretarial position is an example of one that calls for filing and records and database management skills. The secretary is usually responsible for maintaining the employer's files and may in a small organization even have to set up a database or filing system for the organization or reorganize an existing system. The employer depends upon the secretary to find important information quickly. "Please get me a copy of the letter we wrote to Mendenhall Concrete Company about the new parking lot," is a typical request made of a secretary. No secretary should consider secretarial training complete without a thorough knowledge of filing and records and database management procedures.

Office records are used by other office workers as well. Typists, accountants, stenographers, word processing specialists, computer operators, and general clerical workers use paper files and the computer's database frequently. Even if these workers are not directly involved in filing activities, their effectiveness is increased if they understand the importance of systematic filing.

There are offices with centralized paper files which have full-time filing positions. Files are often kept in central locations, especially in larger organizations, because the centralization eliminates the need for duplication of records in separate department files. In this way, records are easily obtained by all departments that may need them for reference purposes. The specialized file worker is an important person in the operation of the office. Filing supervisors are sometimes hired to manage the filing department. Advancement is excellent. The advent of microcomputers has made records and database management a promising career for those with supervisory ability who wish to assume responsibilities.

The office manager should be well enough informed about filing techniques and records and database management to be able to determine such matters as the type of filing system to be used, the equipment to be purchased, and the personnel needed to maintain the files.

CAREERS IN RECORDS AND DATABASE MANAGEMENT

As you study records and database management, you may decide that you would like to specialize in this area of office management.

The *Dictionary of Occupational Titles* provides many job titles and descriptions which deal with classifying, sorting, and filing correspondence, records, and other data. The ones which follow will give you a general idea of the duties and responsibilities of each.

206.362-010 FILE CLERK I Files correspondence, cards, invoices, receipts, and other records in alphabetic or numeric order, or according to subject or other system.

206.137-014 FILE CLERK II Performs duties essentially same as those of FILE CLERK I, except that, in addition to putting material in and removing it from files, performs clerical work in searching and investigating information contained in files, inserting additional data on file records, making out reports, and keeping files current.

206.137-010 SUPERVISOR, FILES Records-section supervisor. Supervises and coordinates activities of workers engaged in maintaining central records files; directs and assists workers in searching for missing records, utilizing knowledge of common errors.

206.387-026 RECORDS CUSTODIAN Stores bank records and oversees destruction of outdated records. Transfers records by truck or other means from banks to storage facility. Stacks or shelves boxed or packaged records according to designated plan.

161.117-014 DIRECTOR, RECORDS MANAGEMENT Plans, develops, and administers records management policies designed to facilitate effective and efficient handling of business records and other information: Plans development and implementation of records management policies intended to standardize filing, protecting, and retrieving records, reports, and other information contained on paper, microfilm, computer program, or other media. Coordinates and directs, through subordinate managers, activities of departments involved with records management analysis, reports analysis, and supporting technical, clerical, micrographics, and printing services.

161.167-018 MANAGER, RECORDS ANALYSIS Directs and coordinates activities of workers involved with analyzing systems of records management: Plans and directs compilation and updating of cost and control records, utilizing knowledge of records inventories, usage, costs, and operating practices. Coordinates activities of personnel engaged in studying such matters as simplification of filing and retrieval systems, protection of vital records, and economical utilization of paper, microfilm, computer program, or other information-bearing media according to organizational and governmental record-keeping schedules and requirements.

Large organizations and businesses often employ one or more records managers in addition to records specialists and supervisors. These individuals usually have a four-year college degree and work as part of the management structure in the business. Their duties may include:

1. Analysis, creation, and coordination of business forms.
2. Analysis, creation, and evaluation of records systems, including database systems.
3. Planning and implementing micrographic systems.
4. Using the principles and techniques of records management to meet the needs of management.

The outlook for records and database management careers is, like that for most office occupations, very good. The current *Occupational Outlook Hand-*

book will give you up-to-date information about the nature of the work, places of employment, training, advancement, employment outlook, and working conditions. There are more than a quarter of a million persons employed in records and database management. Some of these positions can often be held on a part-time basis and are entry-level jobs leading to advancement. Because of business expansion and growing amounts of paperwork, opportunities for employment are plentiful in this type of career.

Records and database managers and other individuals who deal with records and information management may be members of the Association of Records Managers and Administrators, Inc. (ARMA). This is a nonprofit organization to provide guidance and to promote interest, research, and the exchange of ideas concerning records and database management. Many communities have local chapters whose members meet regularly to discuss topics and problems of interest.

GENERAL REVIEW

The following questions will help you to reinforce your learning of the competencies included in this chapter.

1. State why filing and records and database management are important to you. (Competency 1) *Everyone has to know, Employment for the JOB.*
2. Define these terms:
    record   database management
    filing   (Competency 2)
3. State why records are necessary. Give six examples of records needed by business and individuals. (Competency 3)
4. Name the two basic methods of storing and maintaining records. (Competency 4)
5. Define these terms:
    correspondence   database
    filing system   backup
    system   input/output
    procedure   data
    method   field
    caption   file
    (Competency 5)
6. List the four classifications businesses use to value their records and give two examples of each classification. (Competency 6)
7. List and describe the stages in the life cycles of a business record. (Competency 7)
8. Compare the Freedom of Information Act with the Privacy Act. State why each is important in records and database management. (Competency 8)
9. Why is the *need to know* important to the file worker? (Competency 9)

10. Why do office workers need to have a knowledge of records and database management? (Competency 10)
11. Name five job titles in records and database management and list two duties of each. (Competency 11)

CASE PROBLEMS

1. Irene Buckbee is a dentist. She has her own practice. She admitted to her friend, John Martin, that she doesn't keep an organized set of records. John feels Irene should keep well-planned records. He feels she could benefit from a computer for that very reason. With which individual do you agree? Why? (Competencies 1, 3, 7)
2. Jerry Grotowski works for a large government agency. He feels that the keeping of records is more important to a large organization, such as the one where he works, than it is for a small one. Jerry's coworker Jennifer Johnson, disagrees. Who is right? Why? (Competencies 1, 3, 7)
3. Vicki Keller will graduate from college next year. She plans to go to work as a salesperson for her Aunt Rose's firm. She doesn't plan to take a course in records management because she doesn't think it will be of any benefit to her in her job. Do you agree or disagree with her? Why? (Competencies 1, 3, 10)
4. Your employer's motto is "When in doubt, throw it out!" in regard to records. Your former employer felt, "When in doubt, keep it!" when it came to filing correspondence and business records. Who is right? Why? (Competencies 6, 7)
5. Martha Hoffman works in the personnel department of a large retail firm. She needs to refer to employees' files from time to time. She resents the fact that the file worker who controls those files asks for her authorization to see the information she needs. She feels that under the Freedom of Information Act, she has the right to see those files. Is she correct? (Competencies 8, 9)
6. Uncle Henry thinks you should apply for a job in the filing department of the company where he works. Because you would like a career as a secretary or administrative assistant, you feel that working as a records specialist would hurt your chances for another job. Should you apply for the job as a file worker? (Competencies 1, 10)
7. When you started your college career, you were surprised to find that you would have a course in records and database management. You have been wondering why filing is so important that you must spend that much time learning about it. What have you learned in this chapter to convince you that records and database management is necessary to your career as an office employee? (Competencies 1, 3, 10, 11)

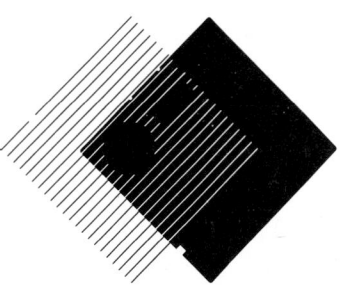

2

ALPHABETIC INDEXING OF
PERSONAL NAMES

COMPETENCIES

Upon completing this chapter, you will be able to:

1. Define the terms *alphabetizing, case, unit,* and *indexing.*
2. Arrange names of persons into correct alphabetic order using the unit-by-unit method.
3. Write or keyboard names of individuals on cards using the rules for alphabetic indexing. Alphabetize, file, and find the cards.
4. Prepare alphabetic cross-reference cards containing personal names and arrange them in sequence with alphabetic cards.

TERMS YOU WILL USE

Arranging names or items in alphabetic order according to the sequence of their letters is called *alphabetizing.* The names on a class roll and in a telephone directory, for example, have been alphabetized. In modern business, much of the information that is used in day-to-day operations is arranged in this way.

When you put names in alphabetic order, you start by comparing the first letter of each name. For example, you would arrange the names *Arnold, Balkus, Chong,* and *Davis* according to *A, B, C, D.* If the first letters are the same, as in the names *Eaves, Echols, Eckel,* and *Eckert,* you must compare second, third, and even last letters to determine the order of the names.

The *case* of a letter of the alphabet refers to whether it is capitalized *(A)* or written in small letters *(a)*. When you alphabetize, it makes no difference whether a letter is capitalized, called *uppercase,* or written as a small letter, called *lowercase*. Thus when you alphabetize, an uppercase letter *(A)* is considered to be identical to its lowercase counterpart *(a)*.

Each part of a name is called a *unit.* For example, the name *Elaine R. Mead* has three units: *Elaine, R.,* and *Mead*.

Indexing is the process of deciding under which name to file a record and then deciding the proper order of the units in that name. You will learn the rules for alphabetic indexing in this chapter and in Chapter 3.

ALPHABETIZING UNIT BY UNIT

Before you learn the rules for indexing, it is important to be able to alphabetize names correctly. Names are alphabetized by using the unit-by-unit method which is explained below. Note the following names, which are divided into units. The units are printed in all capital letters to emphasize the fact that the case of the letters is not considered in alphabetizing.

NAME	UNIT 1 (Key)	UNIT 2	UNIT 3
Mayflower	MAYFLOWER		
Parker Company	PARKER	COMPANY	
Parker Manufacturers	PARKER	MANUFACTURERS	
Rainero Insurance	RAINERO	INSURANCE	
Rainero Lumber Mart	RAINERO	LUMBER	MART
Rainero Lumber Yard	RAINERO	LUMBER	YARD

Follow these steps in alphabetizing using the unit-by-unit method. Refer to the chart above as you read the numbered steps below.

1. Look at the first units. The first unit of a name is called the *key* because it is the unit under which the record is filed. Arrange the first units in alphabetic order.
2. Some of the first units are identical. In the example above, PARKER appears twice and RAINERO appears three times in the Unit 1 column. If first units are identical, alphabetize the second units. Thus, *Parker Company* comes before *Parker Manufacturers*.
3. Some of the first and second units are identical. In the example above, RAINERO LUMBER appears twice. If first and second units are identical, alphabetize the third units, and so on. Thus, *Rainero Lumber Mart* comes before *Rainero Lumber Yard*.

Alphabetizing names is not always as easy as the above examples illustrate. You may have to alphabetize names such as the ones in this chart.

NAME	UNIT 1	UNIT 2	UNIT 3
Brandau	BRANDAU		
Brandau Lumber	BRANDAU	LUMBER	
Collins Rest Stop	COLLINS	REST	STOP
Collins Restaurant	COLLINS	RESTAURANT	

Note the following about the above names.

1. Under Unit 1 the name BRANDAU appears two times and the name COLLINS appears twice. BRANDAU comes before COLLINS.

2. One BRANDAU has no second unit; the other BRANDAU has a second unit, LUMBER. If a name has no second unit, it comes before the same name that has a second unit. Thus *Brandau* comes before *Brandau Lumber*. This is called the "nothing comes before something" rule for arranging names in alphabetic order.

3. One COLLINS has the second unit REST; the other COLLINS has the second unit RESTAURANT. Again, because "nothing comes before something," REST comes before RESTAURANT. Thus *Collins Rest Stop* precedes *Collins Restaurant*.

WHY INDEXING RULES ARE NEEDED

If the names in your files consisted only of letters of the alphabet, alphabetizing would be easy and most indexing rules would not be necessary. But what if you had such names in your files as these?

Mr. Jorge DuPont-Kenny
The Ackney & Boone Co.
O'Hare Restaurant, Inc.
3M Corporation
WTOP Radio
Donna St. Clair

The above contain punctuation, a symbol, a number, a title, and abbreviations. Indexing rules are needed to help you decide how to arrange these and countless other names in correct alphabetic order.

RULES FOR ALPHABETIC INDEXING

To standardize the way names are indexed and filed, the Association of Records Managers and Administrators (ARMA) has published a set of rules for alphabetic filing. The twelve indexing rules which you will learn in Chapters 2 and 3 are compatible with the ARMA standards.

When indexing the name of a person, arrange the units in this order: last name, first name or initial, and middle name or initial.

NAME	UNIT 1	UNIT 2	UNIT 3
T. R. Adkins	ADKINS	T	R
Kim Berg	BERG	KIM	
Kim S. Berg	BERG	KIM	S
Arcel M. Castillo	CASTILLO	ARCEL	M
B. Sonia Castillo	CASTILLO	B	SONIA
Bernard Arthur Castillo	CASTILLO	BERNARD	ARTHUR

Note   Rearranging the units in a person's name into indexing order is called *transposing* the name. If two names are identical, use the address. (See Rule 12.)

Can You Apply Rule 1?

In each of the following pairs, which name will be filed first and why?

1. Donna Lin   D. R. Lin ✓   *nothing comes before something*
2. Larry R. Pavlik ✓   Larry S. Pavlik
3. Marcia Selvey ✓   Marcia Silvey

Turn to page 25 to check your answers.

KEYBOARDING NAMES FOR CARD FILING

Card filing is the storage of names, addresses, and other information on cards which are placed in a file container. In an alphabetic card file, the cards are arranged alphabetically according to the name of the person or organization. You will learn more about the various kinds of card filing in Chapter 5.

Now that you have learned the first indexing rule, let's see how names are keyboarded in indexed order onto file cards. Using a standard format for cards makes the job of filing easier because the information will be located in exactly the same place on each card. Follow these steps in formatting file cards:

1. Begin the name three or four spaces from the left edge of the card on the second or third line from the top.
2. Keyboard the units of the name in all capitals in indexing order. For example, the name *Donald B. Guthrie* should appear as follows:

Note that there is no comma after *GUTHRIE* and no period after *B*.

3. On address cards, type the name and address three lines below the indexed name as shown here:

GUTHRIE DONALD B

DONALD B GUTHRIE
217 FREMONT DRIVE
RADFORD VA 24141–2315

Note that uppercase letters are used and that the only punctuation used is the hyphen in the nine-digit ZIP code. The standard two-letter state abbreviation is used. This address format is recommended by the U.S. Postal Service for addressing mail.

ROUGH AND FINE SORTING

Unarranged cards should be sorted into alphabetic order before they are filed. Sorting saves time and energy and reduces filing errors. If you have a large number of items to sort, start by rough sorting; then fine sort.

Rough Sort: Sort all of the items according to a range of letters, such as *A–H; I–P; Q–Z*.
Fine Sort: Sort the *A–H* group into exact alphabetic order; then *I–P;* then *Q–Z*.

FILING PRACTICE

You should complete Job 1 of the *Practice Materials*.

RULE 2   Personal Names With Prefixes

Consider a prefix, such as *Mc* in *McDonald,* as part of the name it precedes. Ignore any apostrophe or space that appears within or after the prefix.

Commonly used prefixes are *d', D', de, De, Del, De la, Di, Du, El, Fitz, La, Le, M, Mac, Mc, O', Saint, St., Van, Van de, Van der, Von,* and *Von der.*

NAME	UNIT 1	UNIT 2	UNIT 3
Frances S. D'Atre	DATRE	FRANCES	S
Lloyd G. De Hart	DEHART	LLOYD	G
Marilyn Dehart	DEHART	MARILYN	
Brian Lee MacDowell	MACDOWELL	BRIAN	LEE
Brian McDowell	MCDOWELL	BRIAN	
Maureen O'Day	ODAY	MAUREEN	
Roberta Saint John	SAINTJOHN	ROBERTA	
Cynthia R. St. Jean	STJEAN	CYNTHIA	R
Anthony VanAllen	VANALLEN	ANTHONY	
Christiana L. Van Balen	VANBALEN	CHRISTIANA	L

Can You Apply Rule 2?

In each of the following pairs, which name will be filed first and why?

1. Patricia MacAllen   Pat McAllen
2. Terry O'Grady   Teresa Ogle
3. Carmen St. Martin   Carlos E. Saint Torrence

[handwritten: mc Allen Patricia / ogle Teresa / saint Torrence Carlos E.]

Turn to page 26 to check your answers.

HOW TO FORMAT NAMES IN RULE 2 ON A FILE CARD

NAME—Frances S. D'Atre

```
DATRE FRANCES S
```

FILING PRACTICE

Complete Job 2 of the *Practice Materials.*

RULE 3   Hyphenated Personal Names

Consider a hyphenated first, middle, or last name as one unit.

NAME	UNIT 1	UNIT 2	UNIT 3
Wolfgang E. Glasser-Fox	GLASSERFOX	WOLFGANG	E
Jane-Scott Gomez	GOMEZ	JANESCOTT	
Juliano Maranto	MARANTO	JULIANO	
Anthony Y. Maranto-Valdez	MARANTOVALDEZ	ANTHONY	Y

Can You Apply Rule 3?

In each of the following pairs, which name will be filed first and why?

1. Shawn-Della Rosswell   Shawn Della Rosswell
2. Beth Rose Noland   Beth Rose-Noland
3. A. Grande   George W. Grand-Abernathy

Turn to page 26 to check your answers.

HOW TO FORMAT NAMES IN RULE 3 ON A FILE CARD

NAME—Wolfgang E. Glasser-Fox

```
GLASSERFOX WOLFGANG E
```

FILING PRACTICE

Complete Job 3 of the *Practice Materials*.

RULE 4 Abbreviations of Personal Names

Abbreviated and shortened forms of personal names are indexed as written.

NAME	UNIT 1	UNIT 2	UNIT 3
Jos. R. Randolph	RANDOLPH	JOS	R
Liz Ritchie	RITCHIE	LIZ	
Billy Dee Rowland	ROWLAND	BILLY	DEE
Geo. Catlin Rutland	RUTLAND	GEO	CATLIN

Can You Apply Rule 4?

In each of the following pairs, which name will be filed first and why?

1. Susan Graham   Sue L. Graham
2. Jas. Samborsky   James Samborsky
3. Chas. Wills   Charles Wills

Turn to page 26 to check your answers.

HOW TO FORMAT NAMES IN RULE 4 ON A FILE CARD

NAME—Jos. R. Randolph

RANDOLPH JOS R

FILING PRACTICE

Complete Job 4 of the *Practice Materials*.

RULE 5   Personal Names with Titles and Suffixes

When used with a person's name, a title or a suffix is the last indexing unit when needed to distinguish between two or more identical names. Titles and suffixes are indexed as written.

Titles include *Capt., Dr., Mayor, Miss, Mr., Mrs., Ms.,* and *Senator.* Suffixes include seniority terms *(III, Jr., Sr.)* and professional designations *(CPA, MD, Ph.D.).*

NAME	UNIT 1	UNIT 2	UNIT 3	UNIT 4
Karen Kahn, CPA	KAHN	KAREN	CPA	
Dr. Karen Kahn	KAHN	KAREN	DR	
Miss Nancy E. Lambe	LAMBE	NANCY	E	MISS
Mrs. Nancy E. Lambe	LAMBE	NANCY	E	MRS
Barry R. Liskey, II	LISKEY	BARRY	R	II
Barry R. Liskey, III	LISKEY	BARRY	R	III
Barry R. Liskey, Jr.	LISKEY	BARRY	R	JR
Barry R. Liskey, Sr.	LISKEY	BARRY	R	SR
Capt. Alison D. Lux	LUX	ALISON	D	CAPT

Note: Numeric seniority terms *(II, III)* are filed before alphabetic terms *(Jr.* and *Sr.)*

Can You Apply Rule 5?

In each of the following pairs, which name will be filed first and why?

1. Senator Anne Duffy   Anne Duffy, Ph.D.
2. Ralph Thomas, III   Ralph Thomas, Jr.
3. Miss Emily C. Butler   Mrs. Emily C. Butler

Turn to page 26 to check your answers.

HOW TO FORMAT NAMES IN RULE 5 ON A FILE CARD

NAME—Karen Kahn, CPA

> KAHN KAREN CPA

FILING PRACTICE

Complete Job 5 of the *Practice Materials*.

CROSS-REFERENCING PERSONAL NAMES

A record should always be filed under the caption by which it is most likely to be requested. When a record may be requested under more than one caption, it is then necessary to cross-reference the record under one or more alternate captions.

Cross-referencing of personal names may be necessary in the following circumstances:

1. When it is difficult to tell which unit is the individual's last name and which is the first name.

NAME	FILED UNDER	CROSS-REFERENCE
Carter Andrew	ANDREW CARTER	CARTER ANDREW
Nam Ling	LING NAM	NAM LING
Scott May	MAY SCOTT	SCOTT MAY

2. When an individual has a name change. The cross-reference will be necessary only until all records appear in the new name and reference to the former name is no longer necessary.

PRESENT NAME	FORMER NAME	FILED UNDER	CROSS-REFERENCE
Raymond Katz	Raymond Burger	KATZ RAYMOND	BURGER RAYMOND
Chris Logan-Wells	Chris Logan	LOGANWELLS CHRIS	LOGAN CHRIS
Ahman Rashad	William Jackson	RASHAD AHMAN	JACKSON WILLIAM
Marjorie L. Spicer	Marjorie E. Lyons	SPICER MARJORIE L	LYONS MARJORIE E

3. When an individual uses one name for professional purposes and an alternate one for legal or social purposes.

NAME MOST FREQUENTLY USED BY YOUR BUSINESS	ALTERNATE NAME	FILED UNDER	CROSS-REFERENCE
Tony Fox	Antonio Forcelli	FOX TONY	FORCELLI ANTONIO
Vickie Grant	Victoria Collins	GRANT VICKIE	COLLINS VICTORIA

4. When records of two or more individuals need to be kept in the same file. Examples are medical records for members of a family, apartment lease records for roommates, and cochairpersons of a committee.

NAME	RELATED NAMES	FILED UNDER	CROSS-REFERENCE
Beatrice Caruci	Roswell Caruci Annette Caruci (Medical records for family members)	CARUCI BEATRICE	CARUCI ROSWELL CARUCI ANNETTE
Mason Gearhart	Pat Donnelly Donald Wright (Cosigners on a lease)	GEARHART MASON	DONNELLY PAT WRIGHT DONALD
Cagney Zimmer	Don-Joe Keeling (Cochairperson)	ZIMMER CAGNEY	KEELING DONJOE

The illustration below shows an acceptable format for an alphabetic cross-reference card.

HOW TO FORMAT AN ALPHABETIC CROSS-REFERENCE CARD
NAME—Tony Fox
Cross-reference—Antonio Forcelli

```
FOX TONY
SEE FORCELLI ANTONIO
```

Can You Cross-Reference Individual Names?

Indicate the file and cross-reference captions for each of the following names:

1. An Wong   *WONG AN   AN WONG*
2. Michael David   *DAVID Michael Filed*
3. Irene O'Conner changes her name to Irene Brooks. *Brooks, Irene Conner   Irene*
4. Larry Lamonte, an actor with whom you do business under that name, has the legal name Lamonte Worthington. *Lamonte Larry   worthington Lamonte*
5. Angela Ridgeway, a practicing attorney you deal with under that name, has the legal name Angela Greenspan. *R A   G A*
6. Dorothy Miller, Carol Pryor, and Adrienne Wilson lease an apartment together.   *Miller D   Pryor Carol   Wilson Adrienne*

Turn to page 26 to check your answers.

FILING PRACTICE

Complete Jobs 6 and 7 of the *Practice Materials.*

GENERAL REVIEW

1. Define the following:
   a. alphabetizing *arranging names or items in alphabetic order*
   b. case; upper case; lower case
   c. unit
   d. indexing
   (Competency 1)
2. Using the names given in the *Practice Materials,* demonstrate how names should be keyboarded on index and cross-reference cards. Following your instructor's directions, you may state orally or in writing or keyboard to illustrate the proper method. (Competencies 2, 3, 4)
3. Using the cards contained in the *Practice Materials* demonstrate correct rough and fine sorting techniques for putting cards in alphabetic order. If you do not have these materials available, list orally or in writing the steps you should follow. (Competencies 2, 3)

You practiced Competencies 2 and 3 in the *Practice Materials.* The following indexing review will reinforce your ability to select indexing units.

INDEXING REVIEW

A. What is the *first* indexing unit of each of the following names?

1. R. L. Webb
2. R. L. Benson-Webb
3. Mr. Benson Webb
4. Mrs. Dot Webb
5. Shirley-Anne Benson
6. Webb, Robert L.
7. Robert L. Webb, Jr.
8. Geo. Webb
9. Dr. Robert L. Webb
10. Shirley A. Webb, Ph.D.

B. What is the *second* indexing unit of each of the following names?

1. K. T. Odom
2. K. Odom
3. Mr. Bud Odom
4. Nancy-Lee Odom
5. Nina Odom
6. Nancy Odom-Sutherland
7. K. P. Odom, III
8. Chas. Odom
9. Martin Odom Van Camp
10. Butch Odom

C. What is the *third* indexing unit of each of the following names? (If there is no third indexing unit, the correct answer is *none*.)

1. Lori MacDonald
2. Josh L. Bayberry
3. Cora Belle Cooper
4. Jane D. Peele, MD
5. Meghan St. James
6. Nancy-Lee Turner-Betz
7. Amelia G. Croft-Withers
8. Paul James D'Amito, Jr.
9. Dr. Ruth Ellen Craft-Reese
10. Joe Thos. Sellers, II

D. Alphabetize the names in each of the following groups. On separate sheet of paper, list the letters to indicate the correct alphabetic order.

1. a. Caroline Young
   b. C. Young
   c. Carolyn Young
2. a. Pamela York
   b. Mike York
   c. Mr. Mike C. York
3. a. Donovan Trent
   b. Major Timothy F. Donovan, Jr.
   c. Tim Donovan
4. a. J. Norcross
   b. R. Mercer
   c. G. O'Hearn
5. a. Marvin O'Neill
   b. Marv O'Neal
   c. Marvin O'Neal

6. a. Arthur Gray
   b. Gilbert Hackett
   c. Glenna Gray-Hackett
7. a. Mary-Allen Winslow
   b. Mary Allen Winslow
   c. Mary Allen-Winslow
8. a. Bill Pickens
   b. Dr. Bill Perkins
   c. Bill Perkins, Jr.
9. a. Benjamin Reid, Jr.
   b. Col. Ben S. Reid, Sr.
   c. Benjamin Reed, Sr.
10. a. Morris Cook
    b. Maurice Cook
    c. Melinda Cooke

CASE PROBLEMS

1. You are employed by a small business which has the files set up in alphabetic order according to the names of the customers. One of them,

Janet Burgess, recently changed her name to Janet McLellan. When you wanted to file a letter from Janet McLellan, referring to a previous transaction, you could not find a folder for her. This letter was stored in *change the name* the folder with the caption *Burgess, Janet.* (a) What had not been done that should have been done? (b) What steps can you take to find her file? (c) When you do find Janet's file, what will you do to avoid this problem in the future? (Competency 4) *Write a note name chg.*

2. You keep a file of the names and addresses of your clients. Three of the cards have been keyboarded as shown below: (a) What is wrong with this system? (b) What should be done in the future as new cards are keyboarded? (Competency 3)

```
Jones, James L.
99 Terrace Road
Rochester, NY 14624-2112
```

```
LAMAR GRACE N
203 MEADOW LANE
ROCHESTER NEW YORK 14618-1021
```

```
MARCHACK, Eugene Frank, 1206 Burgundy Street
        Rochester, NY 14624-4112
```

3. As part of your daily job routine, you have been asked to file cards in their proper locations. File drawers are set up with alphabetic ranges as guide captions, with some letters of the alphabet taking up two or three drawers. You are given stacks of 100 or more cards to file at a time. What is a more efficient method for you to store the cards than to take the stack as given to you, pick up each card one at a time, and place it in the proper drawer? Describe the steps you would follow. (Competency 3)

ANSWERS TO CAN YOU APPLY THE RULES?

RULE 1

1. D. R. Lin. *D* comes before *Donna*; nothing comes before something.
2. Larry R. Pavlik. *R* precedes *S*.
3. Marcia Selvey. *SELVEY* precedes *SILVEY*.

RULE 2

1. Patricia MacAllen. *MACALLEN* precedes *MCALLEN*.
2. Teresa Ogle. *OGLE* precedes *OGRADY*.
3. Carlos E. Saint Torrence. *SAINTTORRENCE* precedes *STMARTIN*.

RULE 3

1. Shawn Della Rosswell. *SHAWN* precedes *SHAWNDELLA*.
2. Beth Rose Noland. *NOLAND* precedes *ROSENOLAND*.
3. George W. Grand-Abernathy. *GRANDABERNATHY* precedes *GRANDE*.

RULE 4

1. Sue L. Graham. *SUE* precedes *SUSAN*.
2. James Samborsky. *JAMES* precedes *JAS*.
3. Charles Wills. *CHARLES* precedes *CHAS*.

RULE 5

1. Anne Duffy, Ph.D. *PHD* precedes *SENATOR*.
2. Ralph Thomas, III. *III* precedes *JR*.
3. Miss Emily C. Butler. *MISS* precedes *MRS*.

ANSWERS TO CAN YOU CROSS-REFERENCE INDIVIDUAL NAMES? (p. 23)

FILED UNDER	CROSS-REFERENCE
1. WONG AN	AN WONG
2. DAVID MICHAEL	MICHAEL DAVID
3. BROOKS IRENE	OCONNER IRENE
4. LAMONTE LARRY	WORTHINGTON LAMONTE
5. RIDGEWAY ANGELA	GREENSPAN ANGELA
6. MILLER DOROTHY	PRYOR CAROL and WILSON ADRIENNE

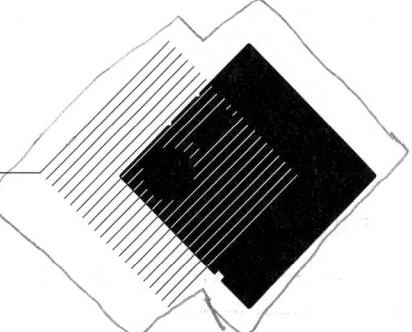

3

ALPHABETIC INDEXING OF BUSINESS AND ORGANIZATION NAMES

COMPETENCIES

Upon completing this chapter, you will be able to:

1. Write or keyboard business and organization names on cards using the rules for alphabetic indexing. Alphabetize, file, and find the cards.
2. Prepare alphabetic cross-reference cards containing business and organization names and arrange them in sequence with alphabetic cards.
3. State examples in which cross-referencing of business and organization names may be necessary.
4. State examples in which the indexing rules might be varied or changed in special circumstances.

INDEXING RULES 6–12

This chapter presents seven rules for indexing business and organization names that are used in addition to the five rules for personal names presented in Chapter 2. When you have completed your study of these rules and have done the related practice, you will have mastered the twelve rules in accepted usage to keep personal, business, and organization names filed in an organized and consistent way.

Consider the units in business and organization names in the order in which they are normally written. To determine the order in which a business or organization name is normally written, use the letterhead of the business or organization. If the letterhead is not available, use such alternate sources as directories, advertisements, and computer databases. When *the* is the first word of the name, it is treated as the last unit. Names with prefixes are considered one unit, just as with personal names.

NAME	UNIT 1	UNIT 2	UNIT 3	UNIT 4
Arrowwood Realty	ARROWWOOD	REALTY		
Arthur Abraham Florist	ARTHUR	ABRAHAM	FLORIST	
Bank of the South-east	BANK	OF	THE	SOUTHEAST
The Bank of Utah	BANK	OF	UTAH	THE
C W Camper Sales	C	W	CAMPER	SALES
CRG Finance Company	CRG	FINANCE	COMPANY	
Dr. Pepper Bot-tling Company	DR	PEPPER	BOTTLING	COMPANY
Dunsmore and Barringer	DUNSMORE	AND	BARRINGER	
Edge Water Fun Park	EDGE	WATER	FUN	PARK
Edgewater Devel-opment Com-pany	EDGEWATER	DEVELOPMENT	COMPANY	
El Toro Manufac-turers	ELTORO	MANUFACTURERS		
Hospital of Tor-rence	HOSPITAL	OF	TORRENCE	
The Hudson Daily News	HUDSON	DAILY	NEWS	THE
Margaret Beeks Elementary School	MARGARET	BEEKS	ELEMENTARY	SCHOOL
Mr. Cotton Sports-wear	MR	COTTON	SPORTSWEAR	
South East Motel	SOUTH	EAST	MOTEL	
St. Louis Office Supply	STLOUIS	OFFICE	SUPPLY	
University of Rich-mond	UNIVERSITY	OF	RICHMOND	
WKEX Radio Sta-tion	WKEX	RADIO	STATION	

Can You Apply Rule 6?

In each of the following pairs, which name will be filed first and why?

1. Cheryl Quillen Computer Store   Quillen and Adams
2. T G Market   TGL Heating Company
3. Eldorado Springs Hotel   El Rancho Golf Resort

Turn to page 41 to check your answers.

HOW TO FORMAT NAMES IN RULE 6 ON A FILE CARD

NAME—Arrowood Realty

ARROWOOD REALTY

FILING PRACTICE

Complete Job 8 of the *Practice Materials*.

RULE 7   Abbreviations in Business and Organization Names

Abbreviations in business and organization names are indexed as written.

NAME	UNIT 1	UNIT 2	UNIT 3	UNIT 4
Kars Ltd. of NY	KARS	LTD	OF	NY
Microsystem Specialists, Inc.	MICROSYSTEM	SPECIALISTS	INC	
Prof. Shell Catering Co.	PROF	SHELL	CATERING	CO
R. L. Robinson Agy.	R	L	ROBINSON	AGY
Royal Mfg. Corp.	ROYAL	MFG	CORP	
The Rug Company	RUG	COMPANY	THE	

Note: Cross-reference between an abbreviation and the complete name when necessary to ensure that records can be located.

Can You Apply Rule 7?

In each of the following pairs, which name will be filed first and why?

1. Central Lumber Co. Inc.   Central Lumber Corp.
2. The Lyons Agency   Lyons Agy. Inc.
3. D. L. Marie Insulation Co.   Marie and Alex Landscapers

Turn to page 41 to check your answers.

HOW TO FORMAT NAMES IN RULE 7 ON A FILE CARD

NAME—Kars Ltd. of NY

```
    KARS LTD OF NY
```

FILING PRACTICE

Complete Job 9 of the *Practice Materials*.

RULE 8   Punctuation in Business and Organization Names

Ignore any punctuation marks that appear in business and organization names. Just as with personal names, hyphenated business and organization names are treated as one unit.

Punctuation marks include the apostrophe ('), colon (:), comma (,), dash (—), exclamation point (!), hyphen (-), parentheses (), period (.), question mark (?), quotation marks (" "), and semicolon (;).

NAME	UNIT 1	UNIT 2	UNIT 3
"Doc" Roberts Tires	DOC	ROBERTS	TIRES
Eller-Wyrick Auto Parts	ELLERWYRICK	AUTO	PARTS
Freedom Rent-a-Car	FREEDOM	RENTACAR	
Oh Joy! Footwear	OH	JOY	FOOTWEAR
Tennis, Anyone? Inc.	TENNIS	ANYONE	INC
Victoria's Country Kitchen	VICTORIAS	COUNTRY	KITCHEN

Can You Apply Rule 8?

In each of the following pairs, which name will be filed first and why?

1. Dalton TV Center   Dalton's Appliances
2. G-Z Computer Software   G Z Company
3. Rub-a-Dub Coin Laundry   Charlene D. Ruben

Turn to page 41 to check your answers.

HOW TO FORMAT NAMES IN RULE 8 ON A FILE CARD

NAME—"Doc" Roberts Tires

```
DOC ROBERTS TIRES
```

FILING PRACTICE

Complete Job 10 of the *Practice Materials*.

RULE 9   Numbers in Business and Organization Names

Arabic numerals (2, 17) and Roman numerals (II, IV) are considered one unit and are filed in numeric order before alphabetic characters. All Arabic numerals precede all Roman numerals. Hyphenated numbers (7–11) are indexed according to the number before the hyphen (7); the number after the hyphen (11) is ignored. The letters *st, d,* and *th* following an Arabic numeral are ignored. Thus 1st is indexed as 1, 2nd as 2, 4th as 4, and so on.

If a number in a business or organization name is spelled out (*First* Street Pizza), it is filed alphabetically as written. Hyphenated numbers that are spelled out (*Twenty-One* Restaurant) are considered one unit (*TWENTYONE* RESTAURANT). An Arabic numeral followed by a hyphen and a word (7-Gable) is considered one unit (7GABLE).

NAME	UNIT 1	UNIT 2	UNIT 3	UNIT 4
7 Dwarfs Fun Park	7	DWARFS	FUN	PARK
7-11 Food Store	7	FOOD	STORE	
7th Heaven Waterbed Co.	7	HEAVEN	WATERBED	CO
12 Drummers Music Shop	12	DRUMMERS	MUSIC	SHOP
101 Frozen Yogurt Parlor	101	FROZEN	YOGURT	PARLOR
1200 Abernathy Apts.	1200	ABERNATHY	APTS	
Forty-Four Frozen Flavors, Inc.	FORTYFOUR	FROZEN	FLAVORS	INC
Four Score Miniature Golf	FOUR	SCORE	MINIATURE	GOLF
Fourteen and Under Sportswear	FOURTEEN	AND	UNDER	SPORTSWEAR
The Fourth Dimension Studio	FOURTH	DIMENSION	STUDIO	THE

(continued)

(continued)

NAME	UNIT 1	UNIT 2	UNIT 3	UNIT 4
Gloria's 7-Gable Restaurant	GLORIAS	7GABLE	RESTAURANT	
Gloria's Action Video Room	GLORIAS	ACTION	VIDEO	ROOM
Harrisburg 6 Screen Cinema	HARRISBURG	6	SCREEN	CINEMA
Harrisburg Five Star Cinema	HARRISBURG	FIVE	STAR	CINEMA

Can You Apply Rule 9?

In each of the following pairs, which name will be filed first and why?

1. 110-210 Garden Apartments   110 Trombones Music Outlet
2. Nine Hole Pitch and Putt   9 Knights Motel
3. 1st Security Corp.   1-Fine Pastry Shop

Turn to page 41 to check your answers.

HOW TO FORMAT NAMES IN RULE 9 ON A FILE CARD

NAME—7 Dwarfs Fun Park

```
7 DWARFS FUN PARK
```

FILING PRACTICE

Complete Job 11 of the *Practice Materials*.

RULE 10   Symbols in Business and Organization Names

If a symbol is part of a name, the symbol is indexed as if spelled out, as shown here:

Symbol	Indexed As
&	AND
¢	CENT *or* CENTS
$	DOLLAR *or* DOLLARS
#	NUMBER *or* POUNDS
%	PERCENT

NAME	UNIT 1	UNIT 2	UNIT 3	UNIT 4
89th Sun & Tan	89	SUN	AND	TAN
The 89¢ Freezie Stop	89CENT	FREEZIE	STOP	THE
A & J Deli	A	AND	J	DELI
$ Way Discount Center	DOLLAR	WAY	DISCOUNT	CENTER
We're # One Books	WERE	NUMBER	ONE	BOOKS

Note: If the $ sign is used with a number, file first under the number.

Can You Apply Rule 10?

In each of the following pairs, which name will be filed first and why?

1. A #1 Used Cars   A Nifty Hair Salon
2. C & J Oil Co.   C and B Draperies
3. 99 Hot Dog Stand   The 99 Bayshore Townhouses

Turn to page 42 to check your answers.

HOW TO FORMAT NAMES IN RULE 10 ON A FILE CARD

NAME—89th Sun & Tan

```
89  SUN  AND  TAN
```

FILING PRACTICE

Complete Jobs 12 through 14 of the *Practice Materials*. Information about cross-referencing business and organization names appears on page 37.

RULE 11   Government Names

Government names are indexed first by the name of the country, state, county, or city. The distinctive name of the department, bureau, or board is considered next. U.S. federal government names are indexed first under *United States Government.*

Federal Government Names. In each of the following examples of federal government names, Unit 1 is *United,* Unit 2 is *States,* and Unit 3 is *Government.*

NAME	NAME AS INDEXED
Forest Service U.S. Department of Agriculture	UNITED STATES GOVERNMENT AGRICULTURE DEPARTMENT OF FOREST SERVICE
Customs Service U.S. Treasury Department	UNITED STATES GOVERNMENT TREASURY DEPARTMENT CUSTOMS SERVICE
Internal Revenue Service U.S. Treasury Department	UNITED STATES GOVERNMENT TREASURY DEPARTMENT INTERNAL REVENUE SERVICE

State and Local Government Names. Following are examples of state and local government names.

NAME	NAME AS INDEXED
Police Department Fairborn, OH	FAIRBORN POLICE DEPARTMENT FAIRBORN OH
Department of Recreation Montgomery County Christiansburg, VA	MONTGOMERY COUNTY RECREATION DEPARTMENT OF CHRISTIANSBURG VA
Division of Motor Vehicles Department of Transportation Commonwealth of Virginia Richmond, VA	VIRGINIA COMMONWEALTH OF TRANSPORTATION DEPART- MENT OF MOTOR VEHICLES DIVISION OF RICHMOND VA
Department of Education State of Georgia Atlanta, GA	GEORGIA STATE OF EDUCATION DEPARTMENT OF ATLANTA GA
Public Works Department Town of Peru Peru, IN	PERU TOWN OF PUBLIC WORKS DEPARTMENT PERU IN

Foreign Government Names. Following are examples of foreign government names.

NAME	NAME AS INDEXED
Commonwealth of Australia Ministry of Finance Federal Republic of Brazil Department of Natural Resources	AUSTRALIA COMMONWEALTH OF FINANCE MINISTRY OF BRAZIL FEDERAL REPUBLIC OF NATURAL RESOURCES DEPARTMENT OF

Can You Apply Rule 11?

In each of the following pairs, which name will be filed first and why?

1. United States Mining Corporation *Government*   3. State of Alaska High-
   U.S. Department of Transportation X   way Commission
2. Chicago Finance Department   State of Alaska, De- *parks*
   Town of Chester Planning Department X   partment of Parks *Department*
                                                                       OF
Alaska State of
Highway Commission

Turn to page 42 to check your answers.

HOW TO FORMAT NAMES IN RULE 11 ON A FILE CARD

NAME—Forest Service
U.S. Department of Agriculture

```
UNITED STATES GOVERNMENT
    AGRICULTURE DEPARTMENT OF
    FOREST SERVICE
```

FILING PRACTICE

Complete Job 15 of the *Practice Materials*.

RULE 12   Addresses

When names are otherwise identical, they may be filed by address. The elements of the address are considered in the following order: city, state, street name, and house or building number.

NAME	UNIT 1	UNIT 2	UNIT 3	UNIT 4	UNIT 5	UNIT 6
Pizzahouse	PIZZAHOUSE					
Bennington		BENNINGTON				
Vermont			VERMONT			
Pizzahouse	PIZZAHOUSE					
Charleston		CHARLESTON				
South Carolina			SOUTH	CAROLINA		
Pizzahouse	PIZZAHOUSE					
Charleston		CHARLESTON				
West Virginia			WEST	VIRGINIA		
Pizzahouse	PIZZAHOUSE					
1800 Todd Avenue		NEWARK				
Newark, Delaware			DELAWARE	TODD	AVENUE	1800

(continued)

(continued)

NAME	UNIT 1	UNIT 2	UNIT 3	UNIT 4	UNIT 5	UNIT 6
Pizzahouse 237 Victor Boulevard Newark, Delaware	PIZZAHOUSE	NEWARK	DELAWARE	VICTOR	BOULEVARD	237
Pizzahouse 23000 Victor Boulevard Newark, Delaware	PIZZAHOUSE	NEWARK	DELAWARE	VICTOR	BOULEVARD	23000

Note: When addresses are otherwise identical, the house or building number is considered in numeric order. Therefore, for the last two names in the above examples, *237* is filed before *23000*.

Can You Apply Rule 12?

In each of the following pairs, which name will be filed first and why?

1. Hamburger Heaven, Allendale, Pennsylvania
   Hamburger Heaven, Billings, Montana
2. Richfood Stores, Sterling Boulevard, Tampa, Florida
   Richfood Stores, 427 Tuckahoe Way, Tampa, Florida
3. Latham Servicenter, 742 Axton Parkway, Sacramento, California
   Latham Servicenter, 18090 Axton Parkway, Sacramento, California

Turn to page 42 to check your answers.

HOW TO FORMAT NAMES IN RULE 12 ON A FILE CARD

NAME—Pizzahouse
        Bennington
        Vermont

PIZZAHOUSE BENNINGTON VERMONT

FILING PRACTICE

Read pages 37 and 38. Then complete Jobs 16 through 21 of the *Practice Materials*.

CROSS-REFERENCING BUSINESS AND ORGANIZATION NAMES

As with individual names, a record should be filed under the caption by which it is most likely to be requested. Cross-referencing business and organization names may be necessary under the following circumstances:

1. When an organization is best known by its initials or other abbreviated name, it should be filed under the initials and cross-referenced under the complete name.

NAME	FILED UNDER	CROSS-REFERENCE
IBM	IBM	INTERNATIONAL BUSINESS MACHINES

2. When the business may have some records under the name of an individual with the designation *d/b/a* (doing business as), while other records are filed according to the name of the business.

NAME	FILED UNDER	CROSS-REFERENCE
Jones' Auto Repair	JONES AUTO REPAIR	JONES JOHN (d/b/a Jones' Auto Repair)

3. When the name of the business or organization contains the complete name or initials of an individual and the last name has been commonly used to refer to the business.

NAME	FILED UNDER	CROSS-REFERENCE
J. C. Penney	J C PENNEY	PENNEY J C COMPANY

4. While many records are filed under the name of a business or individual, a subject heading may be more appropriate. For example, an office may have one or more sources of computer repairs, and keeping the information filed under a subject heading would be more logical than dividing it among the companies that actually do the work.

FILED UNDER	CROSS-REFERENCE
COMPUTER REPAIRS	ACE COMPUTER SERVICE
COMPUTER REPAIRS	SPEEDY COMPUTER SERVICE

5. When the business is known by a coined name or a name which differs from the dictionary spelling, the business would be filed according to the spelling it uses and cross-referenced under the dictionary spelling.

NAME	FILED UNDER	CROSS-REFERENCE
Bill's U-Rent	BILLS URENT	BILLS YOURENT
Bilt-In Cabinets	BILTIN CABINETS	BUILTIN CABINETS
Cap'n Doss Surf'n Shop	CAPN DOSS SURFN SHOP	CAPTAIN DOSS SURFING SHOP

6. When a business has a name change because of sale, incorporation, or other reason, you may need to cross-reference it under the old name until all records have been changed to the new name.

PRESENT NAME	FORMER NAME	FILED UNDER	CROSS-REFERENCE
Food Lion	Food Town	FOOD LION	FOOD TOWN
Dorsey & Will, Inc.	Dorsey Products Co.	DORSEY AND WILL INC	DORSEY PRODUCTS CO

The illustration below shows an acceptable format for a business or organization cross-reference card.

```
IBM

SEE INTERNATIONAL BUSINESS MACHINES
```

Can You Cross-Reference Business and Organization Names?

Indicate the file and cross-reference captions for each of the following names:

1. American Automobile Association, best known as AAA
2. Foliage & Flowers (formerly The Blossom Shop)
3. Geneva Phillips d/b/a Geneva's Country Inn
4. Office Supplies obtained from Newton Company and Office Design, Inc.
5. R U Hungry Deli
6. George Washington University

Turn to page 42 to check your answers.

VARYING THE INDEXING RULES

While the twelve rules you have learned are used by businesses and organizations in the United States, it is sometimes necessary to make modifications.

For example, if your business deals with numerous professionals, such as doctors and lawyers, you may choose to file by last name, as shown in the third column.

BUSINESS NAME	INDEXED AS	ALTERNATE INDEXING
Donald Irons, Attorney, Inc.	DONALD IRONS AT-TORNEY INC	IRONS DONALD AT-TORNEY INC

Whatever variations are developed, it is important that they be followed consistently by everyone who uses your files.

GENERAL REVIEW

1. Give six examples in which the cross-referencing of business and organization names may be necessary. (Competency 3)
2. Give an example in which the indexing rules might be varied or changed in special circumstances. (Competency 4)

You practiced Competencies 1 and 2 in the *Practice Materials*. The following indexing review will reinforce your ability to identify indexing units.

INDEXING REVIEW

A. What is the first indexing unit of each of the following names?
   1. U.S. State Department, Washington, D.C.
   2. Sun Shade Awning Co.
   3. Mrs. Dove's Modeling School
   4. The Pie Shop, Ltd.
   5. 2-Way Truck Rental
   6. "Blue Horizons" Motel
   7. 55th Street Bakery
   8. First National Bank
   9. K & B Equipment Company
   10. University of Alabama

B. What is the *second* indexing unit of each of the following names?
   1. Casa DelMar Apartments
   2. Chester, Dunn, & Lewis, Attorneys
   3. Department of Education, State of Illinois
   4. Dominion of Canada, Finance Department
   5. United Van Lines
   6. Union 86 Oil Co.

7. Jose Corillo Elementary School
8. Rath-Vermilyea Agy.
9. North Gate Shopping Ctr,
10. # 1 Credit Co.

C. What is the *third* indexing unit of each of the following names?

1. Dell-Green Mobile Park
2. We-Guard-Your-Life Security Service
3. Eddie's Upholstery of Chicago
4. University of North Carolina
5. KXTV Television Station
6. Cayuga County Board of Health
7. Dr. Wells' 2-4 One, Inc.
8. 1900 Product Lines
9. Hotel Sun & Sand
10. Rid a Bug Exterminators

D. Alphabetize the names in each of the following groups. On a separate sheet of paper, list the letters to indicate the correct alphabetic order.

1. a. Heart's Department Store
   b. Hearts 4-U
   c. Jack of Hearts Card Shop
2. a. Memorial Hospital
   b. Memorial High School
   c. Mayor's Restaurant
3. a. Canadian Imports
   b. Dominion of Canada, Department of Trade
   c. Domestic Imports, Inc.
4. a. U.S. Interstate Commerce Commission
   b. Inter State Trucking Co.
   c. Inter-State Movers
5. a. First National Bank
   b. First Avenue Bank
   c. 1st National Bank
6. a. Triangle Steel & Supply
   b. Tri-City Shopping Center
   c. Tricycle and Toy Shop
7. a. KNOR Radio Station
   b. KTAZ Television Station
   c. K-9 Obedience School
8. a. Dulany's Spuds, 13 Third Avenue, Garden Grove, Kansas
   b. Dulany's Spuds, 98 Third Avenue, Garden City, New York
   c. Dulany's Spuds, 1136 Third Avenue, Garden City, New York
9. a. Hotel Jamestown

    b. Hotel James-Kelly *2*

    c. The Hot-1, Inc. *1*

10. a. Hodges High School *3*

    b. Hodges City Police Department *2*

    c. Andrew Hodges Art Supplies *1*

CASE PROBLEMS

1. You work for an insurance agency that writes policies for small local businesses. Your clients are primarily small firms, many of which have unique names such as U R #1 (a fast-food hot dog stand), Whatta Resta Rant, and A Reel World (fishing equipment store). You have trouble finding some of these files. What suggestions do you have to make these unusual names easier to locate? (Competencies 3, 4)

2. You have a co-worker, Ali, who decides to file many pieces of correspondence his own way rather than following the rules. As a result, several important papers have been lost. How can you convince Ali to follow the rules? What will you do if you find that Ali never learned the indexing rules?

ANSWERS TO CAN YOU APPLY THE RULES?

RULE 6

1. Cheryl Quillen Computer Store. *CHERYL* precedes *QUILLEN*.
2. T G Market. *T* precedes *TGL*.
3. Eldorado Springs Hotel. *ELDORADO* precedes *ELRANCHO*.

RULE 7

1. Central Lumber Co. Inc. *CO* precedes *CORP*.
2. The Lyons Agency. *AGENCY* precedes *AGY*.
3. D. L. Marie Insulation Co. *D* precedes *MARIE*.

RULE 8

1. Dalton TV Center. *DALTON* precedes *DALTONS*.
2. G Z Company. *G* precedes *GZ*.
3. Rub-a-Dub Coin Laundry. *RUBADUB* precedes *RUBEN*.

RULE 9

1. 110-210 Garden Apartments. *GARDEN* precedes *TROMBONES*.
2. 9 Knights Motel. *9* precedes *NINE*.
3. 1st Security Corp. *1* precedes *1FINE*. (1st is indexed as 1.)

RULE 10

1. A Nifty Hair Salon. *NIFTY* precedes *NUMBER1*.
2. C and B Draperies. *B* precedes *J*.
3. The 99 Bayshore Townhouses. *BAYSHORE* precedes *HOT*.

RULE 11

1. U.S. Department of Transportation. *GOVERNMENT* precedes *MIN-ING*.
2. Town of Chester Planning Department. *CHESTER* precedes *CHICAGO*.
3. State of Alaska Highway Commission. *HIGHWAY* precedes *PARKS*.

RULE 12

1. Hamburger Heaven, Allendale, Pennsylvania. *ALLENDALE* precedes *BILLINGS*.
2. Richfood Stores, Sterling Boulevard, Tampa, Florida. *STERLING* precedes *TUCKAHOE*.
3. Latham Servicenter, 742 Axton Parkway, Sacramento, California. *742* precedes *18090*.

ANSWERS TO CAN YOU CROSS-REFERENCE BUSINESS AND ORGANIZATION NAMES?

FILED UNDER	CROSS-REFERENCE
1. AAA	AMERICAN AUTOMOBILE ASSOCIATION
2. FOLIAGE AND FLOWERS	BLOSSOM SHOP THE
3. GENEVAS COUNTRY INN	PHILLIPS GENEVA (d/b/a Geneva's Country Inn)
4. OFFICE SUPPLIES	NEWTON COMPANY and OFFICE DESIGN INC
5. R U HUNGRY DELI	ARE YOU HUNGRY DELI
6. GEORGE WASHINGTON UNIVERSITY	WASHINGTON GEORGE UNIVERSITY

4

INDEXING FOR COMPUTER DATABASES

COMPETENCIES

Upon completing this chapter, you will be able to:

1. Define the terms *database, file, record, field, character, ASCII,* and *case sensitivity.*
2. Establish name fields for computer databases.
3. Index names of individuals for computer databases.
4. Index names of businesses and organizations for computer databases.
5. Index subject names for computer databases.

In Chapters 2 and 3 you learned the rules for indexing the names of individuals, businesses, and organizations. These rules apply whether records are kept on paper or on computers. However, there are some special procedures that must be followed in indexing names that will be stored and processed by computer. In this chapter you will learn these procedures and be prepared to enter names into a computer as well as design a record that will be stored on a computer.

TERMS YOU WILL USE

A group of computer files is called a *database.* For example, if a company keeps its customer, vendor, and employee files on a computer, the three groups of files are referred to as a database.

A computer *file* is a group of related records. For example, records of all

✶ DATABASE – a group of computer files
FILE – a group of related records, records of all customers

customers compose the customer file. A *record* contains information about one individual or item. For example, an employee record contains information about one employee; an inventory record has information about one product.

Each record is divided into parts called *fields*. A field is a group of *characters* (letters, numbers, special characters, or spaces) that make up an item of information. In an employee record, for example, there will be a field for social security number and a field for the employee's name, among others.

FOUR LEVELS OF INFORMATION IN A DATABASE

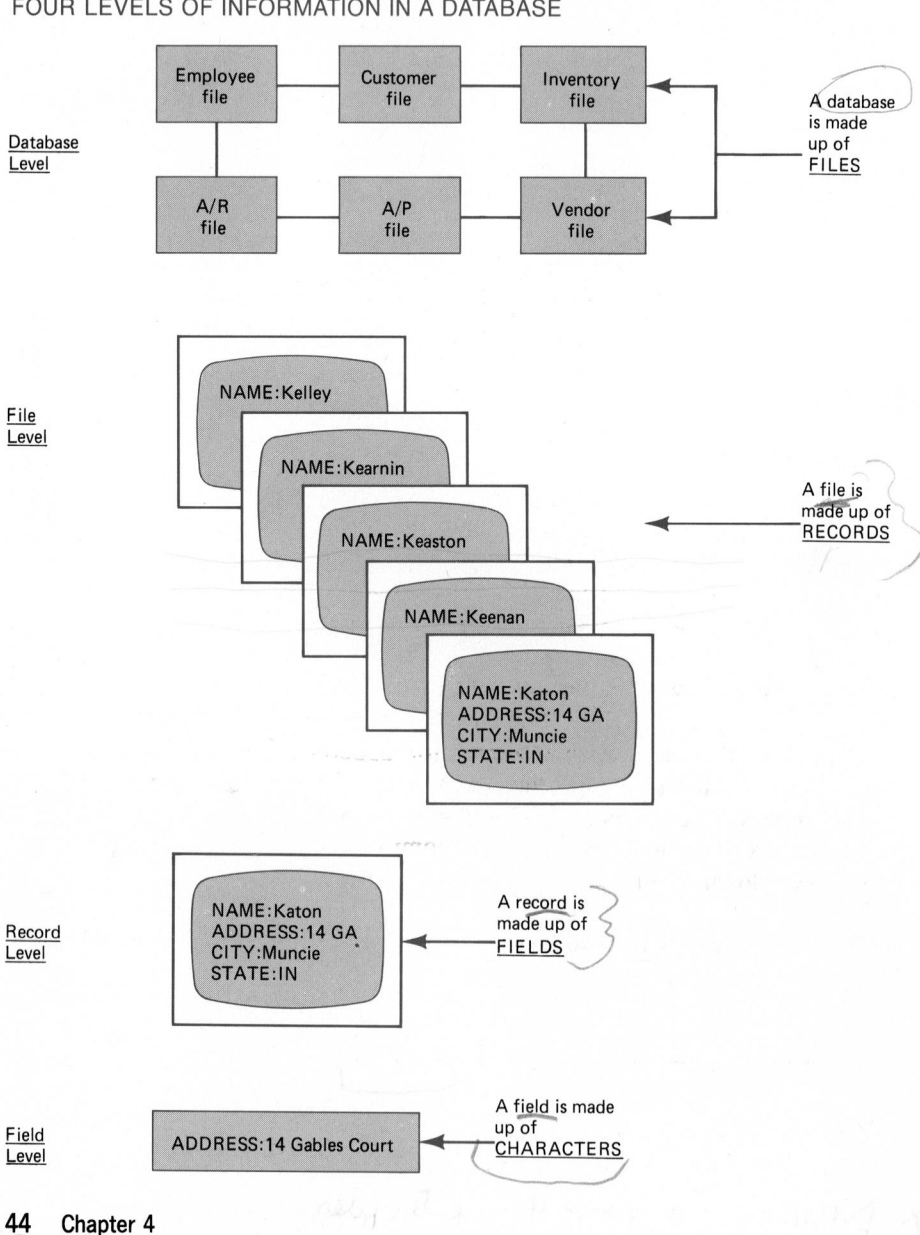

Database Level — A database is made up of FILES

File Level — A file is made up of RECORDS

Record Level — A record is made up of FIELDS

Field Level — A field is made up of CHARACTERS

44   Chapter 4

ASCII - CODE - all characters that are keyboarded
into computer are recorded by a code.
American Standard Code for Information Interchange

All characters that are keyboarded into a computer are immediately recorded by the computer as a code. The code is called *ASCII,* which stands for American Standard Code for Information Interchange. (ASCII is pronounced ask-ee.) It probably will not be necessary for you to learn the specific codes in ASCII. It is important that you know these facts about ASCII:

1. Most computer database programs sort information according to ASCII.
2. The codes are different for uppercase letters and lowercase letters.
3. In ASCII, the general sequence for sorting is:
   a. Space
   b. Special characters and punctuation marks *, ' * : ; - @*
   c. Numbers, 0–9
   d. Uppercase letters, *A–Z*
   e. Lowercase letters, *a–z*

```
        6-12 Department Store
        Anderson Tiles
        Dietrich-Yano
        Dietrichson
        MacGruder Paints
        Macadonia Trucking
        Smith & Larson
        Smith and Breslow
        Tolleson Electronics
        Tolleson and Bretano
        Cummins advertising
```

These names have been sorted according to the ASCII code.

Case sensitivity — computer is sensitive to, aware of difference between

Because ASCII codes are different for uppercase letters and lowercase *R, r* letters, we say that *case sensitivity* exists. That is, the computer is sensitive to, or aware of, the difference between, say, an *R* and an *r*. Case sensitivity can cause problems when we instruct a computer to sort names alphabetically. Note the following example:

NAMES AS ENTERED IN COMPUTER	NAMES AS SORTED BY COMPUTER
MacWilliams	MacWilliams
Mackey	Mackey

Due to case sensitivity, *MacWilliams* is incorrectly sorted before *Mackey.* This is because all of the uppercase letters, including the *W* in MacWilliams, have a smaller ASCII code value than all of the lowercase letters, including the *k* in Mackey. One solution to this problem is to enter database names in all uppercase letters. Note this example:

NAMES AS ENTERED IN COMPUTER	NAMES AS SORTED BY COMPUTER
MACWILLIAMS	MACKEY
MACKEY	MACWILLIAMS

Now, because all letters have the same "case," the names are sorted into correct alphabetic order.

ALPHABETIZING VS. INDEXING

Computers *can* alphabetize, or sort, names very quickly and accurately if you have correctly allowed for case sensitivity. However, most of the computers with which you will work *cannot* index names. You must do the indexing by applying the twelve indexing rules when entering names into a computer database.

ESTABLISHING DATABASE FIELDS FOR INDIVIDUAL NAMES

Before you enter individuals' names into a computer database, consider how the names are to be used. For example, if the names are to be used in a word processing system to address letters, then you want them to be printed on the inside address with the first name first, or in standard form. The standard form of a name may be keyed with upper- and lowercase letters like this:

Judith G. Merriweather

or in all uppercase letters and without punctuation as in the envelope address form recommended by the U.S. Postal Service:

JUDITH G MERRIWEATHER

For word processing, you would *not* use this form:

Merriweather, Judith G.

The above form, of course, is quite acceptable if the names are to be listed in alphabetic order on a class roll or other roster containing only a few names.

In a computer database, then, there are different ways to key names into name fields for different applications. Several examples are:

1. NAME:Ralph R. Reid } Standard form
2. NAME:RALPH R REID }
3. NAME:Reid, Ralph R. } Indexed, or transposed, form
4. NAME:REID RALPH R }

5. LAST NAME:Reid   FIRST:Ralph   MI:R.
6. LAST NAME:REID   FIRST:RALPH   MI:R

Examples 1 and 2, in which the name appears in standard form, might be useful for word processing but will not permit sorting other last names should you want an alphabetized list. Examples 3 and 4, which are in indexed form, would not be useful for word processing but will permit sorting by last name. However, Example 3 could cause sorting problems because the name contains punctuation and both upper- and lowercase letters.

If a record contains only the name of an individual, multiple name fields such as Examples 5 and 6 may be used. The advantage of multiple name fields is that sorting may be done on last name *and* the name can be printed in standard form for use in word processing applications. However, Example 5 may cause sorting problems due to punctuation and case sensitivity. Also, multiple name fields cannot be used if individual and business or organization names are mixed in the same file.

As a general rule, enter names of individuals into a database as follows:

- If names must be printed out in standard form *(Ralph R. Reid),* as in the inside address for correspondence, *and* do not need to be sorted by name, enter the name in standard form (Example 1 or 2).
- If names must be sorted alphabetically *and* do not need to be printed out in standard form, enter the names in indexed form with all uppercase letters and no punctuation (Example 4).
- If names must be printed in standard form *and* sorted alphabetically, use multiple name fields (Examples 5 and 6).
- If names of individuals will be mixed with names of businesses and organizations and the names must be printed in standard form *and* sorted alphabetically, set up *two* name fields for each record:
  1. A name field (titled NAME) for the standard form (Example 1 or 2). *Lisa A. Cain*
  2. A name field (titled INDEXED NAME) for the indexed form (Example 4). *CAIN, LISA A.*

A payroll application may lend itself to this kind of name field for some database software:

NAME: R. R. Reid

Because only the initials appear before the last name, it is possible to sort on last name because all last names begin in the same position. The name can also be printed in standard form on a paycheck. *Caution:* if an employee does not have a middle name, spaces must be inserted to take the place of the second initial.

If you are designing a database record which contains a name field for an individual, you will have to decide how many spaces to allow for any one name. If a name is too long to fit in the spaces allowed, the name will have to be *truncated,* or chopped off at the end. Note the following examples in which the name *Marybella R. Rosencrantz* has been entered into fields which contain 22 spaces for the name:

1. NAME:ROSENCRANTZ MARYBELLA   (Indexed form)
2. NAME:MARYBELLA R ROSENCRANT   (Standard form)

In example 1, the middle initial, *R*, has been truncated. This truncation is acceptable because it is very likely that the person can be identified without the middle initial. In example 2, the last letter of the person's last name has been truncated. This truncation is probably not acceptable because the person's complete last name does not appear in the field. For this reason, you should plan to allow more space in a name field if the names are to be entered in standard form.

ESTABLISHING DATABASE FIELDS FOR BUSINESS AND ORGANIZATION NAMES

The name of a business or organization may be entered in a name field in several ways:

1. NAME:The Boston Travel Agency, Inc.
2. NAME:THE BOSTON TRAVEL AGENCY INC
3. NAME:Boston Travel Agency, Inc., The
4. NAME:BOSTON TRAVEL AGENCY INC THE

Examples 1 and 2, known as letterhead form, are satisfactory for word processing. Example 1 shows how many businesses prefer a name to appear on the inside address of a letter. Example 2 shows the form preferred by the U.S. Postal Service for mail address. Neither Example 1 nor Example 2 will permit alphabetic sorting according to the indexing rules, which say the *The* at the beginning of a name is indexed at the end. Example 3 may cause sorting problems due to punctuation and case sensitivity but will, at least, be sorted with the *B*s rather than the *T*s. Example 4, which is in indexed form, will sort correctly but may not look right as part of the inside address of a letter. None of the four examples is a perfect way to enter the name into a database. As a general rule, enter business and organization names into a database as follows:

- If names must be printed out in letterhead form, as in the inside address for correspondence, and do not need to be sorted by name, enter the name in letterhead form (Examples 1 and 2).
- If names must be sorted alphabetically and not printed out in letterhead form, enter the names in indexed form with all upper case letters and no punctuation (Example 4).
- Just as with individual names, if there are times when business and organization names must be printed in letterhead form *and* alphabetic sorting must be done, enter names into *two* name fields:
  1. A name field (titled NAME) for the letterhead form (Example 1)

2. A name field (titled INDEXED NAME) for the indexed form (Example 4)

INDEXING NAMES OF INDIVIDUALS FOR COMPUTER DATABASES

The rules for indexing the names of individuals for a computer database are basically the same as Rules 1 through 5 which appear in Chapter 2. The only one of the five rules that is not entirely "computer friendly" is Rule 5.

RULE 5:   Personal Names With Titles and Suffixes—*Titles*

Rule 5 states that a title or suffix is used only to distinguish between two or more identical names. Because computers do not distinguish between a name and a title or suffix, Rule 5 may not always be applied consistently when a computer database is instructed to sort names alphabetically. Two ways to deal with this problem are:

1. Allow a title or a suffix to be the last indexing unit whether two names are identical or not. Note these two examples:

RULE 5, CHAPTER 2	UNIT 1	UNIT 2	UNIT 3
Martha Huff, CPA	HUFF	MARTHA	(No third unit because names are not identical)
comes before			
Martha A. Huff	HUFF	MARTHA	A
because nothing comes before something			

RULE 5 MODIFIED FOR COMPUTER	UNIT 1	UNIT 2	UNIT 3
Martha A. Huff	HUFF	MARTHA	A
comes before			
Martha Huff, CPA	HUFF	MARTHA	CPA
because A precedes CPA			

2. Set up a separate field for titles and, perhaps, for suffixes. Use the address, social security number, or other information to distinguish between two identical names.

Another problem that computers might have with Rule 5 is the note that says: Numeric seniority terms *(II, III)* are filed before alphabetic terms. Luckily, the uppercase letter *I* in *II* and *III* comes before the *J* in *Jr.* However, if the seniority term goes as high as *V,* you will need to establish a rule to enter numeric seniority terms in computers as 2d, 3d, 4th, and 5th. As a general rule, it is a good idea to avoid using Roman numerals in computer databases. The reason is that Roman numerals, which are written with letters of the alphabet, will be sorted alphabetically, not numerically.

DATABASE MANAGEMENT PRACTICE

You should complete Project 1 of the *Computer Database Simulations* if they are available.

INDEXING NAMES OF BUSINESSES AND ORGANIZATIONS FOR COMPUTER DATABASES

As with individual names, the rules for indexing the names of businesses and organizations for a computer database are essentially the same as those you learned previously. Of the seven rules that deal with business and organization names, only Rules 9 and 11 are not completely "computer friendly."

RULE 9:   Numbers in Business and Organization Names

When a computer is sorting and encounters a number in a name field, the computer considers the number to be just another character but with a lower value than any of the letters of the alphabet. So, just as Rule 9 says, numbers come before letters. With computers, however, the difference is that *if numbers that are first units are to be arranged in correct order, they must be lined up at the right.* Note this example:

RULE 9, CHAPTER 3
14 Day Weight Loss, Inc.
comes before
121 Brands Foods
because 14 precedes 121

Now, notice what happens when the same two names are sorted in a computer database:

COMPUTER SORT
121 BRANDS FOODS
comes before
14 DAY WEIGHT LOSS INC
because
The first different digit at the left determines the order. (2 and 4 are different, and 2 precedes 4.)

The numbers sorted incorrectly because they are aligned at the left. They must be aligned at the right to sort correctly on a computer.

If you decide when you design your database record that you will have first-unit numbers with as many as, for example, four digits, you can align numbers at the right by inserting one or more zeros before numbers containing fewer than four digits. Note this example of the right-hand alignment of numbers.

COMPUTER SORT
0014 DAY WEIGHT LOSS INC
comes before
0121 BRANDS FOODS
because
The first different digit at the left determines the order. (0 and 1 are different, and 0 precedes 1.)

Note: It is usually not necessary to add leading zeros to numbers that are not first units.

RULE 11   Government Names

Depending upon the type of software used for your database, you may also have a problem with Rule 11. The first three units of all U.S. Government names are *United States Government* (24 characters). Some database software sorts on only the first several characters of a field, so government names and others that are identical beyond 8 to 15 characters should be abbreviated. The abbreviation *US GOV* takes only six characters, a savings of 18 characters for sorting and a great savings in computer entry and processing time. If names are similar beyond 18 to 24 characters, it may be efficient to assign additional fields for parts of the names. This suggestion applies especially to state and local government names and addresses.

> **DATABASE MANAGEMENT PRACTICE**
>
> You should complete Project 2 of the *Computer Database Simulations* if they are available.

INDEXING SUBJECTS FOR COMPUTER DATABASES

Some computer databases store information about products, processes, functions, and other topics. These topics or names of items are called *subjects*, and filing by topic is called *subject filing*. You will learn more about subject filing in Chapter 8.

Remember that if subject names in computer records have to be sorted, the same principles that you learned about establishing name fields for individuals, businesses, and organizations will apply.

Note the following product names from the files of a toy wholesaler:

MAC Skygazer Set
McDougal's Skateboard
Mr. Chef Cookset
Ms. Action Skydiver
The Real Deal Game

How should these names be entered into the product field of a computer inventory file? If an alphabetic printout of these and hundreds of other products will be needed, it is probably best that the subjects be entered in all capitals without punctuation marks. In addition, the rule about *The* at the beginning of a business name should apply. The five names, then, would be entered as follows:

MAC SKYGAZER SET
MCDOUGALS SKATEBOARD
MR CHEF COOKSET
MS ACTION SKYDIVER
REAL DEAL GAME THE

DATABASE MANAGEMENT PRACTICE

You should complete Projects 3 and 4 of the *Computer Database Simulations* if they are available.

GENERAL REVIEW

1. Define the following (Competency 1):
   a. database   e. character
   b. file   f. ASCII
   c. record   g. case sensitivity
   d. field
2. What should you consider before you enter names into a computer database? (Competency 2)
3. List four ways to key the name Yolanda G. Gomez into a field titled NAME. (Competency 2)
4. What is the advantage of multiple name fields for individual names? (Competency 2)
5. How might your name be entered in a name field in a payroll application? (Competency 2)

6. Distinguish between the standard form and the indexed form of an individual's name. (Competency 2)
7. Why might a person's name be truncated in a computer field? (Competency 2)
8. Distinguish between the letterhead form and the indexed form of a business name. (Competency 2)
9. Under what circumstances should a business or organization name be entered into a name field in letterhead form? (Competency 2)
10. Under what circumstances should a business or organization name be entered into a name field in indexed form? (Competency 2)
11. Under what circumstances should a business or organization name be entered into two name fields on the same record? (Competency 2)
12. What are two ways to deal with the fact that computers do not distinguish between a name and a title or suffix? (Competency 3)
13. Into what order will a computer sort the following Roman numerals? I, II, III, IV, V, VI, VII, VIII, IX, X (Competency 3)
14. What must be done to ensure that numbers which are first units will sort correctly? (Competency 4)
15. Why might government names sort incorrectly for some database software? (Competency 4)
16. In what format should subject names be entered into a computer field? (Competency 5)

CASE PROBLEMS

1. A university directory contains an alphabetic listing of all students—a total of more than 20,000 names. Under the letter *O*, several students whose last name is *O'Neil* are listed before students whose names are *Oakes, Obenchain,* and *Odom.* What might be the reason for the names not being in correct alphabetic order? What suggestion can you make to correct this situation? (Competency 2)
2. Consult your local telephone directory and answer the following questions:

   a. How are numbers which are part of business names indexed and sorted?
   b. Are all names arranged according to the filing rules presented here? If not, give examples of differences.
   c. Can you think of reasons why names in a telephone directory might appear in a different order from names in a sorted listing of the computer files of a business? (Competency 2)

3. For each situation listed below, write the field title or titles and the name *Darlene R. Honeycutt* the way it should be entered into the fields of a database. The first one has been answered as an example.

a. The person's name does not need to be sorted, and the name must be printed in standard form as part of the inside address of a letter.
Answer   NAME:Darlene R. Honeycutt

b. The name does not need to be sorted, and the name must be printed as part of the envelope address for a mailing.

c. The name needs to be sorted and listed alphabetically on a class roll containing 20 names.

d. The name must be printed in standard form and sorted alphabetically. (Note: Show two ways to enter the name for this situation, using multiple name fields.)

e. The name will be mixed with names of businesses and organizations. In addition, the name must be printed in standard form and sorted alphabetically.

f. The name will be entered in a single name field in indexed form. The field has room for only eighteen characters. (Competency 3)

4. For each situation listed below, write the field title or titles and the name *The Willoughby Advertising Agency, Inc.* the way it should be entered into the fields of a database.

a. The name does not have to be sorted, and the name must be printed as part of the inside address of a letter.

b. The name does not have to be sorted, and the name must be printed as part of the envelope address for a mailing.

c. The name must be sorted alphabetically but not printed in letterhead form.

d. The name must be printed in letterhead form and sorted alphabetically.

e. Using abbreviation, truncation, or both, how would you enter the name in a field titled INDEXED NAME if the field had room for only 17 characters? (Competency 4)

5. As a rental management company, Douglas Management Services requires listings of all property arranged first by house or apartment number, then by the street name, and finally by the name of the owner. The house or apartment numbers range in length from one digit to five digits. What general rule should be followed when entering house or apartment numbers into the database of Douglas Management Services? (Competency 2)

6. List at least ten subject captions that could be used to organize all of your personal records. Then write the captions the way they should be entered into a computer database. (Competency 5)

USING MANUAL SYSTEMS

COMPETENCIES

When you have completed this chapter, you will be able to:

1. State the differences among incoming, outgoing, and internal paper correspondence.
2. Give examples of how businesses organize paper records according to alphabetic, numeric, subject, and geographic filing.
3. Describe how to set up file drawers and list the equipment necessary.
4. Prepare file folder labels.
5. List and describe the steps in the path of incoming paper correspondence.
6. List and describe the steps in the manual filing process.
7. List and describe the steps for storing paper correspondence in a manual alphabetic filing system.
8. Index and code paper correspondence for filing, prepare cross-references, and practice filing and finding correspondence.
9. State what is meant by *card records,* list the advantages of card records, and give examples of uses of card records.
10. Name and describe the categories and sizes of card records.
11. Compare vertical and visible files.
12. State what is meant by *printed guide words* and *variable information* on business forms.
13. State the purposes and uses of business forms and give examples of forms used in business.

Manual systems of records management are used extensively in the business world. There are a number of standard procedures which apply to paper correspondence as well as to records on cards and forms commonly used by business.

CLASSIFYING CORRESPONDENCE

Correspondence in a manual system may be classified according to whether it is incoming, outgoing, or for internal distribution.

Letters, mailgrams, contracts, reports, or employment applications are considered incoming correspondence. Catalogs, price lists, brochures, newspapers, and magazines and other third-class mail pieces are also incoming correspondence, though most of these items are kept temporarily and discarded without filing.

Outgoing correspondence includes the same items as incoming except, of course, they are sent rather than received.

Mail for internal distribution will include many memos, in addition to other business papers.

ORGANIZING RECORDS FOR STORING

The four main manual filing systems, alphabetic, subject, numeric, and geographic, are mentioned in Chapter 1. These systems define the basic ways records are organized and stored for efficient retrieval of needed information. For example, in a school system where data on students is needed, an alphabetic system with students' names as folder captions would be selected. However, a purchasing agent responsible for buying hundreds of products would select a subject system with product names for folder captions. A real estate agent would select a geographic system with cities or districts or street names as captions, depending upon the area served. An insurance company would select a numeric system, because insurance policies are identified by number. As you can see in all of these examples, records are organized so that they are easy to find, or retrieve, when needed.

Whatever the needs of business or the organization, records are filed in a manual system according to the rules for indexing individual, business, and special names, which you studied in Chapters 2 and 3.

SETTING UP FILE DRAWERS IN A MANUAL SYSTEM

You have probably seen paper records housed in file cabinets or on open shelves in businesses you have visited. Nonpaper records, such as magnetic tape reels, microfilm, or floppy disks for computers, are housed in specially designed equipment. Whatever the type of equipment used, however, the main purpose is to make it easy to retrieve information when necessary. In this chapter, you will consider the basic arrangement of paper records stored in a file drawer. Basic equipment necessary for setting up a file drawer consists of file drawer labels, guides, folders, and folder labels.

File Drawer Labels. Each drawer should be properly labeled so that the contents can be identified quickly. Remember, the objective is retrieval. The caption on the label indicates the alphabetic range of the records housed there. Suppose the drawer contains records that begin with the name *Labarge* and end with the name *Myers.* The label or caption can be written either (1) as a single caption, with the single letter *L* to indicate where the alphabet records begin, or (2) as a double, or closed caption, with the two letters *L* and *M,* usually hyphenated *L–M,* to indicate where the sequence begins and ends.

File Drawer Guides. In correspondence files, cardboard or pressboard sheets called *guides* serve two purposes:

1. They separate the file drawer into distinct labeled sections which make it easier to locate specific records.
2. They support the records to prevent them from bowing and sagging.

Guide Tabs, Cuts, and Positions. Extending above the top edge of a correspondence guide is a *tab,* which identifies the alphabetic range of the records to be stored behind it. The guides are somewhat larger than the file folder and are described by the width of the tab, commonly called the *cut.* A *one-fifth cut* means that the tab extends along one-fifth of the top edge of the guide. A *one-third cut* means that the tab occupies one-third of the guide's top edge, and so on. A tab occupying the first one-fifth of the left edge of the guide as you face the file is said to be in *first position;* the second tab in the second one-fifth position from the left is said to be in *second position;* the third tab from the left in *third position,* and so on. Guides are said to be in a staggered arrangement when their tabs are in successive positions reading from left to right.

Guide Captions. Guide captions which are written or printed on the guide tabs identify the records filed behind them. In some systems, the caption can be typed or printed on a small strip of paper which is then placed into a metal or plastic holder on the guide.

On guides, the captions may be either single or double just as they appear on the file drawer. Captions may be words as well as letters. They should, however, be kept short for quick, easy reading. Single captions indicate where each section begins. The records to be filed after a single caption are those beginning with the caption on the guide tab up to, but not including, the caption on the next guide tab. The use of single guide captions makes expansion of the file easy because additional guides can be inserted wherever another subdivision is needed. Single captions may be easier to read than double

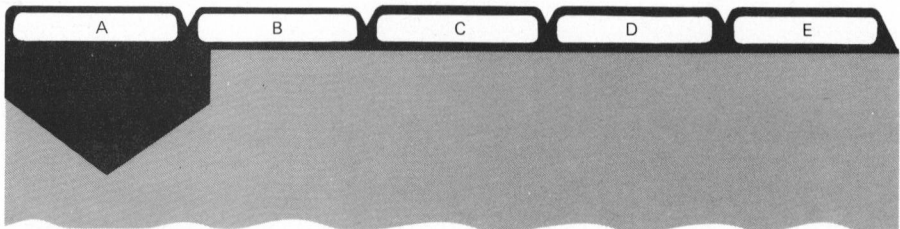

One-fifth cut staggered guides with single captions. Starting at the left, guides are in first, second, third, fourth, and fifth positions.

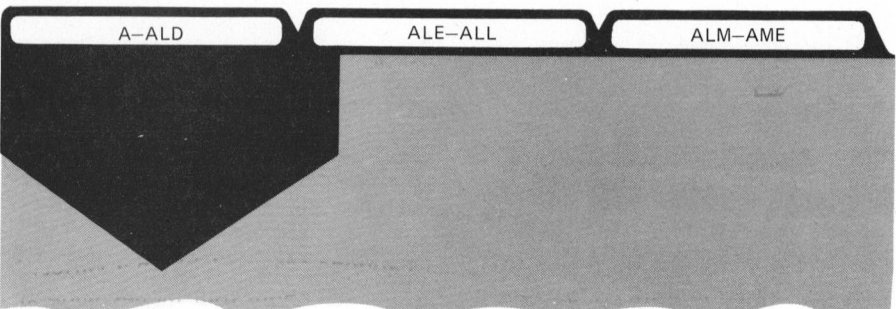

One-third cut staggered guides with double captions. Starting at the left, guides are in first, second, and third positions.

captions because they can be larger and thus more legible on the tabs. The advantage of the double caption is that it allows you to see the entire range of the section covered by a guide without looking at the next guide.

File Folders. File folders serve as containers for correspondence in the files. They are made of heavy paper that is folded so that all or part of the top edge of the back extends one-half inch or more above the front to form a tab. At the bottom of the folder are several horizontal creases called *scores* that permit expansion of the folder to hold up to 100 sheets of correspondence. (See illustration.) The first score on a folder should be broken for the first fifty sheets of paper; the second score should be broken to accommodate an additional fifty sheets in the folder.

Folder Tabs. The extended tab on the back of the folder provides a place for the title, or caption, of the folder contents. This caption is usually typed on a folder label, and the label is attached to the tab. Folders, like file guides, are available with tabs of various widths, or cuts. Folders can also be obtained with tabs in any one of the several positions along the top edge of the folder. Files can be arranged so that the tabs are in a staggered arrangement, or they can be arranged so that the tabs are all in the same position.

BREAKING THE FIRST SCORE ON A FILE FOLDER

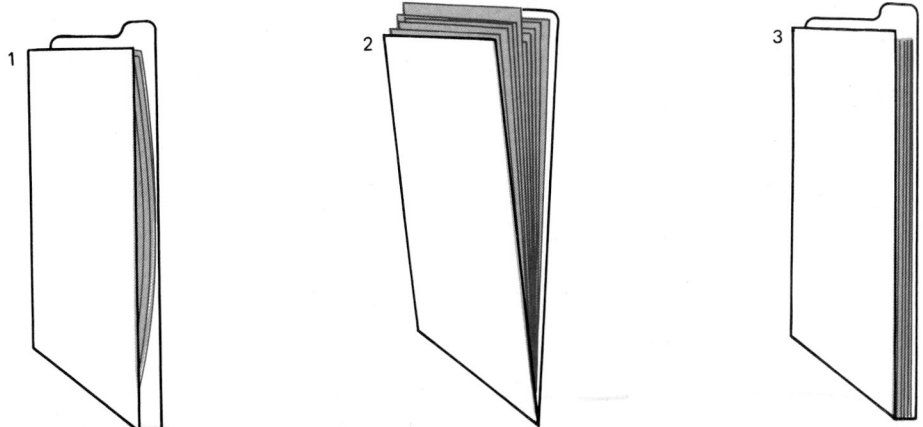

(1) Papers curl if scores on a file folder are broken too soon. (2) Papers ride up if scores are not broken soon enough. (3) When about 25 papers are filed, break the first score, and papers will stand straight.

Folder Labels. Gummed labels for folder captions are available in a variety of colors or in white with colored borders. They are about four inches wide and come in perforated strips, adhesive strips, or continuous rolls. High-speed computer equipment is able to print captions on long strips of file labels, or

TAB CUTS ON FILE FOLDERS

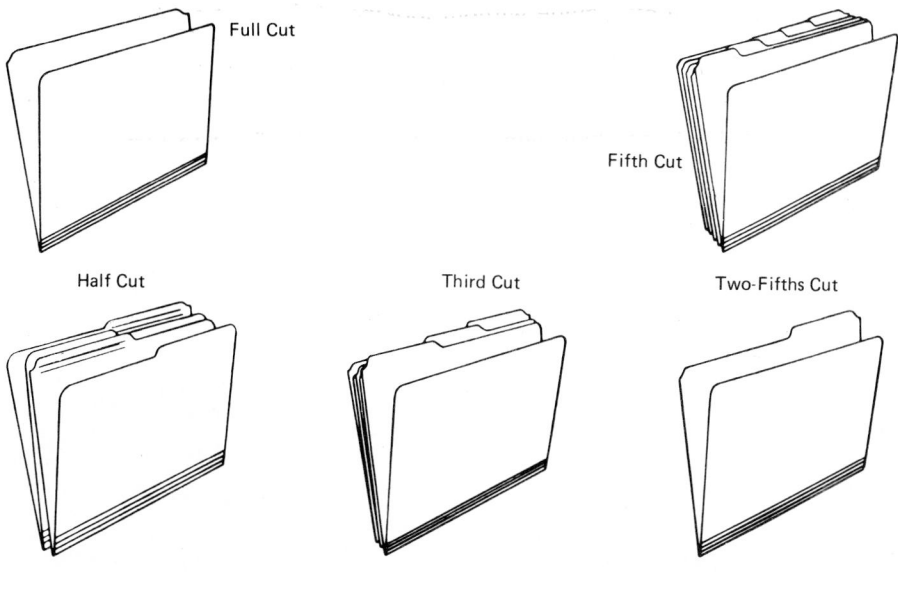

Full Cut

Fifth Cut

Half Cut

Third Cut

Two-Fifths Cut

the captions can be typed individually. If you don't have ready-made labels, you will find the suggestions below and on page 61 helpful in the preparation of file folder labels. You may at some time use labels which are folded into a front and back portion. The wider portion, if there is a difference, is always the front of the label and is the one on which the caption is typed.

Here are some suggestions for typing folder labels:

1. Begin typing the caption on the third space from the left edge of the label and on the second line below the top edge or crease. The caption should begin at the same place on every tab. Some tabs, particularly those that are white with a colored border, have small white marks in the border to indicate typing alignment. You may use these marks to achieve consistent placement of information on the label. Thus all first words on tabs of the same position will be in a straight line when they are placed in a file drawer. This makes it easier to read the labels and locate the file you need. It also creates a neater and more uniform appearance.

TWO OF MANY STYLES OF COLORED BORDER FOLDER LABELS

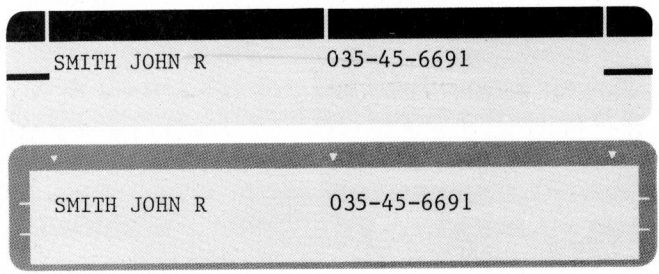

Notice how they are printed to follow the markings on the label.

2. The words of the items in the caption are typed in uppercase letters in indexing order. For example, the name *Jennifer Anne Allen* would be typed, ALLEN JENNIFER ANNE.
3. In most offices, punctuation, including the period after abbreviations, is omitted entirely.
4. Block style is preferred if the caption includes more than one item. If any item in the caption runs over to a second line, these words should be indented three spaces for clarity. Correctly typed and aligned folder captions are shown in the illustrations on page 61.

FILING PRACTICE

Complete Job 22 of the *Practice Materials*.

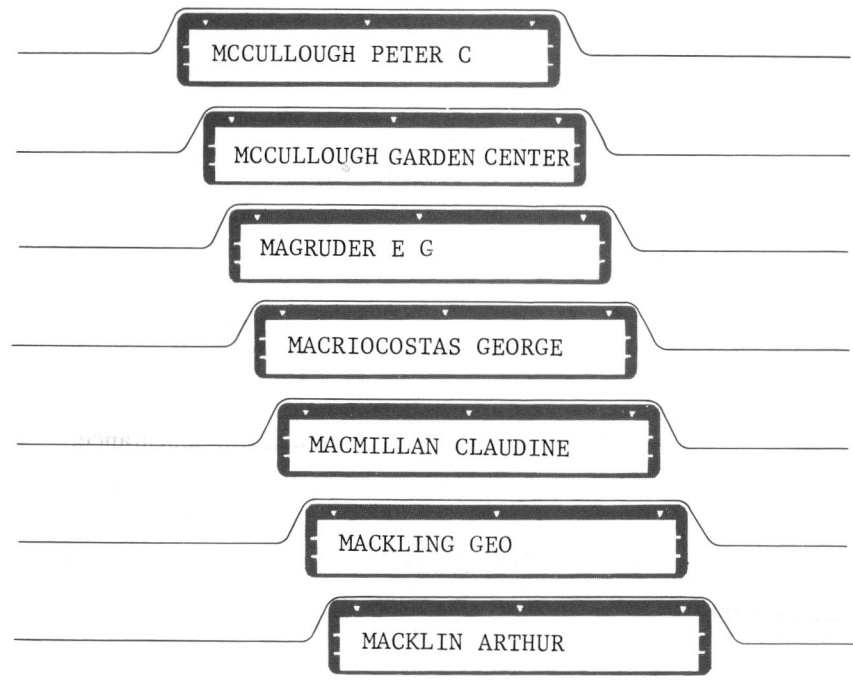

MCCULLOUGH PETER C

MCCULLOUGH GARDEN CENTER

MAGRUDER E G

MACRIOCOSTAS GEORGE

MACMILLAN CLAUDINE

MACKLING GEO

MACKLIN ARTHUR

ORGANIZING GUIDES AND FOLDERS

Alphabetic correspondence files generally have these elements: (1) primary guides; (2) special guides, also known as secondary or auxiliary guides; (3) individual folders; and (4) miscellaneous folders. These parts are shown in the illustration on page 62.

Primary Guides. Primary guides are placed at the beginning of each section in order to divide the file drawer into major alphabetic sections. If a file is small, it might be divided into only twenty-six sections, the first being *A*. In large filing systems, you might find several primary guides for each of the twenty-six alphabetic divisions. For example, the primary guides under the letter *A* could be *Aa, Ae, Ai, Ao, Au*. The *A* primary guide tells the file worker that all records behind it, up to the primary guide for *B*, concern those correspondents whose names begin with *A*. The tabs for primary guides are usually at the extreme left.

The advantages of rapid location and proper support of the folders are lost when there are too many folders behind one guide. As a general rule, each primary guide should have at least five, but not more than ten, folders behind it. Files become cumbersome and expensive to maintain where there are fewer than five folders behind each guide.

BASIC ALPHABETIC CORRESPONDENCE FILE DRAWER ARRANGEMENT

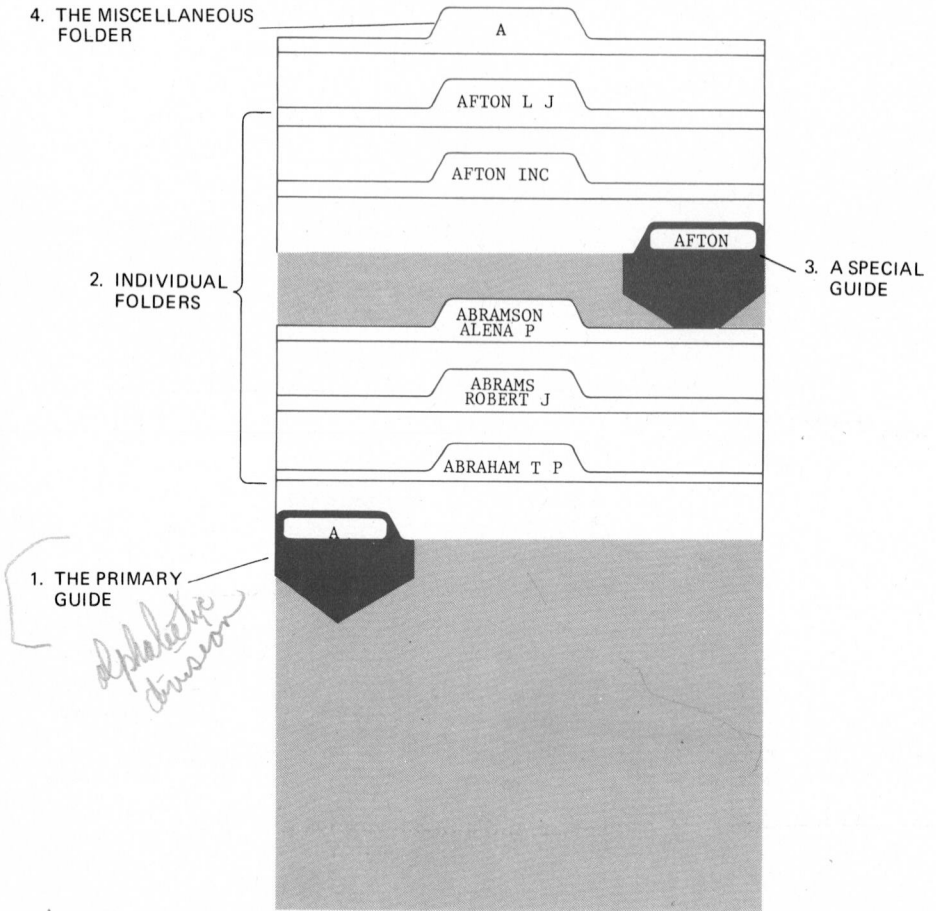

4. THE MISCELLANEOUS FOLDER

A

AFTON L J

AFTON INC

AFTON

2. INDIVIDUAL FOLDERS

3. A SPECIAL GUIDE

ABRAMSON ALENA P

ABRAMS ROBERT J

ABRAHAM T P

1. THE PRIMARY GUIDE

A

(1) The *primary guide* is located in front of the group of folders and special guides it controls. (2) *Individual folders* come *after* the guide and are arranged alphabetically. (3) A *special guide* is located in front of frequently consulted individual folders. (4) The *miscellaneous folder* comes *after* the individual folders. It has the same caption as the primary guide.

Special Guides. Special, auxiliary, or secondary guides are used after a primary guide to subdivide that section or to highlight names that are frequently needed. A special or auxiliary guide may be placed in any of the "cut" positions, depending on the arrangement of the file and the purpose of the guide.

Individual Folders. Individual folders are arranged alphabetically after each guide. Individual folders are not prepared until at least five records relating to a particular correspondent or subject have been received. You will recognize individual folders quickly in an alphabetic correspondence file because their tabs contain the full names of correspondents and because the tabs are usually wider than those on guides and miscellaneous folders. The tab position of an individual folder is generally in the center or to the right of center. The records in individual folders are arranged chronologically with the most current date in front so that the most recent correspondence will be easy to locate.

Miscellaneous Folders. Miscellaneous folders appear at the end of every group of individual folders. These folders are for correspondents who fall within the area defined by the primary guide but who do not have a sufficient number of records to warrant an individual folder. Miscellaneous folder tabs are usually to the left of the individual folder tabs. Within the miscellaneous folder, records are arranged alphabetically according to the name of the correspondent. If there is more than one record for a correspondent in the miscellaneous folder, these records are arranged chronologically with the most current first as in an individual folder.

PATH OF A LETTER

When a piece of correspondence is first received by the office staff, what happens? First, the incoming mail is processed. Then the letter is used for business purposes. When the individual using the letter is finished, the letter is "released" for filing. The last step before the actual filing process is the collection of the correspondence that is to be filed. (See the illustration on page 65.)

Processing Incoming Correspondence. Most organizations have a procedure for handling incoming correspondence. This procedure usually includes the following steps:

1. Correspondence received in a central mail department is sorted and distributed unopened to the various offices. Mail which is not identified is opened and then routed to the proper location.
2. Within each office, the administrative assistant or another individual will open and process the mail by:
   a. Checking to see that a return address is on the correspondence or the envelope
   b. Stamping the correspondence with the date and time to verify receipt
   c. Checking for enclosures
   d. Checking to see whether it can be handled by that office or needs to be routed to another office

Releasing Correspondence for Filing. After the mail has been processed, it is used by someone to conduct the business of the organization. After it has

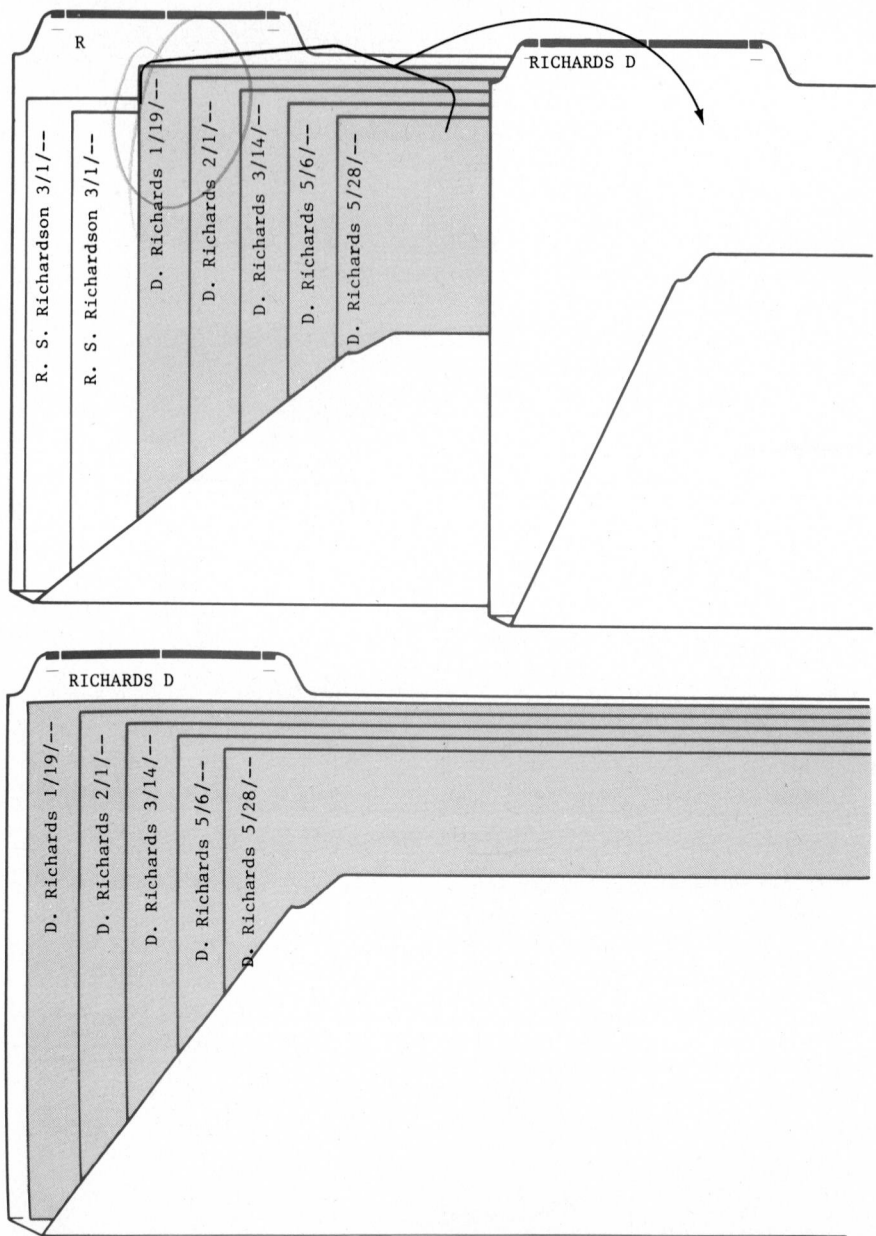

Since there are five letters from Don Richards in the Miscellaneous *R* folder, an individual folder is opened for that company and the letters are transferred to it. Letters in the individual folder are arranged by date, with the latest date in front.

PATH OF A LETTER FROM RECEIPT TO RELEASE OF FILING

Incoming correspondence is opened. The paper is then date-stamped and delivered to the user.

The user attends to the correspondence, places release marks on the paper to be filed, and places the paper in the out basket for delivery to the files.

been used, the correspondence is released for filing. A *release mark* is a notation that a letter is ready to be filed. A common release mark is the initials of the person using the record for the first time. These initials are placed in the upper left corner of the letter. Other release marks can be used, but it is important that the same mark be used consistently. Release marks are not necessary on photocopies of outgoing letters and interoffice memorandums.

Not all items of incoming correspondence or photocopies of outgoing correspondence will be filed. Many routine acknowledgments and relatively unimportant communications are discarded after they have been read or answered. The decision of whether or not to file should be made by the executive who handles the correspondence. (Detailed information about records control, backup, and retention is discussed in Chapter 10.)

Collecting Correspondence for Filing. A definite routine for collecting correspondence to be filed should be developed so that materials will be available in the files when needed. A special folder, out basket, or other means of designating material ready for filing should be used. This policy is especially important in a large corporation where thousands of pieces of correspondence are handled every day and where the work of hundreds of people is affected by the availability of records.

STEPS IN THE FILING PROCESS

Once correspondence has been released for filing, it travels through five distinct steps: (1) inspecting, (2) indexing, (3) coding, (4) sorting, and (5) storing. These steps are illustrated on page 67. All these steps will be followed by the individual who works with the files, whether an administrative assistant in a small office or a filing specialist in a large company.

Inspecting. Because the release mark is the authority to file, each piece of correspondence must be checked for it before being filed. If it has not been released, it should be returned to the person to whom it was assigned.

Indexing. When you learned the rules for filing in a manual system in Chapters 2 and 3, you practiced indexing the names you filed in your practice jobs or exercises. Indexing, as you learned, is the mental process by which you determine the name, subject, or other caption under which a piece of correspondence is to be filed.

There are several different clues to help you determine the caption:

1. The name on the letterhead (incoming correspondence)
2. The name of the person or organization addressed (outgoing)
3. The name in the signature (incoming)
4. The name of the subject discussed (incoming or outgoing)
5. The name of the geographic location about which the correspondence is concerned (incoming or outgoing)

STEPS IN CORRESPONDENCE FILING

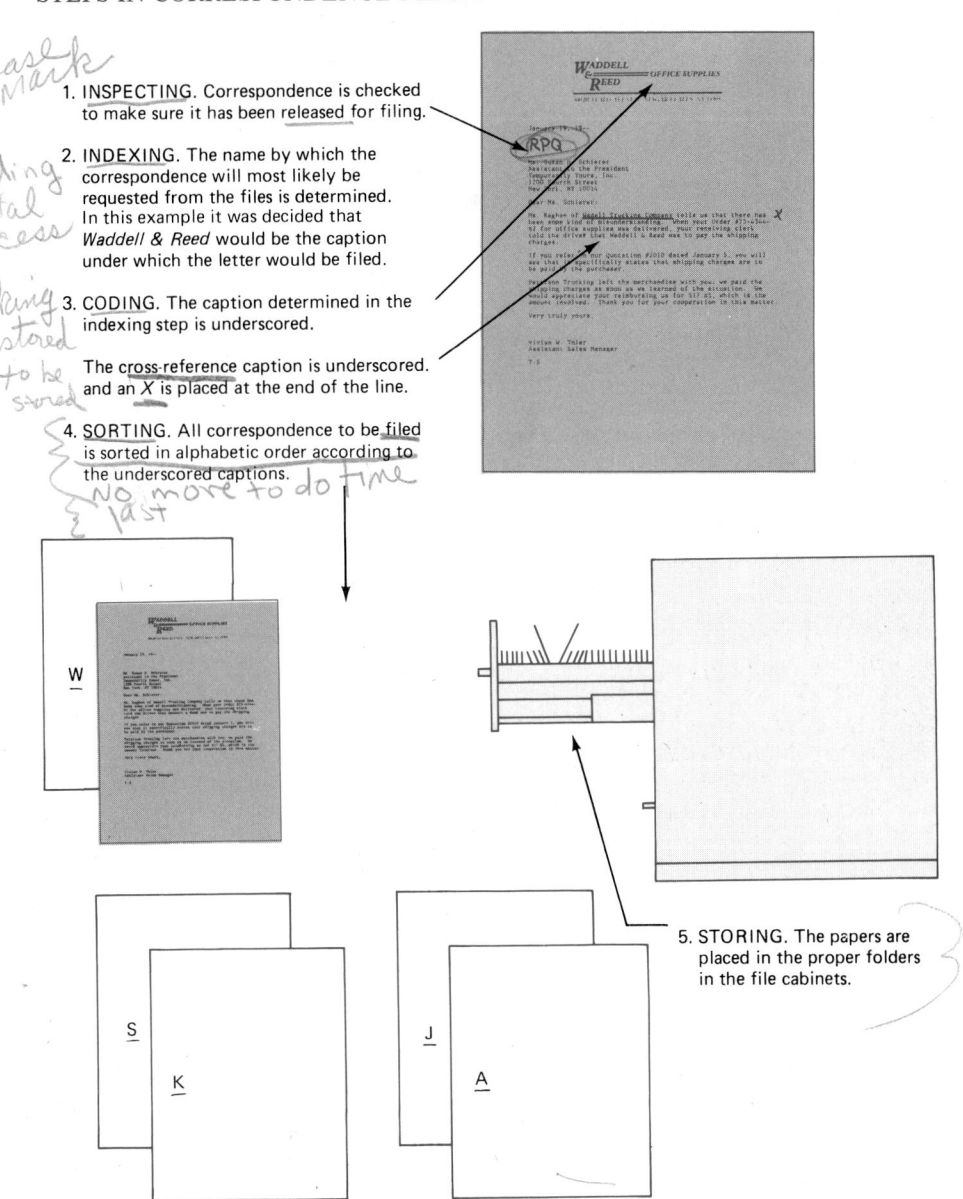

1. INSPECTING. Correspondence is checked to make sure it has been released for filing.

2. INDEXING. The name by which the correspondence will most likely be requested from the files is determined. In this example it was decided that *Waddell & Reed* would be the caption under which the letter would be filed.

3. CODING. The caption determined in the indexing step is underscored.

   The cross-reference caption is underscored. and an *X* is placed at the end of the line.

4. SORTING. All correspondence to be filed is sorted in alphabetic order according to the underscored captions.

5. STORING. The papers are placed in the proper folders in the file cabinets.

Coding. Indexing is the mental process of determining the caption under which the correspondence is to be filed. Writing or otherwise indicating the caption on the correspondence is known as *coding*. In alphabetic systems, there are two common methods of coding correspondence:

1. The caption, or name to be indexed, can be underlined, preferably with a colored pencil.
2. If the caption under which the correspondence should be filed is not mentioned in the body of the message or does not appear anywhere on the paper, the caption is written in the upper right corner of the correspondence.

Cross-Referencing. Correspondence should always be indexed and coded by the caption under which it is most likely to be requested from the files. It is possible that a piece of correspondence may be requested in one or more different ways. It should be filed under the most frequently used caption and cross-referenced under the others. You will recall that cross-referencing means placing a sheet of paper containing information about the actual location of a document (or a copy of the document) in all places in a file where a person might want to look for it. When it is necessary to cross-reference a piece of correspondence, the caption under which it is actually placed in the file should be underlined or written as explained in 1 and 2 above. The caption selected for the cross-reference should also be underlined or written, and in addition, an *x* should be placed at the end of the line or after the written caption to indicate that it is a cross-reference. A cross-reference sheet or a copy of the correspondence should be prepared at the same time. Most offices use a form such as the cross-reference sheet shown in the illustration on page 69 so that complete information is recorded in a consistent manner.

Sorting. Sorting is the process of arranging the records in alphabetic order after they have been coded, thereby speeding up the process of actually filing the records. Both rough and fine sorting of cards is explained in Chapter 2. The same procedure is used for sorting correspondence. In offices where there is a large volume of correspondence to be readied for the files, special sorting devices and equipment are used to simplify and speed up sorting.

Storing. The last step in this procedure, storing, is the actual placement of the records in the files. Correspondence is normally stored in file folders. Follow these step-by-step directions for storing records in file folders:

1. Take the sorted records to the proper file drawer, cross-check the label with the sorted record, and open the file drawer.
2. Using the guide captions as locators, scan the folder tabs until the caption under which the correspondence is to be stored is located. Guides, even those with metal tabs, should be handled as much as possible from the sides so that the tabs do not become bent and smudged. Occasionally, you should straighten the contents of the file drawer by pulling the bottoms of small groups of folders forward until they stand upright in the drawer.
3. Raise the folder (do not pull the tab of the folder because this will cause it to break off eventually) and rest it on the edge of the drawer.

A TYPICAL CROSS-REFERENCE SHEET

CROSS-REFERENCE SHEET

Name or Subject

REID TRUCKING COMPANY

Date

1/19/19--

Regarding

SHIPPING CHARGES ON ORDER 73-4344-82

SEE

Name or Subject

WADDELL & REED OFFICE SUPPLIES, INC.
300 BUFFALO AVENUE
NIAGARA FALLS, NY 14300

File cross-reference sheet under name or subject at top of the sheet and
by the latest date of papers. Describe matter for identification purposes.
The papers, themselves, should be filed under name or subject after "SEE."

Made in U.S.A.

4. Be sure that you have the proper folder. Compare the caption on the folder with the caption on the record being stored and with the caption on the top record already in the folder. Checking will take only a few seconds—time that may prevent many records from being misfiled and thus lost.

5. Place the record carefully in the folder with the heading to the left as you face the file so that the left side of the record will rest on the bottom of the folder. Within the individual folder, the most recent correspondence is placed on top; in other words, a letter dated May 22 would be placed on top of a letter dated May 15 of the same year. Placing the letterhead to the left of the folder ensures that it will be in correct reading position when the folder is pulled from the file and opened. Remember, overcrowding a folder causes the contents to ride up and obscure the caption and makes the folder difficult to handle.

STORAGE OF CORRESPONDENCE IN A FILE DRAWER

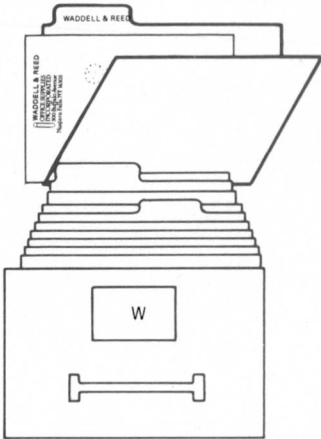

1. Locate the proper file drawer, using the guide captions as locators. Raise the desired folder and rest it on the drawer side.

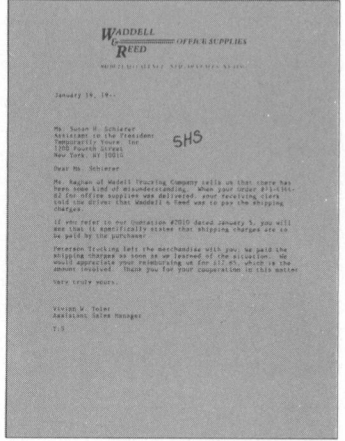

2. Compare the caption on the record to be filed with the caption on the record in the folder.

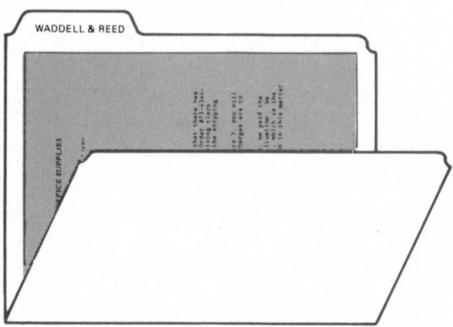

3. Place the record in the folder with the heading to the left.

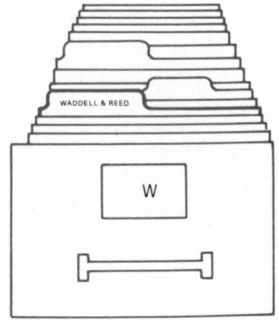

4. Carefully slide the folder back to the original position. Close drawer.

6. Make sure that the folder rests on the bottom of the drawer with the sides in a vertical position and that the caption is fully visible when you replace it.

7. If there is no individual folder for the record, all the individual folders in the section are pulled forward, exposing the miscellaneous folder for the section. The record is then placed inside the miscellaneous folder. The miscellaneous folder is placed behind the individual folders so that time is not lost looking for it if there is no individual folder for that particular record. Within the miscellaneous folder, correspondence is

filed alphabetically. If there are two or more pieces of correspondence for the same name, the most recent is placed on top as in the individual folder. When five pieces of correspondence for the same name accumulate, usually an individual folder is set up and the correspondence is removed from the miscellaneous folder and placed in the proper location in the file drawer.

There are file workers who like to use the bookmark method of removing file folders. In this procedure, the folder is lifted, but instead of being removed completely, it is raised at one end until the end rests on the edge of the drawer with about one-third of the folder exposed. In this position the file worker can insert the piece of correspondence in the folder and return it to its proper location. The bookmark method has the advantage of maintaining the folder's proper position in the file, thereby saving time.

FILING PRACTICE

Complete Jobs 23 through 27 of the *Practice Materials*.

CARD RECORDS

In addition to correspondence, much information is recorded and stored on cards. Card records and business forms are used for both internal and external purposes to tabulate, record, or transmit information as briefly and quickly as possible in a standardized, understandable format.

Card records are distinguished from correspondence in two ways: (1) They are smaller in size, and a heavier weight of paper is used for them. (2) They are not kept in folders as is correspondence. Card files are used both as indexes to correspondence filing systems and as independent records.

Advantages of Card Records. For organizing information, a card file has the following advantages:

1. Information can be inserted easily by the preparation of a new card.
2. Information can be deleted quickly by the destruction of an old card.
3. Information can be rearranged in any sequence—alphabetic, geographic, numeric, or subject.
4. A group of cards can be used by several workers simultaneously.
5. Some cards are designed so that they can be placed in certain business machines for automatic sorting, posting of data, and processing.

Purposes of Card Records. According to the purpose they serve, card records are classified as *index card records* or *posted card records*.

Index Card Records. Cards that are used to provide reference information are called *index card records*. The information on them does not change frequently. For example, the office address file, the index to numeric correspondence files, and the card index in a library are all forms of index card records. Much of this information is frequently kept on computers, but there are still numerous offices which use index card records.

Posted Card Records. Cards on which information is continually recorded are called *posted card records*. They too provide reference information, but the information on posted card records frequently changes. Posted card records are usually consulted for up-to-date information. Again, a great deal of information which was once kept on posted card records is now kept on computers. However, it is still to your advantage to understand posted card records. (There is an illustration of posted card records on page 75.)

Posted card records are used in business whenever there is a large number of products, customers, facts and figures, or other items to be referenced. For example, many firms have card files in their purchasing departments. On the cards in these files are names of suppliers and purchases made from them.

Sales records are often kept on cards. From these cards, management can easily determine sales volume according to territory, product, department, or salesperson. The cards need only to be rearranged to produce various categories of information. Likewise, computer database systems can be called upon to produce such categories of information. Sometimes customer accounts can be kept on cards that are placed in a machine for daily posting of both sales and receipts. A computer database system can also be designed to handle that task. A copy of the card may be sent to the customer at the end of the month as a bill. Inventory records are kept on cards so that records about new products can be easily added, records about discontinued products can be removed, and the quantity of a product on hand can be kept up to date on an independent record. The inventory record is also a part of many computer database systems.

Payroll records are another example of posted card records. A separate card for each employee contains such information as the names and ages of dependents, current salary, job title, and date of employment. (See Chapter 6 for a description of this process as part of a database system.)

TYPES OF CARD FILES

Card records may be stored in *vertical* card files or in *visible* card files (frequently referred to simply as *visible files*).

In vertical card files, cards stand upright in file drawers, like correspondence. In visible files, cards are stored in such a way that information may be read without handling the cards.

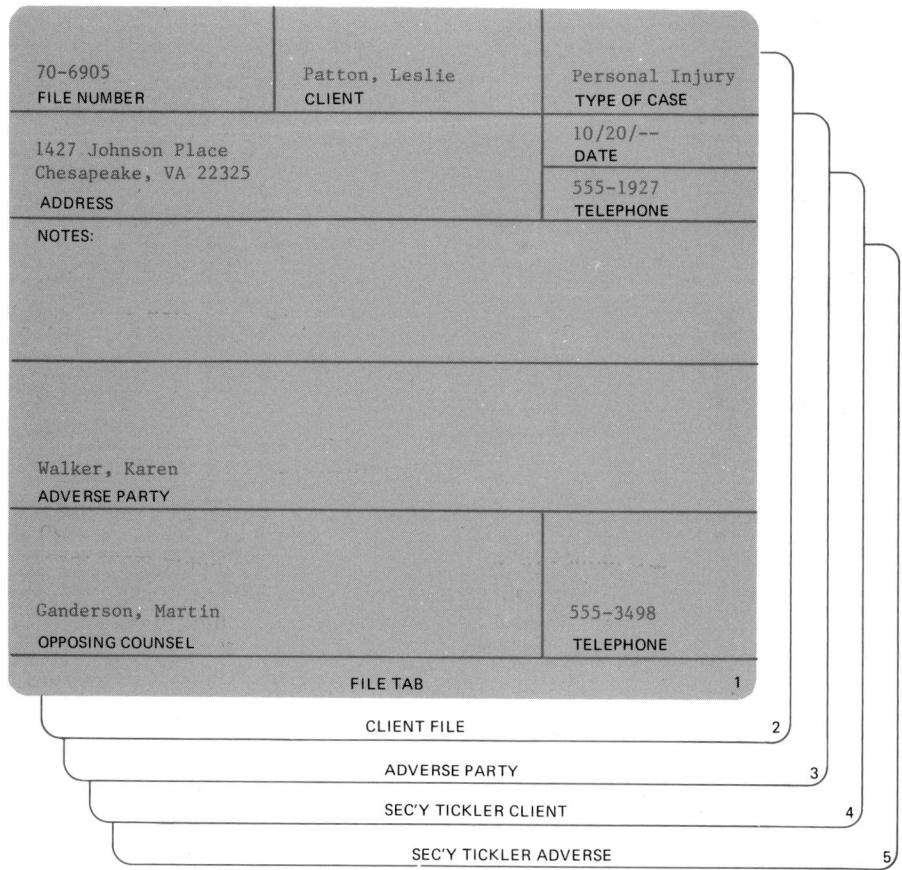

70-6905 **FILE NUMBER**	Patton, Leslie **CLIENT**	Personal Injury **TYPE OF CASE**
1427 Johnson Place Chesapeake, VA 22325 **ADDRESS**		10/20/-- **DATE** 555-1927 **TELEPHONE**

NOTES:

Walker, Karen
ADVERSE PARTY

Ganderson, Martin
OPPOSING COUNSEL

555-3498
TELEPHONE

FILE TAB	1
CLIENT FILE	2
ADVERSE PARTY	3
SEC'Y TICKLER CLIENT	4
SEC'Y TICKLER ADVERSE	5

A legal secretary might use this form with carbons for reference information to be placed in various files, as indicated at the bottom of each copy. The first form is attached to the client folder so that the top part serves as a folder tab.

Vertical Card Files. Vertical card files do not require folders because each card is an independent record that contains information about one name, address, location, topic, or product. Cards are relatively heavy, do not curl, and therefore stand vertically in the file without much support.

Standard Card Sizes. There are several standard sizes for cards. The first dimension given is the side on which the card rests when stored. They are generally 5 × 3 inches, 6 × 4 inches, and 8 × 5 inches.

The size of the card selected will depend on its use and the amount of information to be recorded on it. Cards used to record names and addresses of individuals need only be 5 × 3 inches to provide adequate space. A card

HOOD JAMES P
Nunnelly Insurance Co.
998 W. 47th Street
Norfolk, VA 23507

HOOD JAMES P Nunnelly Insurance Co., 998 W. 47th St.

The top card is for use in vertical files; the bottom, for use in visible files.

have guide   *no guide*

used to record health examination information, however, would normally need to be 8 × 5 inches, both sides being used to record all the necessary information in a compact format.

Information Placement. When cards are prepared for storing, the caption should be typed on the second line from the top of the card. All other key data should be as close to the caption as possible so that the card can be read without being removed from its container.

Guides. Whatever the size of the cards, there should be one guide in the file drawer for each twenty-five to fifty cards. For faster finding, vertical card files that are frequently referred to should have one guide for each twenty-five cards. In some vertical card files, in addition to the guides, each has its own tab, usually bearing a number. This greatly speeds up finding when cards are constantly removed from and inserted into the file. In most card systems, though, the cards have no tabs.

Visible Card Files. There are a great many types of visible card files available, such as (1) horizontal trays, (2) vertical racks, (3) open bins or tubs, (4) rotary wheels, (5) loose-leaf visible books. All of these types have an important feature in common, and it is from this feature that visible files get their name: *key information on each record can be seen without handling when the record is in storage* because the information is on a projecting edge. Thus visible files

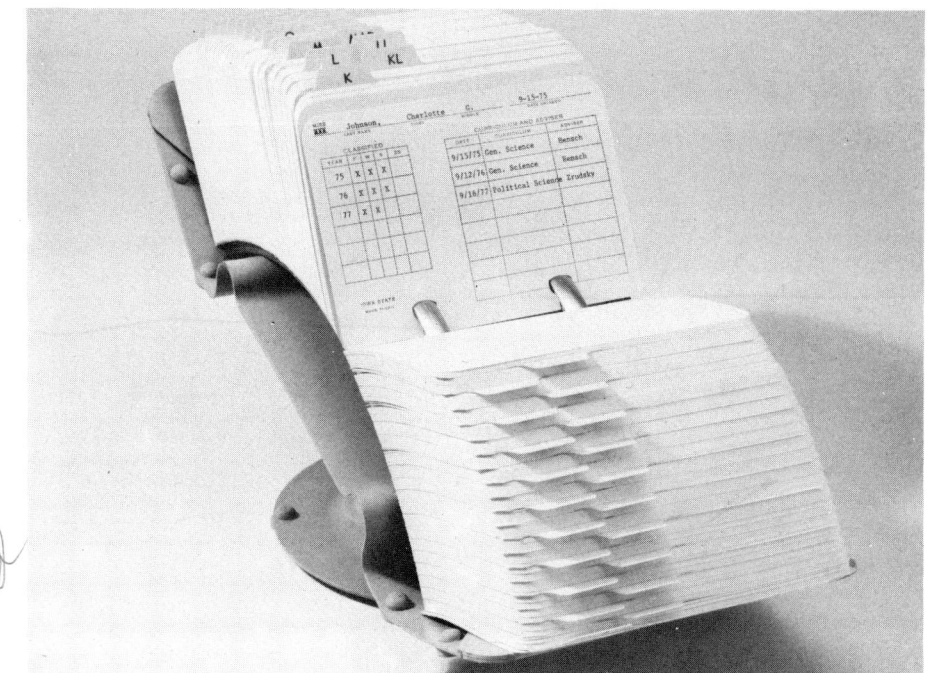

The administrative office of a school might use posted card records to maintain up-to-date data on students enrolled at the school. Courtesy Wheeldex, Division of LeFEBURE

are used when it is essential that information be found rapidly. For incoming calls, the telephone operator of a company might use a visible file to find extension numbers quickly so that important customers would be talking to executives in a matter of seconds. Similar systems are used in hotels so that incoming calls can be quickly connected to the proper room.

Visible files for posted records, such as inventories, are easy to keep up to date. With a drawer-type horizontal file tray, new inventory facts can be quickly posted or handwritten on the card. In addition, the card never has to be removed from its holder.

The requirements of the organization as to volume, location, portability, and use should determine the type of visible file to be used. Horizontal trays are well suited for posted visible records. Vertical racks are handy for quick reference to names, code numbers, and telephone numbers, while bins or tubs make excellent containers for machine-posted records. Rotary wheels provide fast reference to such information as addresses and credit data, and loose-leaf visible books, because they are portable, provide a quick reference to product information for traveling salespeople. It is important to note that all of these

Each of the two wheels on this motorized card file holds 5000 cards. Courtesy Wheeldex, Division of LeFEBURE

business activities have been turned over to computers in many, but not all, instances.

Standard Card Sizes. Cards for visible card files are similar to those used for vertical card files. The difference in the two types lies in the arrangement of the information on the cards.

Information Placement. Placement of the information to be typed or printed on visible cards will be determined by the arrangement of the file.

When visible record cards are being prepared, the caption should be typed as close as possible to the visible edge. Because the cards are often stored with their edges overlapping, the file worker should be certain that the caption is not obscured by another card.

Guides. Guides are not used in most visible files because each acts as its own guide. But certain facts, such as the quantity of a product on hand, can be made to stand out by using signals—colored plastic or paper strips, tabs, or clips that can be placed on the visible portion of a card. The position or color of the signals can be used to classify, schedule, and follow up such records as inventory, sales, accounts receivable, and accounts payable.

A visible file such as this one allows the worker to quickly find the desired card by reading the visible index on each card. It is set up with counterspace for manual posting of information. Courtesy Acme Visible Records, Inc.

BUSINESS FORMS

Most businesses use forms which are documents containing blanks or spaces for the insertion of requested information. They are used in offices to record and process information of a repetitive nature in an efficient way.

Forms are important carriers of business information and are the most frequently used record in many offices. Forms may be printed on paper of approximately the same weight and size as that used for correspondence, or they may be printed on cards.

Types of Information Recorded on Forms. Every business form has information printed on it and space for information to be added. Many computers are able to process and print scores of business forms such as invoices and the like quickly and efficiently by using tractor-fed paper which has previously printed guide words.

Printed Guide Words. The information which is already printed on the form is called *static information.* Examples are *pay to the order of, ship to, sold to, name, address, a*nd *telephone.*

variable

Variable Information. The information which is added to the forms in the blank spaces is called *variable information* because it may change with each form. A good example might be the address to which goods are shipped. When you complete a form, you are supplying variable information. Variable information may also be referred to as *fill-in information* or *fill-ins*.

PURPOSES OF BUSINESS FORMS

There are basically three purposes for the forms used in business.

Source of Input. Every business transaction must have a beginning. The original record of a business event is made on some type of business record. This original record is known as a *source document* or *source record*. For example, the original record for a weekly payroll is usually made on a time card for each employee. Each of these source records is a means for putting information into the business system; hence, the term *input* is used to describe their purpose.

Means of Processing Information. The purpose of a business system is to process, or change the form of, input data so that the information will be useful in the operation of the business. Processing operations include such activities as classifying, sorting, computing, recording, summarizing, and storing.

Information can be processed both manually and automatically, as you have learned. Three methods of processing information automatically that are commonly used in the business world are the following:

1. The equipment used by banks to process checks by means of magnetic ink character recognition (MICR) can also be used by business for processing card records.
2. Cards marked with special pencils can be read by optical scanning devices for computer processing.
3. Information can be entered into a computer, keyboarded by data-entry operators.

Means of Output. The results of processing are of value to the business only when they have been communicated to the proper persons for action. Processed data transmitted out of a system is referred to as *output*. Records that are used to report output data are *action records*. For example, the keeping of a customer's account, an intermediate record, is of no value to a business unless the customer eventually pays the debt. The monthly statement, which ideally prompts the customer to pay, is an action record in a sales system.

Many manual systems within businesses use cards and forms to process information. These may be purchases and accounts payable systems which ensure that merchandise for resale or raw materials are obtained and that

DATE October 12, 19--	PHONE RES. 555-3858				PHONE BUS. 555-1122					

1. John T. Magruder

2.

ADDRESS 1368 West Avenue, New York, NY 10025

STS	FROM	TO	CARR.	FLIGHT	CL.	DATE/DAY	LEAVE	ARRIVE	STATUS	OPTION	CONFIRMED DATE/BY	FARES	
	RIC	LAG	PI	501	Y	11/3/-- Wed	8:01A	9:06A			10/12 rk	66	00
	LAG	RIC	PI	502	Y	11/5/-- Fri	10:40P	11:45P				66	00

HOTEL RESERVATIONS	DATE IN	DATE OUT	NO. OF NIGHTS	RATE	TYPE	TOTAL	COMM.	
New York Hotel	11/3	11/5	2	51.00	single	102.00		
MISCELLANEOUS								
TRANSPORTATION						132.00		
					TOTAL	234.00		
					TAXES			
					TOTAL	234.00		
					DEPOSIT			
					BALANCE			
					PAID ON	11/2--		

This form serves as input since information on it is used to prepare tickets and an itinerary. Since data on it is used to process information, it also serves as an intermediate record. Front (above) and back of the card are shown. Courtesy, Willow Press, Inc.

payment is made for them at the proper time. They may be shipping and receiving records which ensure that outgoing products are sent promptly and economically and that incoming materials are received, checked, and delivered to the using department. They may also be cash records which ensure the proper control of money received and paid by the business. Inventory records are but another example; these records provide information for deciding what items need to be purchased in order to keep the quantity of materials or merchandise at a satisfactory level.

Correspondence, cards, and forms are also used as the input for the computer to maintain the records necessary for the business to operate on a daily

| Billing Date | Plus Current Charges |
| 12-04--- | 42.30 |

| GEO | Great Eastern Oil Company |
| | 127 Hartsdale Avenue, Dover, DE 19901 |

| Previous Balance | | | |
| 38.50 | Install No. | Plus Installments Conv. | Amount |

Less Payments	
38.50	Account Number
	2637322765

JAMES F. MACDONALD
128 HAWLEY ROAD
LATROBE, PA 15650

Payment due upon receipt of statement

Return this portion with your payment

Less Credits	
Past Due Balance	New Balance
Plus FINANCE CHARGE	New Balance
	42.30	42.30

Indicate change of address on return envelope by checking box

To avoid additional FINANCE CHARGES, new balance must be paid within 25 days after billing date except under extended payment arrangements as explained on reverse side.

FINANCE CHARGE SCHEDULE

	Unpaid Balance	Periodic Rate Per Month	ANNUAL PERCENTAGE RATE
To $	500	1-1/2%	18%
Over $	500+	1%	12%

| Account Number |
| 1 2637322765 |

If Not A Credit
Pay This Total

2637322765

This card serves three purposes: to bill the customer; to provide a receipt for the customer; to provide a record of payment by the customer. It is an example of an action record.

basis. Whatever the purpose, without records of this sort, the business could not function efficiently and effectively.

GENERAL REVIEW

The following questions will help you reinforce your learning of the competencies included in this chapter.

1. What items are included in incoming correspondence? Outgoing correspondence? Internal correspondence? What distinguishes each from the other two types? (Competency 1)

2. What are the four basic methods businesses use to organize records? Give an example of each of these uses in the business world. (Competency 2)

3. Describe how to set up a file drawer and list the equipment necessary. (Competency 3)

4. Give an example of a single caption for a file folder label. A double caption. (Competency 4)

5. What is the purpose of *guide captions*? (Competency 3)

6. What purpose do file folders serve? What are *scores*? What information is shown on a folder tab? (Competency 3)

7. How should you type information on file folder labels? (Competency 3)

8. What is the purpose of *primary guides*? What is the purpose of *special guides*? What is the purpose of *miscellaneous folders*? (Competency 3)

9. What is a *tab*? What is a *cut*? What does *first position* mean? (Competencies 3, 4)

10. What are the steps for processing incoming correspondence? (Competency 5)

11. What is a *release mark*? Why is it important in the filing process? Are all items of correspondence filed? (Competency 5)
12. Why is a routine for collecting correspondence for filing necessary? (Competency 5)
13. List and describe the steps in the manual filing process. (Competency 6)
14. List five clues to help you determine the caption of a piece of correspondence. (Competency 6)
15. What are two common methods for coding correspondence? (Competency 6)
16. How do you cross-reference correspondence? (Competency 6)
17. List and describe the steps for storing correspondence in a manual alphabetic filing system. (Competency 7)
18. What is the minimum number of records for an individual folder? How are these records arranged within the folder? (Competency 7)
19. What is the *bookmark method*? (Competency 7)
20. What are card records? Name three examples of card records. (Competency 9)
21. List the advantage of card records. Give examples of uses of card records. (Competency 9)
22. Name and describe the categories and sizes of card records. (Competency 10)
23. Compare vertical and visible files. (Competency 11)
24. State what is meant by *printed guide words* and *variable information* on business forms. (Competency 12)
25. State the purposes and uses of business forms and give examples of forms used in business. (Competency 13)

CASE PROBLEMS

1. You have been working in a small office for several weeks. You are having the following problems with the filing system. See if you can pinpoint the problems and advise your employer as to changes to be made.

   a. You can't read the labels on some folders because the correspondence in the folders rides up and covers them.
   b. Some folders are too low in the drawer and you have been missing them when you are filing. You then have to go back and look through the drawer again.
   c. You have to open two, sometimes three, drawers to find where a particular folder should be stored. The captions on the drawers are a single letter, and there are three or four drawers labeled with the same letter.
   d. You need to go through the entire drawer to find where a folder should be stored.

e. When there is no folder for a piece of correspondence, you have to make a new one even if there is only one letter to put in the folder. Miscellaneous folders are placed immediately after the primary guide for that section of the file drawer; these folders are usually empty.

   f. There seems to be no organization to the contents of the folders.

   What advice and suggestions can you give your employer to make filing easier? (Competencies 2, 3, 4, 6, 7)

2. Fitzgerald's, Inc., is a large wholesale operation with several branches nationwide. Richard Hypes works in the Central Filing Department at their main offices. Many people see correspondence before it is filed. Richard's job is to sort the correspondence, code it, and make sure that it gets stored properly. There have been some problems lately with correspondence which was not replaced in the files after the individual responsible was finished with it and which was therefore not available when needed by others in the firm. In addition, some items have been filed before action was taken. Raymond has been reprimanded for these situations, but since he files only what is brought to him by the various departments, he feels the criticism is unfair. What can he do, if anything, to help avoid these situations in the future? (Competencies 5, 6)

3. Tidewater Psychiatric Hospital uses a card index at its reception desk to supply information about the room locations of the patients. Currently the hospital uses a card index contained in a metal drawer-type file. The receptionist must go through the cards and pull out the one needed. From what you have learned in this chapter, what would be a better system of locating patients? In addition, the hospital would like to determine at a glance which patients are allowed to have visitors during general visiting hours and which patients have restricted visiting hours. Can you suggest a method which would help? Why would a card index be helpful for this kind of information instead of a list or other format? (Competencies 9, 10, and 11)

4. Many retail outlets record their inventory on cards, using a separate card for each item. Why are cards used instead of lists? Can any information be printed on the cards prior to inventory? (Competencies 9, 10, 11, 12, 13)

5. Caroline Wright recently finished college. She was hired to fill a new position as office manager of New Designs, Inc. One of the responsibilities she has been given is to suggest ways to make the files better serve the needs of the office staff. She discovered that no card files were used; all papers were housed in centrally located correspondence file cabinets. She recommended the purchase of card files and suggested five instances in which card files would save time for the employees. What are your ideas about when card files would be more efficient than correspondence files? (Competencies 9, 10, 11)

6. Bill Wiley uses forms in the office where he works. He feels that it would be just as easy to jot down the information he needs and eliminate the form. Do you agree with him? (Competencies 12, 13)
7. Business forms and cards are found in many places. Think of the different forms or cards that you have seen; classify each as a source of input, output, or an intermediate record. Name three source documents that you or someone you know has generated in the business community recently. (Competency 13)

6

MANAGING RECORDS USING ELECTRONIC DATABASE SYSTEMS

COMPETENCIES

Upon completing this chapter you will be able to:

1. Name three types of microcomputer software that may be purchased for filing records. *WP Database   Spreadsheet*
2. Define *hard copy, integrated package, filename, extension, directory, root directory,* and *subdirectory.*
3. List the steps in analyzing a paper system in preparation for creating a database system.
4. Discuss the limitations that must be observed in selecting filenames.
5. Discuss considerations to follow in naming documents.
6. Name four uses of the filename extension.
7. List the kinds of information that appear in a disk directory.
8. Explain why hard disk directories are said to have a tree structure.
9. List three ways to make disks easy to identify.
10. Name four problems associated with a poorly developed electronic database system.
11. Discuss the special requirements associated with invisible files.

12. Discuss guidelines for developing a workable electronic database system. *invisible - can't see hard copy, disk*

In addition to paper, or *hard copy,* files, many of the documents generated in the office today are stored on some type of magnetic or electronic media. Electronic filing systems may be found on mainframe computers, minicomputers, and microcomputers. The electronic media range from magnetic disk packs and magnetic tape to microcomputer disks. Managing these "invisible" filing systems creates unique challenges for the office professional who must file and find information stored on electronic media.

Though there are many types of electronic filing systems, this chapter emphasizes those competencies needed by the office professional who has a microcomputer workstation and deals largely with word processing and database management programs. The principles in this chapter can be applied to other systems using electronic media to store records.

TYPES OF ELECTRONIC DATABASE SYSTEMS

Several types of microcomputer software may be purchased for filing records. The software selected depends on the nature of the documents to be stored. The three major types are:

- *Word processing programs* such as DisplayWrite, Microsoft Word, MultiMate, Volkswriter, WordPerfect, and WordStar. These programs are designed for document preparation and are suitable for the creation of reports, letters, memos, tables, and mailing lists.
- *Database programs,* such as dBase and pfsFile, which are designed to create a form for rapid input of repetitive data. These programs are designed to input, sort, and extract data in a system that has a large number of records.
- *Spreadsheet programs,* such as Lotus 1-2-3 and Multiplan, which are used primarily for mathematical planning. These programs may include payroll, employee, inventory, and other files containing numeric information which may be used in calculations and retrieved for reference or update.

The type of software you select depends on how the records will be used. It is important to select software which has the broadest application and greatest flexibility for the work to be done in your office. Generally, information in one software product can be "imported" to be used with another. For example, a database mailing list may be used for form letters created by word processing software. However, compatibility between the two software packages is mandatory for an interchange to take place.

Another factor to consider in selecting software is the number of different software packages you should use. A software package that works for several applications, such as word processing, database, and spreadsheet, is called an *integrated* package. It may be more efficient for you to use an integrated package than to purchase, learn, and use three or four separate packages that each have a single function.

When selecting database software, ease of creating and completing forms should be considered if that is a frequent application in your office. Remember that labor is the highest cost in creating and maintaining files of any type. Therefore, true database software, rather than word processing or spreadsheet software, may be the most efficient for entering and processing data.

CREATING A DATABASE SYSTEM → to retrieve info.

Most database systems originate from existing paper systems. The need for the electronic system is evident when the paper system becomes too cumbersome for rapid access. To begin an efficient transition, first analyze the paper system for the following: *name – static never changes*

- *What fields are used?* For example, in a payroll record such fields as *last name, social security number, rate of pay,* and *withholding allowances* are used.
- *Which fields are unique in each record?* In an electronic database, each record must have at least one field containing unique data which identifies the record. This field is called the *key* field. Social security numbers are unique to each individual and telephone numbers are unique to each household. However, last names can be common to many people.
- *Which fields are now or could be converted to contain numeric data?* Because the computer uses less space to store numbers and because numbers are easier to read and more accurate to key than letters, electronic records should be planned to include numeric fields whenever possible.
- *How many fields are actually* needed *in the database?* If the business has frequent mailings, the ZIP code should be included as a field for sorting. A doctor may require a list of patients by treatment date, a salesperson may require a list of clients by telephone number. Note, however, that the more fields in the record, the more time it takes to create the record and the greater the risk of error. An analysis should be made of what data is *required* rather than what data would be "nice to have."

To ease the transition from paper to electronic files, a form should be developed to translate the current files to the database. In this way, consistent information, including any limitations on the number of characters for each field, can be specified. Some names may have to be truncated after ten characters, for example, so that several fields can be viewed at one time on the screen, which is usually eighty characters wide. Developing a form and putting the field data on each form will also point out any problems before the system is put in place. In a hospital, for example, while each adult patient may have a social security number, children under five may not. Or the social security number in the file may need to be that of the person responsible for the medical insurance, rather than that of the patient.

FILENAME LIMITATIONS

As with paper files, a caption must be selected for each document to be filed in a database. In an electronic system, a caption is known as a *filename*. The filename is the name assigned by the user to an item in the electronic file. With paper files there is no limit to the length of the name, the number of units, or which words or letter combinations may or may not be used. With electronic media, on the other hand, specific limitations must be observed in selecting the filenames under which documents are to be stored. The limitations restrict the database user to certain combinations and numbers of characters for filenames.

These limitations apply generally to the selection of filenames for documents filed on floppy or hard disks. You should consult the documentation for your specific software for additional guidelines and instructions.

1. A filename has two parts: the *name* and the *extension*. Every file must have a name. The extension is optional. The document name is usually limited to approximately eight characters, which may include letters, numbers, and some of the special symbols found on the keyboard. The extension is usually limited to three characters and may be separated from the name by a period.

2. The software you are using may allow you to use more than eight characters when you are creating a new name. However, it is likely that the long name will be truncated to eight characters for screen display. When you retrieve the document, you may have to key the full name in order to access the file. If a typographical error has been made in the truncated part of the name or the complete name has been forgotten, the document may never be recovered.

3. Certain names which are used by the disk operating system (DOS) may not be used. Consult your software documentation for these restrictions.

4. The extension, which is the part of the filename after the period, consists of up to three letters, numbers, or symbols. Some extensions are reserved for use by DOS or the program. Examples are BAT, BIN, COM, CRF, EXE, LST, MAP, OBJ, and SYS. Consult the documentation for the computer operating system and the programs to determine which extensions are reserved.

5. In Chapter 4 you learned that information may be entered in a database in either upper- or lowercase letters. You also learned that most databases sort uppercase letters ahead of lowercase letters. In other words, the programs are case sensitive. However, with most electronic media,

IBM on DOS

EXAMPLES OF FILENAMES

EXAMPLES OF FILE NAMES

Name	Explanation
ROBINSON	(Full name is 8 characters. No extension.)
SZYMANOW	(For Szymanowicz--truncated at 8 characters. Full name may have to be entered to access the file. Again, no extension is used.)
LETTER.XYZ	(Document type is less than 8 characters. Extension is used to identify the company that will be receiving the letter.)
LTR0130A.JK	("LTR" stands for the type of document--a letter. "0130" is the month and day. "A" means it is the first letter sent that day. "JK", the initials of the sender, make up the 2-letter extension.)

filenames may be keyed using either upper- or lowercase letters. When the filename is entered, the computer records all letters as uppercase. Thus, most programs are *not* case sensitive for filenames. A few word processing programs, however, *are* case sensitive for filenames, and would file *SMITH, Smith,* and *smith* as three separate documents.

6. In most cases, no spaces may be used between the characters of a filename. A space tells the program the name is ended. However, a few word processing programs *do* allow spaces within the names of documents.

HOW TO NAME DOCUMENTS

In spite of the limitations that apply to selecting filenames for documents on electronic media, the process can be relatively simple if the time is taken to establish a system which fits the needs of the organization. A review should be made of the existing files to determine the frequently used captions. Document names, though short, should be as descriptive as possible. While it is easy with paper files to use captions such as *Johnson, Soto, Nissir,* and *Sanchez Brothers,* adapting them to computer guidelines and avoiding duplication is not always easy. Any individual or business name of eight or fewer characters can be used in a database as a filename without change. Names longer than eight characters (unless allowed by the program) must be shortened.

If you, as the originator, send a letter to Maria L. Sanchez, you might decide to name the document SANCHEZ. Or, if you know ahead of time that you will write more than one letter to Sanchez, you might name the first letter SANCHEZ1. Then, the second Sanchez letter can be named SANCHEZ2. If you correspond with more than one person named Sanchez, you might use the first and middle initials after a truncation of the last name. For example, one file might be named SANCHML1 (for the first letter to M. L. Sanchez).

Another procedure is to assign document names which identify the originator. For example, Ali Hassan files his outgoing documents as HASSAN.

Some companies may choose to number consecutively all of their documents with the number appearing as a reference at the bottom of the hard copy. The number can be used to retrieve the document from a disk or other electronic medium. This technique is especially useful when a word processing center has a large number of clients, for example, and when no one client generates a large volume of documents.

USING FILENAME EXTENSIONS

The three-character filename extension can have many uses in the filing process in addition to those restricted to the computer program. Some programs allow for directory displays of documents by extension. Thus the operator can view a list of all documents created by M. W. Henderson, for example, if the initials, MWH, are used for the extension. Other uses of the filename extension are listed here.

1. A combination of three letters or numbers can be used to represent the months of the year and the days of the month. The first character represents the month:

Month		Month	
January	1	July	7
February	2	August	8
March	3	September	9
April	4	October	O
May	5	November	N
June	6	December	D

   A number, 01 through 31, is added to indicate the day of the month. For example, January 15 is represented by 115; November 5 by N05. While many computer programs include the date in the directory display, the date as part of the document name may also be helpful.

2. Extensions may be used to identify the type of document. Examples follow:

THIS TYPE OF DOCUMENT	MIGHT HAVE THIS EXTENSION
Report	RPT
Memorandum	MEM
Letter	LET or LTR
Table	TAB

3. Extensions may be used to identify the retention period of a document, or the length of time it should be kept in the files. Examples are:

THIS RETENTION PERIOD	MIGHT HAVE THIS EXTENSION
Temporary	TEM
Long Term	LTM
Permanent	PRM

4. Extensions may be used to identify the versions of a document as it goes through several stages of editing. For example:

THIS DOCUMENT VERSION	MIGHT HAVE THIS EXTENSION
Creation	V1
First revision	R1
Second revision	R2
Final	FNL

DISK DIRECTORIES

Both floppy-disk and hard-disk systems create a *directory*, which is a list of the documents stored on the disk by filename. As part of the filing process, directories should be set up to maximize the efficient retrieval of the documents. Shown below is a directory from a floppy disk with each item labeled.

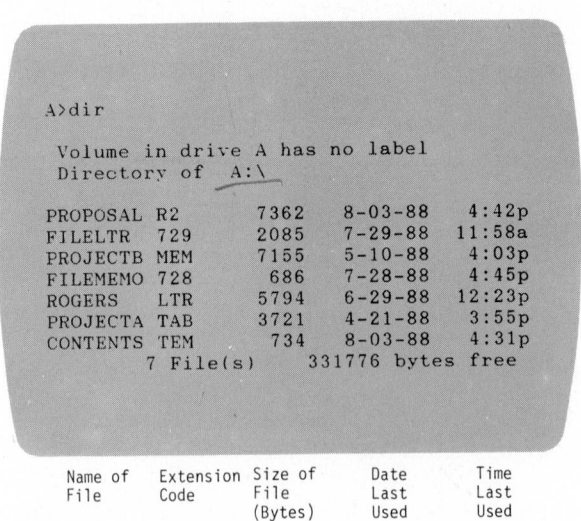

```
A>dir

    Volume in drive A has no label
    Directory of  A:\

PROPOSAL R2       7362    8-03-88    4:42p
FILELTR  729      2085    7-29-88   11:58a
PROJECTB MEM      7155    5-10-88    4:03p
FILEMEMO 728       686    7-28-88    4:45p
ROGERS   LTR      5794    6-29-88   12:23p
PROJECTA TAB      3721    4-21-88    3:55p
CONTENTS TEM       734    8-03-88    4:31p
         7 File(s)      331776 bytes free
```

| Name of File | Extension Code | Size of File (Bytes) | Date Last Used | Time Last Used |

Directory of diskette in A drive, normal format.

To ensure that a directory is usable and to avoid loss of important information, disks should not be filled to capacity. Higher density disks will hold hundreds of pages of documents, increasing the severity of the loss should something happen to the disk. Ideally, the number and type of files stored on any one floppy disk should be limited by factors such as the following:

1. A disk may be assigned to each originator.
2. A disk may be assigned to each major project.
3. A disk may be assigned to work done within a given period of time, such as a week or two.

Backup copies should be made regularly of all important work on disks.

HARD-DISK DIRECTORIES

Hard disks can hold hundreds of files, so the information on the hard disk must be carefully organized for retrieval to be efficient. The main directory of a hard-disk system is called the *root directory*. A root directory is illustrated below with each item labeled.

PARTIAL LISTING FOR A SAMPLE ROOT DIRECTORY

```
SORT        EXE      1911    12-30-88    12:00p
SUBST       EXE      9911    12-30-88    12:00p
SYS         COM      4620    12-30-88    12:00p
TREE        COM      3357    12-30-88    12:00p
VDISK       SYS      3307    12-30-88    12:00p
XCOPY       EXE     11200    12-30-88    12:00p
XYWRITE          <DIR>        5-19-89     2:25p
WORD             <DIR>        8-05-89    10:39a
AUTOEXEC BAT        36       7-28-89     9:13a
WORDSTR          <DIR>        8-17-89    10:21a
CFS              <DIR>       11-20-89     2:49p
MS                8740       2-03-90     5:19p
DBS              <DIR>        5-04-90    11:37a
TEST             <DIR>        6-03-90     2:50p
        47 File(s)   15548416 bytes free
```

```
Name and   Notation   Size    Date       Time
Extention  for
           Directory
```

The root directory should hold only a few files necessary for the operation of the computer. All other files should be assigned to *subdirectories,* which are divisions of a root directory or other subdirectories. A subdirectory is like the branches of a tree. The root directory contains the filenames for several subdirectories, and each subdirectory may be further broken down into more subdirectories. The tree structure of hard-disk directories makes files easier

```
C>cd \wordstr

C>dir

    Volume in drive C has no label
    Directory of  C:\WORDSTR

                   <DIR>        8-17-90   10:21a
    ..             <DIR>        8-17-90   10:21a
    WINSTALL COM    1152        3-02-88
    WINSTALL OVR   38528        3-02-88
    WS       INS   43776        3-02-88
    WSOVLY1  OVR   41216        4-12-88
    WSMSGS   OVR   29056        4-12-88
    WSU      COM   21376        1-01-86   12:06a
    WS       COM   21376        6-05-89    3:49p
    PRINT    TST    3968        4-12-88
    WSCOLOR  BAS    6656        4-12-88
        11 File(s)   15548416 bytes free
```

Program and Data File Names	Size	Date	Time

Directory of "Word" subdirectory showing program
and data files, number of bytes in each file, and
date and time last used.

to find than if hundreds of files were listed in a single directory. A hard-disk
subdirectory is shown below with its parts labeled.

How the root directory and subdirectories are related is shown in the following example, in which one hard disk is assigned to all documents related
to two major projects and two departments in the organization:

ROOT DIRECTORY

PROJECTA   PROJECTB   DEPTA   DEPTB

The DEPTA subdirectory might contain the following:

FILENAME	FOR A SUBDIRECTORY OF
JEAGER	Work for Sandy Jeager
SOTO	Work for Dante Soto
RUGGERA	Work for Doris Ruggera
ANNUAL	Documents for annual report
BUDGET	Documents for budget review
TEMPA	Temporary work first week
TEMPB	Temporary work second week

Each subdirectory can be divided into additional subdirectories. For example:

SUBDIRECTORY	ADDITIONAL SUBDIRECTORIES				
JEAGER	LETTERS	MEMOS	REPORTS	NOTES	DRAFTS
SOTO	LETTERS	MEMOS	MINUTES	AGENDAS	CONFRNCE
ANNUAL	PHOTOS	STATEMNT	COPY	COVER	PRINTER

Each of the additional subdirectories will contain a listing of the filenames of the individual documents it includes.

The subdirectory filenames are also limited as to the number of characters that can be used: one to eight characters and an extension of one to three characters. Consult your software and operating system documentation for limitations.

LABELING AND IDENTIFYING DISKS

Magnetic media, such as disks, should be easy to locate and identify when they are not in the computer. There are several ways to make disks easy to identify:

- *A label with identifying information written on it*. To avoid damaging the disk, the label should be completed before it is attached to the disk. If a label may be changed in the future, space should be allowed for additional writing. Use only a soft-tip marking pen when writing on a label that has been affixed to a disk. Ballpoint pens and pencils or other sharp writing instruments should never be used on disks.
- *Colored jackets and colored labels*. Disks can be purchased with different colored jackets. The colors can be used to identify categories of documents, projects, or originators. Also, different colored disk labels can signify types of information on the disks.
- *Notebooks and folders with disk holders*. Some file folders are constructed with a pocket for a floppy disk as well as room for paper documents. In addition, notebooks are available which have plastic or heavy paper disk holders. The folder tab or notebook label can be used for primary identification of the document.

TAKING CARE OF YOUR DISKS

1. Keep disks away from magnets and telephones.
2. Keep disks away from smoke, dust, and other sources of air pollution.
3. Never touch the open section of the disk and touch the jacket only at the label end to insert the disk into the drive.
4. Keep the disk in its cover when not in use.
5. Store the disk upright in a disk file when not in use.
6. Never lay books, papers, or other items on top of the disk.
7. Keep disks away from food and beverages. Spills and grease make the disk unreadable.
8. Never bend the disk.
9. Never place the disk near a high heat source or in direct sunlight.
10. Never use paper clips, cellophane tape, masking tape, or sticky notes on disks.

PROBLEMS ASSOCIATED WITH A POORLY DEVELOPED SYSTEM

Deciding how to file documents in an electronic database system involves a great deal of planning. Failure to develop an efficient system can cause serious problems such as the following:

- Loss of documents on the electronic medium. Unlike paper documents, the user cannot "see" what is on a disk. If a document cannot be properly identified, it may never be found.
- Time-consuming reorganization of files to keep related documents together. It is extremely inefficient to search in several places for related documents. It is also time consuming and risks document loss to move documents from one file to another in an attempt to keep related items together that should not have been separated in the first place.
- Inability of others to retrieve files. One of the purposes of many database systems is to allow access to documents by more than one person. Documents which are not filed according to carefully planned systems may be difficult or impossible for someone else to locate.
- One feature of an efficient electronic filing system is its ability to distinguish between documents requiring long-term storage and temporary storage. Failure to categorize documents according to retention period during creation may result in a filing system filled with many unnecessary documents. An excess of unneeded documents on your disks will add to the time it takes you to create backups, locate files, and store and locate disks.

SPECIAL REQUIREMENTS FOR "INVISIBLE" FILES

Paper files can be seen, touched, and read. A microcomputer disk can be seen and touched, but the information on it is "invisible" until the disk is loaded into a computer and you look at the screen. Some of the special requirements associated with invisible files include the need for:

- *A backup copy of files on a disk,* which means a second copy of a disk or a disk copy of hard-disk files. Disks can become unusable because of defects, accidents (such as spills or contact with a magnet), or hardware failure. Data on disks can also be deleted by operator error. Hard disks can "crash" due to equipment failure or can be wiped out by operator error. The amount of material that can be stored on any one disk can represent days or weeks of employee time. The amount of material which can be stored on a hard disk can represent months or years of employee time. In addition to the labor cost, the most serious loss is that of the records and information which cannot be replaced.
- *A printed copy, or hard copy, of the electronic file.* While this is not necessary for every record, paper copies should always be made of important documents. However, care should be taken not to clutter paper

files with temporary and relatively unimportant material which should be discarded.

- *Identification of revisions and versions of a document.* It is often a good idea to keep the previous revision of a document as a backup, but it should be identified as such. Otherwise, valuable time will be wasted making corrections and changes which already exist on the later version.
- *A security system* to safeguard the data against accidental loss, hackers, deliberate sabotage, or disasters such as fire and flood. Accidental loss of information in a computer can result from a power failure. Systems which are networked and can be accessed from outside the organization are at risk from computer hackers trying to break into the system. A disgruntled employee familiar with the filing system can destroy months and years of work and millions of dollars worth of records in a few seconds. Fire and flood can destroy computer systems and disks in a matter of minutes. The value of the records to the organization should determine the amount of time and effort to be expended in developing security systems to protect the records from loss.
- *Conserving and monitoring space on the system.* Because it is so easy to store on computer systems and often so hard to know what is stored, unwanted material can quickly build up. This results in loss of needed storage space, compounding the deleting, archiving (saving), and backup process with an excessive number of disks or a decrease in the hard-disk space available.
- *Training users.* Human beings are not infallible, and accidents can happen which change or delete files. On some systems, it is very easy to give a second document the name of another, thus deleting the first. Even systems which give a "replace" prompt can lure the operator into thinking that the correct name has been selected. Thus the first document is replaced by the second, a mistake which may not be discovered for some time. Occasionally a system can be accidentally programmed to renumber or rename all the files. It can take days or even weeks to reconstruct the original file names so that documents can be retrieved as needed. Perhaps the greatest danger to the records of an organization is the inexperienced user of the hardware and software.

GUIDELINES FOR DEVELOPING A WORKABLE SYSTEM

The following guidelines may be useful in developing a workable electronic database system, no matter what hardware and software are used.

1. List the kinds of work created and filed. Include categories such as letters, memos, reports, and tables.
2. Consider what system (alphabetic, numeric, subject, geographic, or a combination) is currently used for paper files.

3. Consider how long documents need to be kept. Documents which will be kept only a short time may be more easily remembered and need less identification than those kept for a long period. Records in short-term storage will probably be organized by date to make the process of purging, or deleting, more efficient.
4. Consider how an item to be revised, reused, or referenced will be requested (by date, name, or subject, for example).
5. Consider whether a hard copy will be kept and whether it can be used as the reference for recalling the document. If so, the identification of the document can be added to the printed copy as a reference line at the bottom or written on the file copy.
6. Consider how many people will need to refer to the document through electronic media. The more people using the documents the more specific and detailed must be the criteria for filing the documents.
7. Study the current filing system to identify patterns for conversion to magnetic media. Formalize these patterns into lists, forms to be used for entering the current files, and ideas for improving on the current system. For example, this is the time to resolve how to file the ten clients named *Smith* who each received fifteen letters a year.
8. Consult others in the organization to review the preliminary system for consistency, possible errors, and any additions which may be needed.
9. Document the system in a procedures manual and distribute it to everyone who will be using the system. Check to make sure each person understands the procedures and follows the system. Determine who has the authority to create, rename, revise, and delete documents.
10. Update the list of filing guidelines periodically. The number of documents generated may outgrow the system more quickly than anticipated.
11. If the computer or program automatically creates backup or duplicate copies, purge them periodically. Try to identify the versions of backup copies so a glance at the first "page" will let the operator know the document version.
12. Take the storage and retrieval process seriously. Computer systems can be very unforgiving when a mistake is made. Learn how to recover documents accidentally deleted. Make sure all users know how to create and save a document and how to retrieve, update, and store the revised version. It is very easy to "kill" a good version and keep a bad one.

CONCLUSION

When planned and used properly, electronic filing systems save time and energy and make the paperwork flow in the office smooth and efficient. Care should be taken to plan the filing system to fit the needs of the organization, keeping in mind the constraints of electronic filing and the need for rapid access. Hard copies of important documents should be made, as should backup copies of each magnetically stored document. The filing system should be carefully documented and followed exactly by all users. If so, electronic records will be located when they are needed in order to make important business decisions.

GENERAL REVIEW

1. What three types of microcomputer software may be purchased for filing records? (Competency 1)
2. Define the following as they were used in this chapter (Competency 2):
   a. hard copy *addition to paper files many of documents generated in office today are stored on some type of magnetic/electronic media*
   b. integrated software *- a software package that works for several applications as word processing, database, spreadsheet*
   c. filename *electronic system the caption*
   d. extension *limit of three characters*
   e. root directory
   f. subdirectory
3. What are the steps in analyzing a paper system in preparation for creating a database system (Competency 3)
4. What is wrong with this filename? (Competency 4)

   HR BR.AUGUST   *HR BR.*

5. How might you name a document that was sent to Paula Burke on November 12? (Competencies 5 and 6)
6. List the kinds of information that appear in a disk directory. (Competency 7)
7. Of the following files on a hard disk, which would most likely be in the root directory? (Competency 8)

   PROJECTA.RPT   PROJECTB.RPT   PROJECTS.LTM

8. What are three ways to make disks easy to identify? (Competency 9)
9. What may happen if you fail to categorize documents according to retention period during creation? (Competency 10)
10. Why should you keep backup copies of computer disks which contain important files? (Competency 11)
11. How should a business decide how much time and effort to expend in developing a security system for electronic media? (Competency 11)

CASE PROBLEMS

1. Obtain a paper form that is used by a business or organization. Draw up a plan to show how data on the form might be entered into an electronic database system. (Competencies 3, 10, 11, and 12)

2. The following are a few of the documents kept by an administrative assistant in an automobile agency. Develop a plan and then assign a specific filename to each document. (Competencies 4, 5, and 6)

   a. Memorandum dated October 1 to all salespersons
   b. Second revision of yearly budget
   c. Table showing sales for the year
   d. Letter dated October 7 to D. L. Carlos
   e. Memorandum dated October 11 to H. A. Stadler
   f. Report to credit bureau, creation
   g. Report to credit bureau, first revision
   h. Letter dated October 21 to G. H. Carlos
   i. Final revision of yearly budget
   j. Letter dated October 28 to W. W. McCoy

3. Develop a plan showing filenames in the root directory and each specific subdirectory for the following situation: A records manager for a financial consulting company has a total of 84 files that are all listed in the root directory of a hard disk. No subdirectories are used, but the manager would like to reorganize the files to make use of subdirectories. The files seem to refer largely to the four departments in the business: Administration, Finance, Marketing, and Operations. Each department deals with the four local branches of the business: Chicago, Kansas City, New York, and Seattle. Each local branch provides four services: loan consolidation, refinancing, second mortgages, and employment seminars. (Competencies 4, 5, 6, 7, and 8)

4. Interview a person who works with magnetic media on a daily basis. Determine how the person protects electronic files from loss of data. (Competencies 9, 10, 11, and 12)

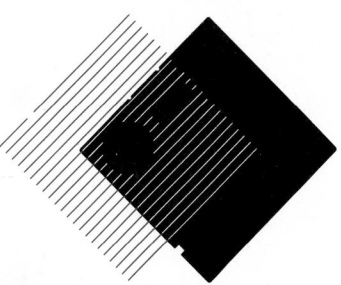

7

NUMERIC SYSTEMS

COMPETENCIES

When you have completed this chapter, you will be able to:

1. Define numeric filing.
2. State the advantages of numeric filing.
3. List and describe the parts of a numeric filing system.
4. File and find cards using a consecutive numeric filing system. (See Jobs 28 to 30 in the *Practice Materials*.)
5. File and find cards using a terminal-digit filing system. (See Jobs 31 to 33 in the *Practice Materials*.)
6. Index and code correspondence for filing, prepare cross-references, and file and find correspondence using a numeric system. (See Jobs 34 to 38 in the *Practice Materials*.)
7. Explain the procedure for transferring papers from a miscellaneous alphabetic file to a numeric file.

NUMERIC FILING

In filing large groups of documents where alphabetizing of all the many names and keeping them in order would be difficult, numeric filing is the most common method of filing. Maintaining records for the many contributors to the social security system is one good example of a need for numeric filing. Other examples include records for credit card holders and owners of vehicles. The only efficient way to keep those records in order is to file them by number.

Definition of Numeric Filing. *Numeric filing* is the arrangement of records according to numbers. The number may be assigned to the record, or it may be a part of the record itself (such as the number that appears on an invoice or a check). Filing records in consecutive order according to these numbers is called *consecutive* or *serial numeric filing*. Other methods of arranging records numerically are discussed later in this chapter.

Numeric filing systems are called *indirect systems* because you must first consult an alphabetic index to determine the code number of a record. Alphabetic filing systems, on the other hand, are *direct systems* because you can go directly to the file drawer and, by means of the name captions, find the records for which you are searching.

If Elaine Whitton were a client in a lawyer's office and a numeric filing system were used, her correspondence might be filed under a case number such as 36-9987. She might also be a client of a major credit card company. In that case her correspondence might be filed under a number such as 622 789 9923 004 553. If Elaine has an insurance policy, her agent might find correspondence relating to her under her policy number such as 09-7766-532-559. It's necessary to understand the basis for the numeric filing system in order to determine where the record should be stored and why it should be stored in that particular location.

Of course, in an alphabetic system, correspondence for Elaine Whitton would be filed under *W* or *Whitton*.

Advantages of Numeric Filing. Numeric filing systems have six basic advantages over alphabetic, subject, and geographic systems.

Sequential Identification of Records. Records that have been identified by number are easy to put in sequential order. Although the process of identifying the record can take time, as you will see later in this chapter, once the number has been assigned, the filing process is speeded up. Names can be similar, even identical, which can cause confusion; numbers assigned according to an established pattern are always different.

Convenient Expansion. Because numeric filing systems allow for the addition of numbers as the need arises, expansion is easier than with alphabetic systems. Additional folders and, as needed, additional storage units can be added without moving any files. In an alphabetic system, if you needed more room in the *A* drawer, you would need to move the folders in all drawers to expand at the beginning.

Permanent and Extensive Cross-Referencing. Some businesses, such as law firms and contractors, deal with records that refer to definite cases, contracts, or operations that are active for relatively long and indefinite periods. Because each case, contract, or operation usually refers to several names or several other cases, an extensive cross-reference is necessary. This can be provided in the card index of a numeric file.

Card Index as an Integral Part of the System. The card index used for locating the assigned number for a correspondent can also be used for other purposes by the business. For example, it provides a list of names, addresses, and telephone numbers; a quick reference check to see if there is a file already for the customer; a reference to previous business which may have been transacted or is in progress; credit information; the names of people to contact about various matters, such as the head of the marketing division, the accounting department, or the repair service. In short, the card index can be as useful to you as you care to make it.

Confidentiality of Information. Numbers are very impersonal. Because the files are referred to by number, there is less temptation to snoop in the files. All alphabetic references to files are contained only in the card index. Hence, if you should meet a stranger in the hall while you're carrying files with only numbers, no conclusions can be reached. However, if that individual saw you carrying files about Braxton Hill or Victoria Keller, the conclusion could be reached, and correctly, that your employer had important business dealings with those individuals. The stranger might gain an advantage from having that knowledge.

Numbers That Are Already Identifying Factors. There are many instances when a number is already the means of identification, such as social security numbers, telephone numbers, invoice numbers, and charge account numbers. If the information to be filed could be (or some day will be) stored in a computer, it makes sense to use a number already available. As an easy numeric system, a store may file telephone orders according to the last two digits of the telephone number. The customer's last name is used to file within each group. For example, Kaitlynn Allen's invoice would be filed according to her phone number which is (804) 555-1055. Within the folder, her invoice would be filed between an invoice for Arthur Akers and one for Luther Alston. Restaurants which offer home delivery of pizza often use the entire phone number to file customers. Hence, if you call to order a pizza, you will be asked your telephone number. The clerk can then tell you your name, your address, and, more often than not, what you ordered the last time you called.

Social security numbers are used by many businesses and institutions for identification of individuals. This is a unique means of identification and one that most people easily remember.

NUMERIC CARD FILES

If information is to be recorded in a limited space, on a 5 × 3 card, for example, or in a computer's memory where access to a specific location is important, numbers are used to standardize caption size and arrangement. Numbers are also unique identifiers of records. Two people can have identical names, but they cannot have identical social security numbers. As a rule, an identification number will be shorter than a name. A vendor number of five or six digits can be used for processing sales records rather than the vendor's

HOW A NUMERIC CARD FILE MAY BE USED

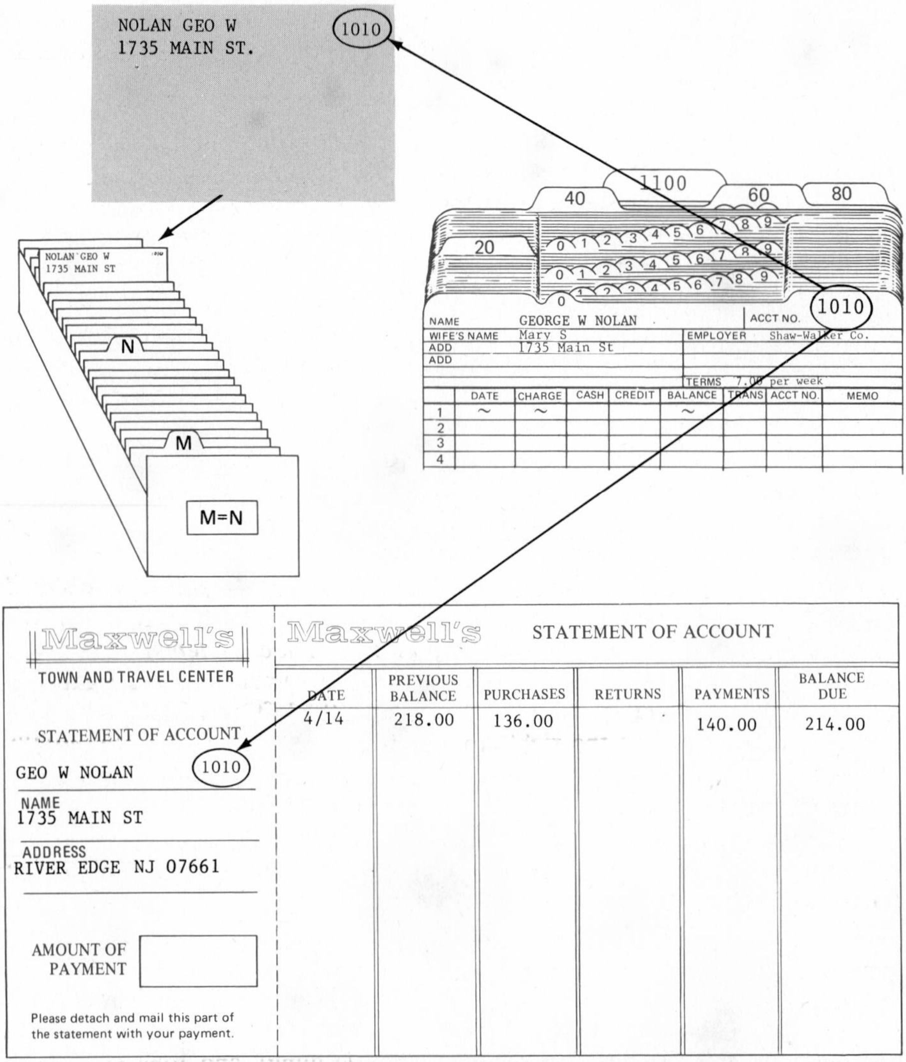

NOLAN GEO W
1735 MAIN ST.

1010

NOLAN GEO W
1735 MAIN ST

N

M

M=N

		1100		
40			60	80
20				

NAME		GEORGE W NOLAN		ACCT NO.	1010	
WIFE'S NAME	Mary S			EMPLOYER	Shaw-Walker Co.	
ADD		1735 Main St				
ADD						
				TERMS	7.00 per week	
	DATE	CHARGE	CASH	CREDIT	BALANCE	TRANS	ACCT NO.	MEMO
1	~	~			~			
2								
3								
4								

Maxwell's   **Maxwell's**   STATEMENT OF ACCOUNT

TOWN AND TRAVEL CENTER

...STATEMENT OF ACCOUNT

GEO W NOLAN   1010

NAME
1735 MAIN ST

ADDRESS
RIVER EDGE NJ 07661

AMOUNT OF
PAYMENT

Please detach and mail this part of
the statement with your payment.

DATE	PREVIOUS BALANCE	PURCHASES	RETURNS	PAYMENTS	BALANCE DUE
4/14	218.00	136.00		140.00	214.00

The numeric card file for customer account cards (upper right) is the source file for the preparation of the monthly statement shown at the bottom. The card file at the upper left is an alphabetic index to customer account numbers.

name, which would have to be written out each time. Office workers find that sorting cards by number is faster than sorting by names. An example of a numeric card filing system is shown on page 102.

Guides are used in card files to divide the cards into workable groups. A file of 100 cards, for example, would probably be divided into groups of 10 for each reference, with the guides 00, 10, 20, 30, 40, 50, 60, 70, 80, and 90.

OTHER NUMERIC CARD SYSTEMS

In addition to the consecutive, or serial, type, other numeric systems used in business are (1) terminal-digit systems, (2) triple-digit systems, (3) middle-digit systems, and (4) duplex-numeric systems.

In *terminal-digit systems,* the numbers are read from right to left. The numbers are generally analyzed in three parts. The last, or terminal, two digits are the drawer number, the next two digits are the folder number, and all the other digits indicate the sequence in the folder. An insurance policy numbered 401185 makes a good example. It would be stored in the drawer number 85 (last two digits) and in the folder numbered 11 (middle two digits), and the 40 (first two digits) would determine its sequence in the folder. Terminal digit systems have the advantages of an even distribution of records in the files at all times and permanent numbering of cabinets and primary guides, even after records have been transferred. The illustration on page 104 compares consecutive-numeric and terminal-digit systems.

Triple-digit systems are similar to terminal-digit systems except that the numbers are broken into two parts, instead of three. The last three digits of a number on the extreme right are called *primary numbers,* and the remaining digits determine the sequence of records in the folder bearing the primary numbers. For example, the same insurance policy No. 401185 would be stored in folder 185. The 401 would determine its sequence in the folder.

In *middle-digit systems* (also called *significant-number systems*), records are separated first according to the third and fourth digits from the right of a number, then according to the first two digits on the left, and finally according to the last two digits on the right. In this case, insurance policy No. 401185 would be stored in drawer 11 (middle two digits), and in folder 40 (first two digits). The 85 would determine its sequence in the folder.

Duplex-numeric systems use digits and letters of the alphabet, separated by hyphens or commas, to code records numerically. This system is discussed further in Chapter 8.

FILING PRACTICE

Complete Jobs 28 to 30 (consecutive-numeric filing), and Jobs 31 to 33 (terminal-digit filing), of the *Practice Materials.*

COMPARISON OF CONSECUTIVE-NUMERIC AND TERMINAL-DIGIT SYSTEMS

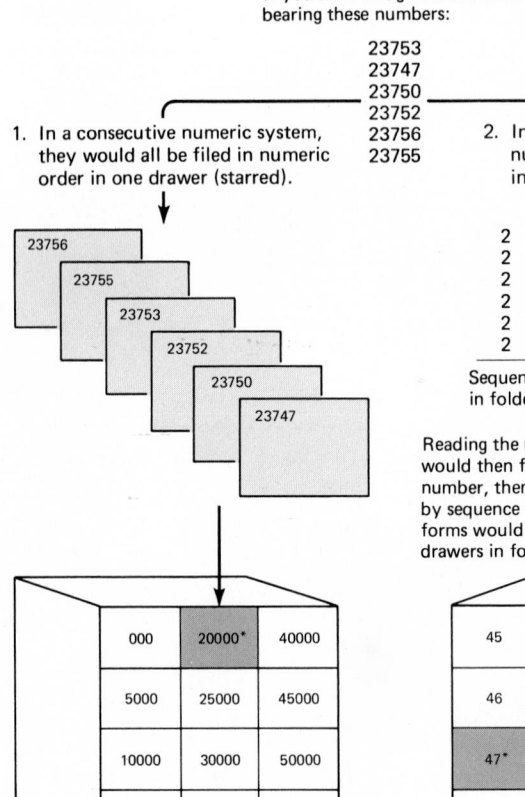

If you were filing business forms bearing these numbers:

```
23753
23747
23750
23752
23756
23755
```

1. In a consecutive numeric system, they would all be filed in numeric order in one drawer (starred).

2. In a terminal-digit system, the numbers would first be broken into these groups:

Sequence in folder	Folder number	Drawer number
2	37	47
2	37	50
2	37	52
2	37	53
2	37	55
2	37	56

Reading the numbers from right to left, you would then file the forms first by drawer number, then by folder number, and finally by sequence within the folder. Thus the six forms would be stored in six separate file drawers in folder number 37.

When many forms have to be filed by several file workers, the terminal-digit system is an advantage because it overcomes crowded working conditions by spreading the work over several file drawers.

NUMERIC CORRESPONDENCE FILING

Lawyers and businesses which deal in contract work often file by number. Numeric correspondence filing is used (1) when the records to be stored will be requested by number, (2) when they would be difficult to classify under one particular name, (3) when confidentiality is facilitated by using numbers for identification, and (4) when rapid expansion of the files may be necessary.

Organization of a Numeric Correspondence File. There are four parts to a numeric correspondence file: (1) main numeric file, (2) miscellaneous alphabetic file, (3) card index, and (4) register for determining the next number to be assigned.

Main Numeric File. The main numeric file contains guides and individual folders that bear numeric captions. Each numbered folder contains records concerning a separate correspondent. As in alphabetic filing, the records within the folder are arranged chronologically with the most recent date on top.

There is a numeric guide for each group of five to ten folders. The guides may be arranged in one of three ways:

1. The guide tabs may be in three positions staggered from left to right.
2. The guide tabs may appear in two or more positions on the left with the folder tabs in the last position on the right.
3. The guide tabs may be in the center only, and the folder tabs may be in two positions to the left and two positions to the right.

Guide tabs are numbered in fives or tens unless the contents of each folder contain ten numbers, in which case the guides are numbered in hundreds.

The records can be subdivided by date or subject, depending on how they will be requested, when a numeric folder becomes full. When the records are subdivided and half of them are placed in a new folder, both the new and the old folders bear the same caption, plus an auxiliary number. The auxiliary number gives further identification. For example, Folder 206, upon being subdivided, becomes 206-2 and the new folder is 206-1. This is illustrated below.

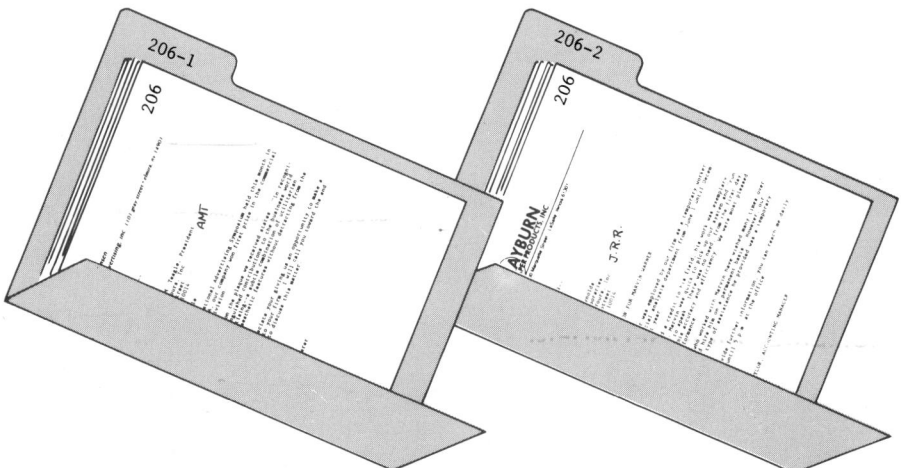

To prevent overcrowding, these numeric folders have been subdivided by date. When enough papers are stored to warrant opening a new folder, the new folder is numbered 206-1—and the existing folder is renumbered 206-2—so that the most recent papers are in the first folder. If another folder is needed, 206-1 then becomes 206-2, 206-2 becomes 206-3, and so on.

Miscellaneous Alphabetic File. The miscellaneous alphabetic file contains guides and folders bearing alphabetic captions. Its purpose is to provide a place to store pieces of correspondence that do not warrant individual folders in the main numeric file. Therefore, every folder in this file is a miscellaneous folder containing the records of several correspondents. Records proceed in strict alphabetic order throughout the file. When five or more records concerning one correspondent accumulate, they are assigned the next unused number, placed in a numeric folder corresponding to this number, and stored in the main numeric file.

The miscellaneous alphabetic file can be in the front of the first drawer of the main numeric file, in a separate drawer of the main numeric file, or in a separate filing cabinet.

Card Index. Arranged alphabetically, the card index contains cards, each with the name (and often the address and other information) of a correspondent, as well as the number assigned to the records of that correspondent. This type of index is necessary in all numeric correspondence systems because the correspondence is usually called for by name rather than by number. If the particular records requested are kept in the miscellaneous alphabetic file, this is indicated on the card by the symbol *M*. The *M* is eliminated and a folder number is written in its place when the correspondent is assigned a folder in the main numeric file.

Register. The register shows the names and numbers already assigned and the numbers available. When a new correspondent warrants an individual folder, the register is consulted and the next available number is assigned. If any correspondence has been placed in the miscellaneous alphabetic file, it is removed, coded with the assigned number, and placed in proper sequence in the folder. The card in the card index is updated to show the assigned number. In some systems, when the file for that particular correspondent is no longer needed, it may be removed from the files and destroyed. The number may then be assigned to another folder.

Cross-Referencing. You will recall that cross-referencing in alphabetic systems is accomplished by placing cross-reference sheets or copies of the original document in the individual and miscellaneous folders. In numeric filing systems, however, cross-referencing is done in the card index. This is discussed at the beginning of the chapter as an advantage of numeric filing systems.

The example in the illustration on page 107 shows a change of billing procedure. A card made up for Shelton Industrial Supplies will contain a notation concerning this company's relationship with Universal Industries, Inc.

Steps in Numeric Correspondence Filing. The steps in numeric correspondence filing are inspecting, alphabetic indexing and coding, alphabetic sorting, nu-

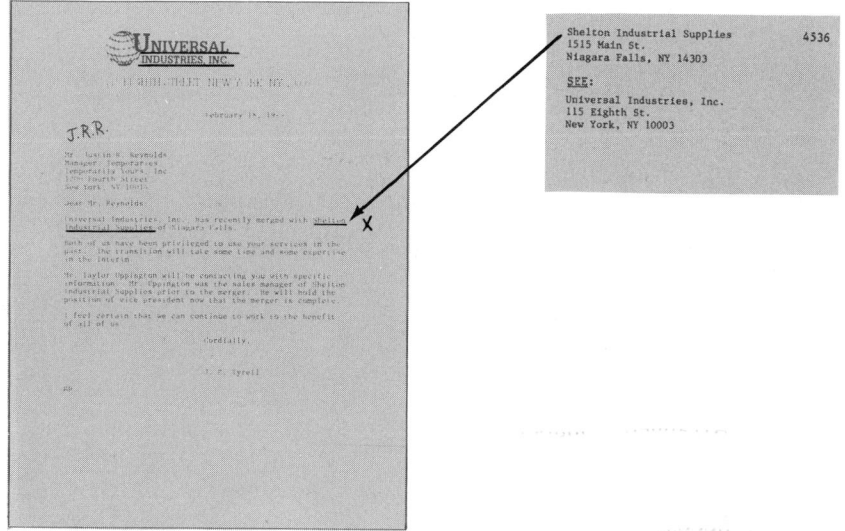

Since records regarding Shelton Industrial Supplies are now filed under
Universal Industries, Inc., a cross-reference card in the card index is needed
to lead the file worker to the proper folder.

meric coding, numeric sorting, and storing. A diagram of this process is shown
on page 108.

Inspecting. As in alphabetic correspondence filing, the correspondence is
checked for a release mark before being filed.

Alphabetic Indexing and Coding. Alphabetic indexing and coding are the same
as for alphabetic card filing. See pages 66–68.

Alphabetic Sorting. The correspondence to be filed is sorted into alphabetic
order so that the card index can be consulted to code each piece with the
proper number. This step is necessary only the first time a record is filed. After
that, because the number has been written on the paper, you can skip all steps
up to the numeric sorting.

Numeric Coding. The card index is consulted for each piece of correspondence. The number is written on the record, usually in the upper right corner.
If there is no number assigned, the record is coded with the letter *M* to indicate
that it is to be stored in the miscellaneous alphabetic file.

Numeric Sorting. After the numeric coding is finished, the papers are sorted
into numeric order. As in alphabetic filing, you should use rough and fine
sorting techniques. The number of piles will depend on the range of numbers

STEPS IN THE NUMERIC FILING OF CORRESPONDENCE

1. INSPECTING. Correspondence is checked to make sure it has been released for filing.

2. ALPHABETIC INDEXING AND CODING. The name or subject under which the record is to be filed is determined and underlined. (Names for cross-referencing should be selected and coded also.)

3. ALPHABETIC SORTING. The papers are arranged alphabetically according to the coded names, to expedite the use of the card index.

4. NUMERIC CODING. The file number, found in the card index, is placed in the upper right corner of each paper.

5. NUMERIC SORTING. The papers are placed in numeric sequence.

6. STORING. The papers are stored in numeric files.

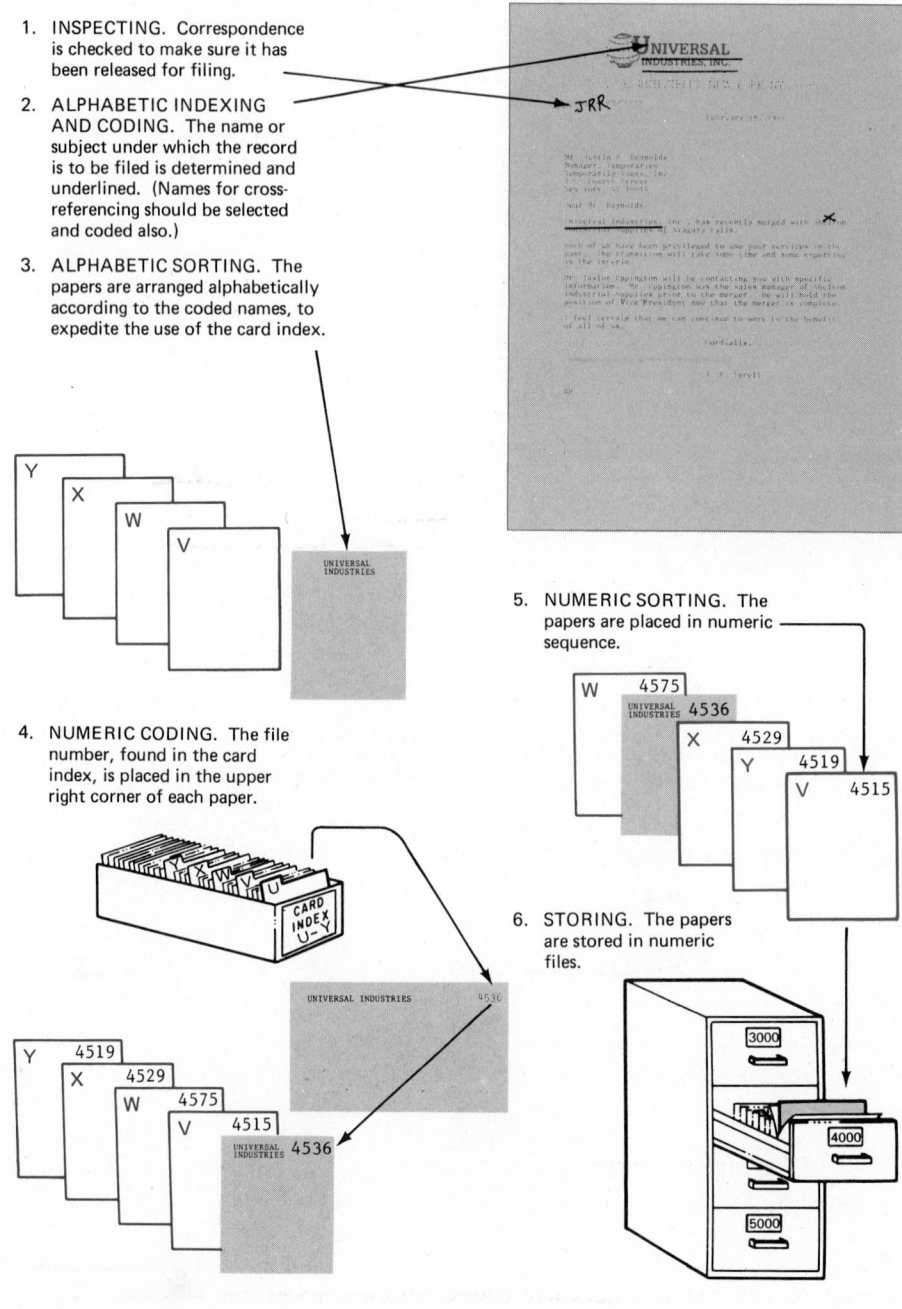

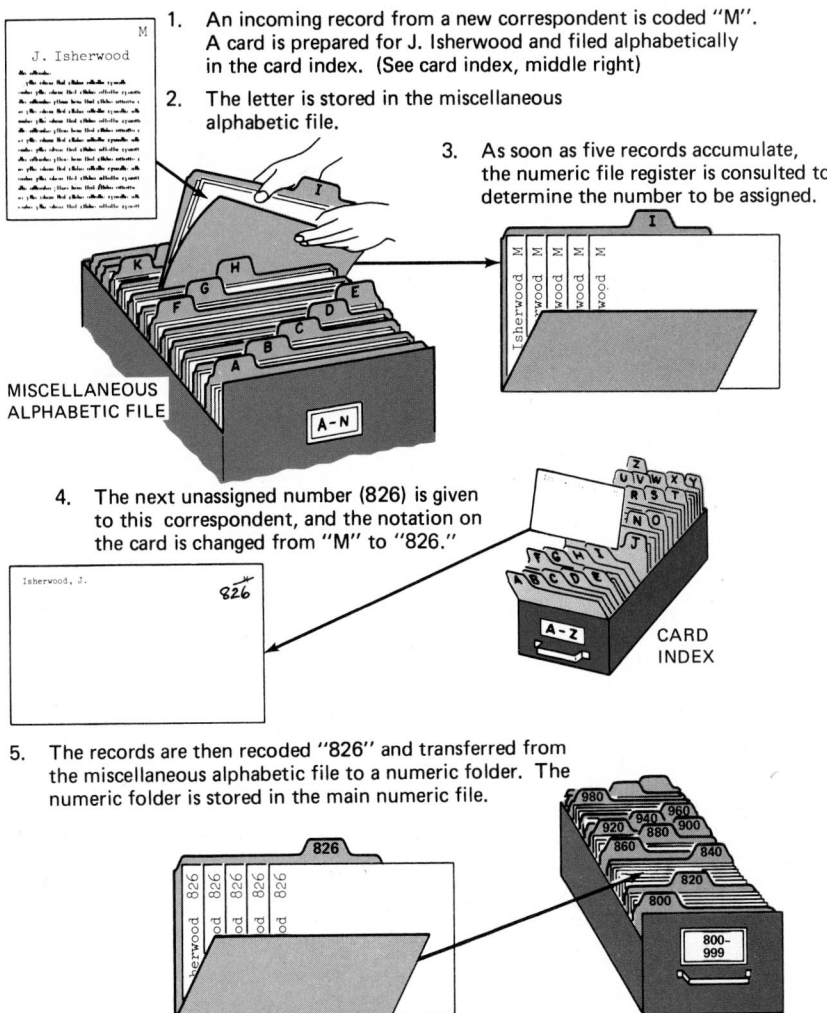

1. An incoming record from a new correspondent is coded "M". A card is prepared for J. Isherwood and filed alphabetically in the card index. (See card index, middle right)

2. The letter is stored in the miscellaneous alphabetic file.

3. As soon as five records accumulate, the numeric file register is consulted to determine the number to be assigned.

MISCELLANEOUS ALPHABETIC FILE

4. The next unassigned number (826) is given to this correspondent, and the notation on the card is changed from "M" to "826."

CARD INDEX

5. The records are then recoded "826" and transferred from the miscellaneous alphabetic file to a numeric folder. The numeric folder is stored in the main numeric file.

with which you need to work, but four to six will fit conveniently on most desk tops.

Storing. The papers are then placed in the proper location in their files in the file drawers as in alphabetic filing.

Using a Miscellaneous Alphabetic File With a Numeric File. In the illustration on page 108, incoming letters wre coded with a number that was found in the card index. Then the letters were stored in correct order according to number. A numeric file only was used.

Another system which some offices use is a combination of a miscellaneous alphabetic file with a numeric file. In the miscellaneous alphabetic file, papers from correspondents are stored until at least five records are accumulated from a correspondent. Then the papers are transferred to the numeric system. The illustration on page 109 explains the process of transferring papers from a miscellaneous alphabetic file to a numeric file.

FILING PRACTICE

Complete Jobs 34 to 38 of the *Practice Materials*.

GENERAL REVIEW

1. What is numeric filing? (Competency 1)
2. List six advantages of numeric filing. (Competency 2)
3. List and describe the parts of a numeric filing system. (Competency 3)
4. What is *consecutive-numeric filing? Terminal-digit? Middle-digit?* (Competencies 4, 5, 6)
5. What are the steps in preparing correspondence to be filed numerically? (Competency 7)
6. How is cross-referencing done in numeric filing systems? (Competency 7)
7. When and how is a folder changed from the miscellaneous alphabetic file to the numeric file? (Competency 8)

CASE PROBLEMS

1. One of your coworkers, Michelle Wilson, does not think that it is necessary to maintain a card index for your numeric files. She feels that the register will provide you with all the necessary information to assign numbers to the daily correspondence. Is this practical? Can you convince Michelle that the card index is necessary? How? (Competencies 2, 3)
2. You have been transferred to another department within your company. You find they currently use an alphabetic system. You note some problems with this system; you feel a numeric system would solve those problems. Here are some of the problems:

   a. It is difficult to locate files which contain records about a project because several individuals are involved. The records are currently filed under the name of one of the individuals.
   b. Retrieving information is slow. Many orders come in over the telephone, and you rush to the files to find out whether the potential customer has an acceptable credit standing and the limit of credit

allowable. Also you want to know whether the customer is a new one or has submitted previous orders.

c. The file drawers are overcrowded. As the number of folders in each drawer increases, you have been taking several file folders from the back of the crowded drawers and moving them to an empty drawer. You have not had the time to redistribute the file folders in all the drawers to keep them in alphabetic order. Thus you have two groups of folders which need to be checked each time you file records.

d. Vendor number mistakes are a problem. Each large-volume supplier has a vendor number assigned, and you use it for identification on several forms instead of the name. Suppliers with small volume, however, do not have numbers; usually these are one- or two-time orders which do not need to be kept in the files with suppliers with large businesses who may have more than one file.

What advantages would numeric filing have over your present system? How are you going to convince your employer that a change would be a more efficient filing method? (Competencies 2, 3)

3. The person who had your job before you cross-referenced information in the main numeric file or not at all. This is very frustrating for you because you have to go to several files to find the files you want. You would like to cross-reference the card index. Should you change the present system? If so, what should you do about cross-references already in the files? (Competencies 2, 3, 7)

8

SUBJECT SYSTEMS

COMPETENCIES

When you have completed this chapter, you will be able to:

1. Define *subject filing*.
2. Give at least two examples of business situations in which subject filing is used.
3. State the advantages of subject filing.
4. List and describe the parts of a subject correspondence file.
5. File and find cards using a subject filing system (See Jobs 39 and 42 in the *Practice Materials*).
6. Index and code correspondence for filing, prepare cross-references, and file and find correspondence using a subject filing system. (See Jobs 43 through 46 in the *Practice Materials*.)
7. Describe the three kinds of subject filing systems.
8. Describe chronological filing and set up a chronological file. (See Job 53 in the *Practice Materials*.)
9. Organize a list of folder captions into a dictionary arrangement and then reorganize them into an encyclopedic arrangement.
10. Select guide and folder captions when given a list of items which are to be filed using a subject system.
11. State why files are needed for personal as well as business use.

12. List documents that individuals need to safeguard.
13. List ways to safeguard personal files.

SUBJECT FILING

Arranging records by names of items or topics rather than by names of people, companies, or locations is called *subject filing*. In subject filing, records related to one subject or area of business activity may be grouped and stored in one place to provide a complete picture of what has transpired on the subject.

Arrangement of Subject File Drawer. The subject file drawer is arranged in the same way as the alphabetic file drawer: the captions determine which system is being used. In alphabetic filing the captions are the names of people or organizations; in subject filing, the captions are names of items, objects, business activities, or functions. Examples of subject captions in a retail store are INVENTORY CONTROL, PERSONNEL POLICIES, PURCHASE ORDERS, and SHIPPING RATES.

Subject Filing Used With Other Systems. It is important to remember that any filing system has to be adjusted to fit the needs of a particular office. An office may choose to adapt any one system or use a combination of systems if that is the way the office wants to organize its records to operate most efficiently. Some records, such as inventory cards, are referred to only by the name of the item, and thus they are filed by subject only. Other records, such as insurance policies, have a policyholder's name, a policy number, and a subject *(Insurance Policies)* and may be filed in any of the three ways.

Subject Filing as a Means of Organizing Related Records. In subject filing, a common element is identified under which several or many papers may be grouped. Such a grouping helps to organize those records and make them easy to find. The following are examples of this application of subject filing.

Information on the care and maintenance of a piece of new equipment, such as an office copier, would probably be stored under the subject *Equipment Repair: Office Copier.* Thus you would not have folders for maintenance of each type of equipment used in the office scattered throughout the files; they would all be behind the guide *Equipment Repair.*

Records relating to the construction of a new building would be stored in one place—probably the name of the building or the site location. Thus papers from many different sources related to that construction—such as different subcontractors—would be grouped in one logical place for reference.

A hotel would probably file contracts for meetings scheduled for the month of January behind a guide labeled: *Bookings: January,* so that all the commitments for that month would be in one place as a help in planning the overall operation of the hotel's meeting facilities.

SUBJECT CARD FILING

Subject card filing serves the same purposes as alphabetic card filing: as an index to complete files or as a handy reference for information that is frequently needed.

If you are researching a topic to write a paper for a class you are taking, you will find the subject card catalog in the library helpful to use when you do not know either the name of an author or the title of a book. So, too, in an office there are kinds of information you may need in your day-to-day activities which are best organized by subject. Many offices have card files which list items such as repair service for machines, emergency telephone numbers, departments in the organization with the name and extension of the individual who can best handle certain matters, and an agenda showing regularly scheduled activities for each month of the year.

Guides in subject card files are the same as guides used in alphabetic card files; however, the captions are subjects rather than names.

SUBJECT CORRESPONDENCE FILING

Organization of Subject Correspondence Files. There are two parts to a subject correspondence file—the main subject file and the relative index. If there are only a few folders with subject captions, they may be filed in alphabetic order in the same drawers as the alphabetic correspondence folders.

Main Subject File. The main subject file contains guides and folders that bear subject captions. The most difficult task when setting up a subject file is determining parallel captions to use in the filing system. For example, you would not have guide captions such as OFFICE SUPPLIES, PENS AND PENCILS, ANNUAL REPORT, ANNUAL REPORT FOR 1990, and ANNUAL REPORT DESIGN AWARD in the same file. Instead, you would select the parallel guide captions OFFICE SUPPLIES: MEMOS; OFFICE SUPPLIES: PENS AND PENCILS; and OFFICE SUPPLIES: STATIONERY PAPER. You would also have as a guide ANNUAL REPORT: 1992; ANNUAL REPORT: 1993; and ANNUAL REPORT: DESIGN AWARD.

Each guide caption should be of equal importance and of a broad enough description that it may be subdivided as necessary. As a general rule, you should outline the headings for a subject filing system as you would outline the topics and subtopics of an English composition.

Relative Index. People do not all reason the same way, and therefore what one person considers the main subject may not be the same as what another person thinks. It may depend on a person's interest in the subject. For example, a staff member who wants to compete for a design award for the cover of the annual report may think the logical place to file information on the award is under ART DEPARTMENT or PUBLIC RELATIONS, whereas the information was filed under ANNUAL REPORT.

To handle a situation where different guide captions might be referenced, subject files need a *relative index*: a listing of all the main headings, divisions, and subdivisions in the main subject file. The relative index will not only help you find the right folder but also guide you in the selection of the subject caption for new items to be filed. It serves the same purpose as the index of a book. There is much decision making in subject filing; therefore, the person who sets up guide and folder captions should be knowledgeable about the business and the manner in which files are requested.

Cross-Referencing. Cross-referencing is done in the relative index in the same way information is cross-referenced in the index of a book. For example, the entry *Design Award* might be followed by *See Annual Report*. This is explained in more detail in the discussion of alphabetic subject files.

Kinds of Subject Correspondence Files. The primary kinds of subject files are combination subject, alphabetic subject, and numeric subject.

Combination Subject Files. A combination subject file contains subject captions mixed in with individual or company name captions. This kind of subject file is used when there is relatively little material to be organized on a subject basis. In such a case it is impractical to set up a separate subject file, and so the subject captions, as described earlier in this chapter, are merged with name

COMBINATION SUBJECT FILE

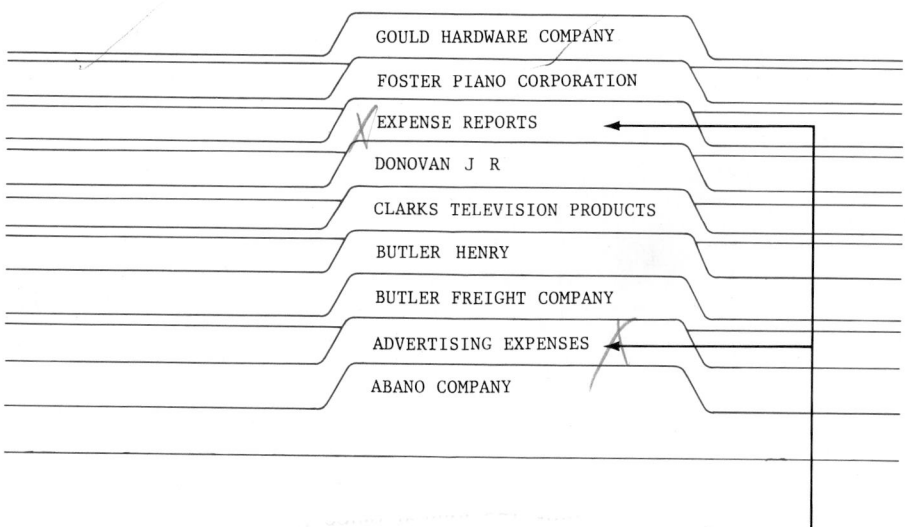

Arrows point to subject folders interfiled with folders for individual and company names.

captions in what would otherwise be an alphabetic correspondence file. Combination subject files are illustrated on page 115 and below.

Alphabetic Subject Files. Alphabetic subject files are similar to alphabetic correspondence files except that all the captions refer to topics instead of people and organizations. There are two arrangements for alphabetic subject files—encyclopedic and dictionary.

COMBINATION SUBJECT FILE

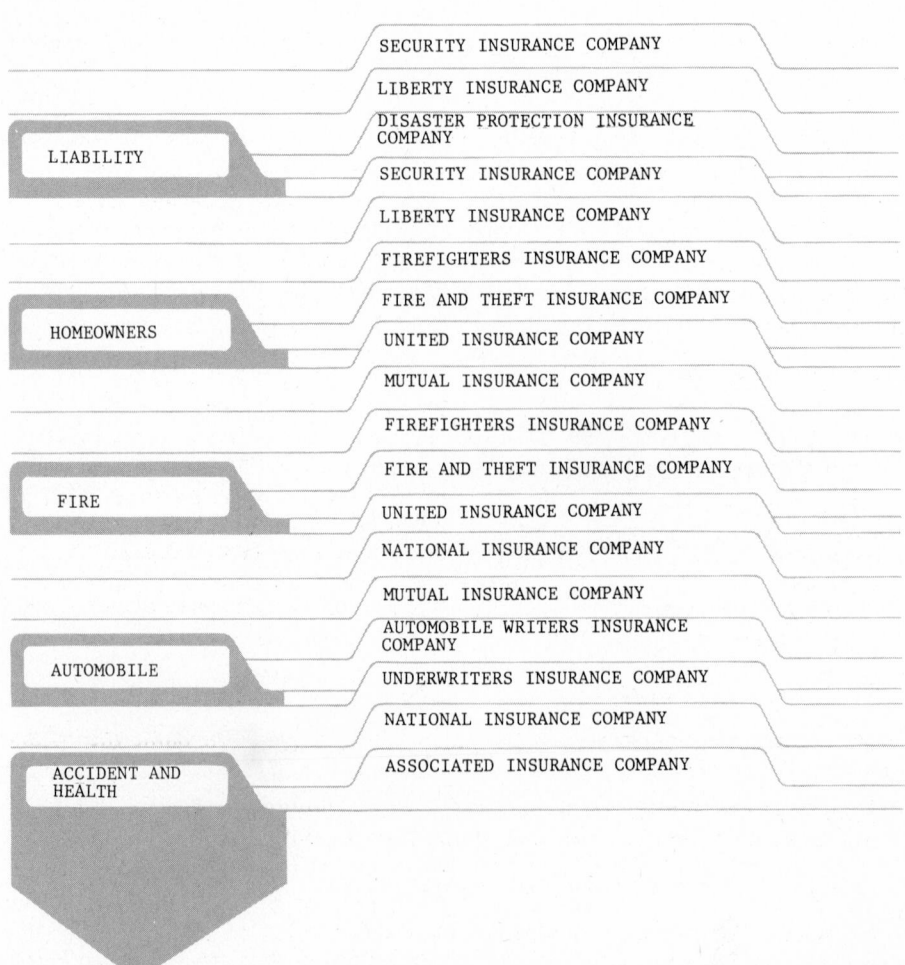

Here is another example of a combination subject file in which main headings are subjects and subheadings are company names. An insurance agency might file forms for new policies first by the type of policy and then by the names of the companies whose policies they write.

A subject file with _encyclopedic arrangement_ has alphabetized major headings, which in turn have alphabetized divisions and subdivisions. The encyclopedic arrangement makes it necessary to create an alphabetic list of all the captions in the subject file, including all the headings, divisions, and subdivisions in the file. A good relative index will also list topics related to the actual captions in the file. For example, the captions listed below are indicative of those which could actually be used by a construction firm to file the wealth of information needed for buildings which the firm constructs. This is a sample of the encyclopedic arrangement for one house under construction. A similar list would be used for each house.

CAPTIONS	EXPLANATIONS
WILLIS HOME	First heading
ARCHITECTURAL DETAILS	First division of Willis Home
CHIMNEY AND FIREPLACES	First division of Architectural Details
DOORS AND WINDOWS	Second division of Architectural Details
LIGHTING FIXTURES	Third division of Architectural Details
ROOFS AND GUTTERS	Fourth division of Architectural Details
VENETIAN BLINDS	Fifth division of Architectural Details
WALLPAPER	Sixth division of Architectural Details
GENERAL	Miscellaneous folder placed after alphabetic breakdowns
BUILDING MATERIALS	Second division of Willis Home
BRICK	First division of Building Materials
GLASS	Second division of Building Materials
HARDWARE	Third division of Building Materials
LUMBER	Fourth division of Building Materials
PAINT	Fifth division of Building Materials
SHINGLES	Sixth division of Building Materials
STONE	Seventh division of Buildings Materials
TILES	Eighth division of Building Materials
GENERAL	Miscellaneous folder

Should a subcontractor come into the firm asking which paint the Willis family selected, the employee could first look under _PAINT_ in the relative index. Because this information is filed by the building, the relative index would have a cross-reference notation as shown below:

PAINT   SEE (Name of homeowner)

Suppose a file worker was trying to find information about the walls in the bathrooms of the Willis home. The cross-reference notation in the relative index would read:

WALL COVERINGS   SEE WALLPAPER
                                          PAINT

A relative index, then, can serve as a cross-reference for related topics as well as direct reference to the captions in the subject file.

The most popular relative index used in the home is found in the back of any large cookbook. When deciding to make chocolate chip cookies, for example, you would look under the major heading *COOKIES* to find the recipe. Food has fancy names, and the relative index helps you find *Original Toll House Cookies*.

A subject file with *dictionary arrangement* has no divisions and subdivisions of subjects. Because the subjects are arranged in alphabetic sequence like the words in a dictionary, a relative index is not necessary. This type of alphabetic subject file is used in small businesses and other situations in which division of topics is not desired. One example of dictionary subject arrangement is the listing of types of businesses in the yellow pages of a telephone directory.

An alphabetic subject file with dictionary arrangement is shown below.

Numeric Subject Files. Code numbers for subject captions are used in numeric subject filing. Numeric subject filing has the advantages of any numeric filing system. (See Chapter 7.) Coding is much easier than with alphabetic subject

ALPHABETIC SUBJECT FILE WITH DICTIONARY ARRANGEMENT

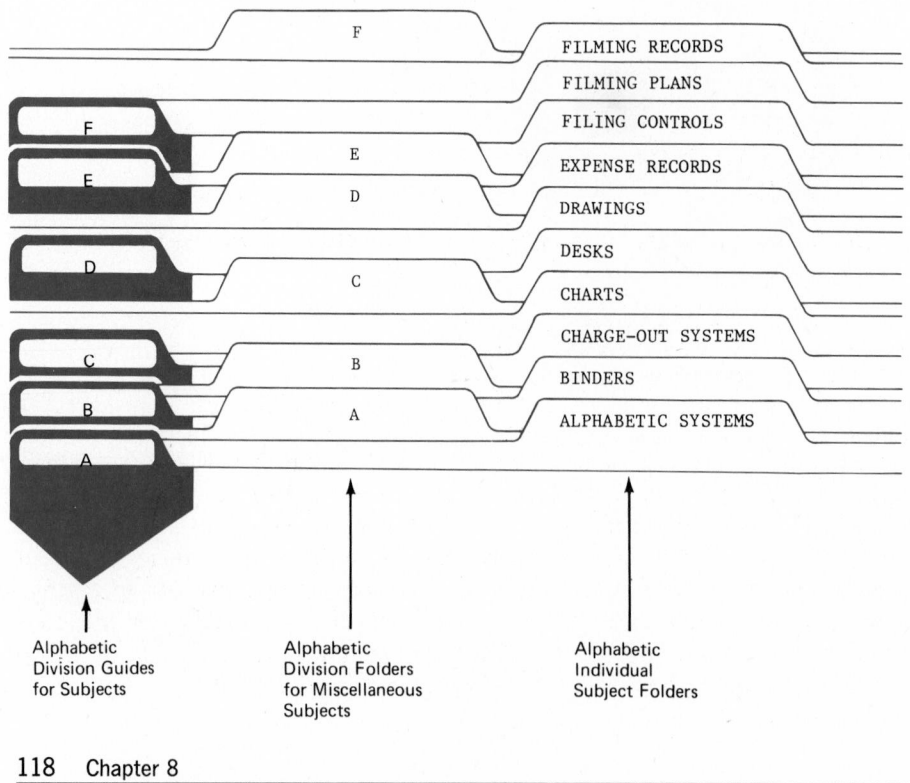

systems because only a number, and not a long subject caption, is recorded on the record. The files are easier to expand because new topics can be placed at the end of the files rather than inserted in the middle, as with alphabetic files. Because all topics have a code number, they do not have to be arranged in alphabetic order. Therefore, another important advantage of numeric subject filing is that related topics can be placed conveniently near each other in the files without regard to alphabetic sequence. Of course, a card index is needed for numeric subject systems, just as it was needed for the numeric systems discussed in Chapter 7.

Three important types of numeric subject systems are simple-numeric, decimal-numeric, and duplex-numeric.

Simple-numeric subject systems usually have three-digit captions. The main headings are usually hundreds and are assigned first, as in this example of a system Addington's Furniture Warehouse, Inc. uses:

BEDROOM	100	KITCHEN	500
DINING ROOM	200	LIVING ROOM	600
FAMILY ROOM	300	PATIO	700
HOME OFFICE	400	PLAYROOM	800

In turn, the divisions of each heading are assigned numbers that are hundreds and tens. For example:

DINING ROOM	300
CHAIRS	310
HUTCH	320
SERVERS	330
SIDEBOARDS	340
TABLES	350

And finally, the subdivisions of each division are assigned numbers. Hence:

TABLES	350
CONTEMPORARY	351
EARLY AMERICAN	352
SCANDINAVIAN	353
TRADITIONAL	354

Notice that some numbers are not assigned, such as 900, 360, and 355. This allows for expansion in the event that new headings, divisions, or subdivisions are added later. The assigned numbers are placed on guides and folders in the file, sometimes together with the subject caption, sometimes alone.

A card is prepared for each heading, division, and subdivision in the file. The cards are arranged alphabetically to provide a reference for the code numbers assigned. The card for *Traditional* is shown on page 120 as an example. It would be filed under *T* in an alphabetic card index.

Decimal-numeric subject systems permit more subdivisions than simple-numeric systems. Up to the first subdivision, the decimal-numeric code numbers are the same as the simple-numeric ones. For example:

SERVERS	330.
FORMAL	331.
INFORMAL	332.

The code 331. (Informal) can be further subdivided by adding one digit to the right of the decimal point, as:

FORMAL	331.
OVAL	331.1
ROUND	331.2
SQUARE	331.3

It is possible to continue the subdivisions by adding more digits to the right of a decimal point. The number 331.2 could be subdivided into 331.21, 331.22, 331.23, and so on.

Duplex-numeric subject systems, which use a number, a dash, and a second number, permit more than ten main headings and more than nine divisions under any one heading. (Simple-numeric and decimal-numeric systems are limited to ten main headings, 000–900, and nine main divisions under any one heading 110–190, for example.) Further subdivisions are possible with the duplex-numeric systems by adding a hyphen and beginning a new series of numbers. Some duplex-numeric systems use a combination of numbers and letters of the alphabet. The table on page 121 shows how a main heading and its eleven divisions would be assigned codes in both simple-numeric and duplex-numeric systems. Note that the tenth and eleventh divisions cannot be coded in the simple-numeric system.

SUBJECT	SIMPLE-NUMERIC	DUPLEX-NUMERIC
FAMILY ROOM	800	8
BOOKCASES	810	8-1
CHAIRS	820	8-2
FIREPLACE ACCESSORIES	830	8-3
GAME BOARDS	840	8-4
LAMPS	850	8-5
LOUNGERS	860	8-6
PLANT STANDS	870	8-7
SOFAS	880	8-8
TABLES	890	8-9
TV STANDS	No provision	8-10
WALL UNITS	No provision	8-11

The following tables summarize the numbering system for simple numeric, decimal-numeric, and duplex-numeric systems.

SIMPLE-NUMERIC

500 ADMINISTRATION
  510 MEETINGS
    511 STAFF MEETINGS
    512 OPERATIONS MEETINGS
    513 REVIEW MEETINGS
    514 TECHNICAL MEETINGS

DECIMAL-NUMERIC

550 ADMINISTRATION
  551. MEETINGS
    551.1 STAFF MEETINGS
    551.2 OPERATIONS MEETINGS
    551.3 REVIEW MEETINGS
    551.4 TECHNICAL MEETINGS

DUPLEX-NUMERIC

5 ADMINISTRATION
  5-1 MEETINGS
    5-1-1 STAFF MEETINGS
    5-1-2 OPERATIONS MEETINGS
    5-1-3 REVIEW MEETINGS
    5-1-4 TECHNICAL MEETINGS

Steps in Subject Correspondence Filing. You should follow these steps when you are filing papers according to subject.

Inspecting. As in alphabetic correspondence filing, the correspondence is checked for a release mark before filing.

Indexing and Coding. In alphabetic subject filing systems, it is usually necessary to write the subject classification in the upper right corner of the correspondence. In numeric subject filing, the records are coded by writing the number in the upper right corner as in numeric filing.

Because subject captions are not always apparent, the indexing of correspondence by subject is more difficult than indexing by individual or company name. Often the indexing step is performed by the executive who handles the correspondence. If the indexing is performed by a records specialist, the relative index is frequently consulted to determine the exact folder caption under which the correspondence is to be filed. If a piece of correspondence refers to more than one subject, a cross-reference sheet is prepared for the secondary subject.

Sorting. The coded records are sorted into piles using rough and fine sorting techniques as for other filing systems. In subject filing, the first sort is done by the main heading. The successive sorts are done according to the subdivisions as many times as necessary.

Storing. The records for each folder are arranged chronologically with the most recent date on top. If the records are not dated, you might want to stamp or write the date on them to indicate which is most recent. You may file alphabetically within each folder instead of by date depending on the subject. If the order of the contents is not a critical factor in the organization of the materials for their use, filing the most recent on top is the most efficient method to use. The steps in the subject filing of correspondence are shown on page 123.

Cross-Referencing. When a piece of correspondence may be needed under more than one subject heading, a cross-reference sheet may be completed. Some businesses prefer to make a photocopy of the document instead of a cross-reference sheet. An example of a letter which may be filed by subject and cross-referenced is shown on page 124.

STEPS IN THE SUBJECT FILING OF CORRESPONDENCE

1. INSPECTING. Correspondence is checked to make sure it has been released for filing.
2. INDEXING AND CODING. In an alphabetic-subject system it is usually necessary to write the subject classification in the upper right corner. (In a numeric-subject system, the records are coded by writing the folder number in the upper right corner.)
3. SORTING. The coded records are sorted into piles by main and then subheadings, whether they are alphabetic or numeric.

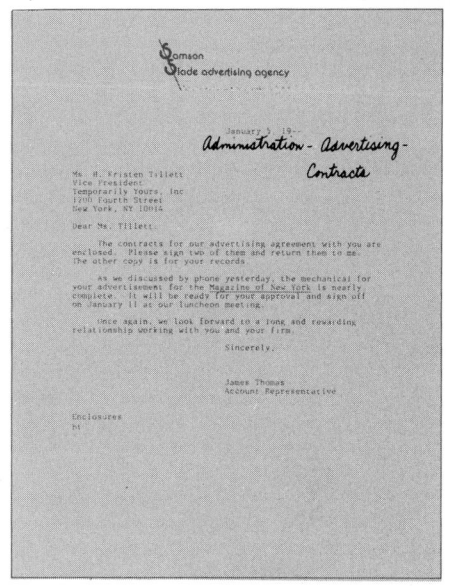

Next, these piles are sorted according to the divisions of the subheading.

4. STORING. Records for each folder are arranged chronologically with the latest date in front and stored in file drawers.

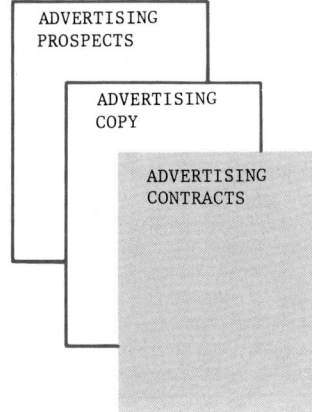

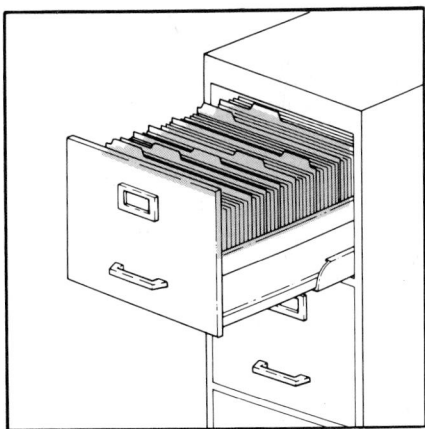

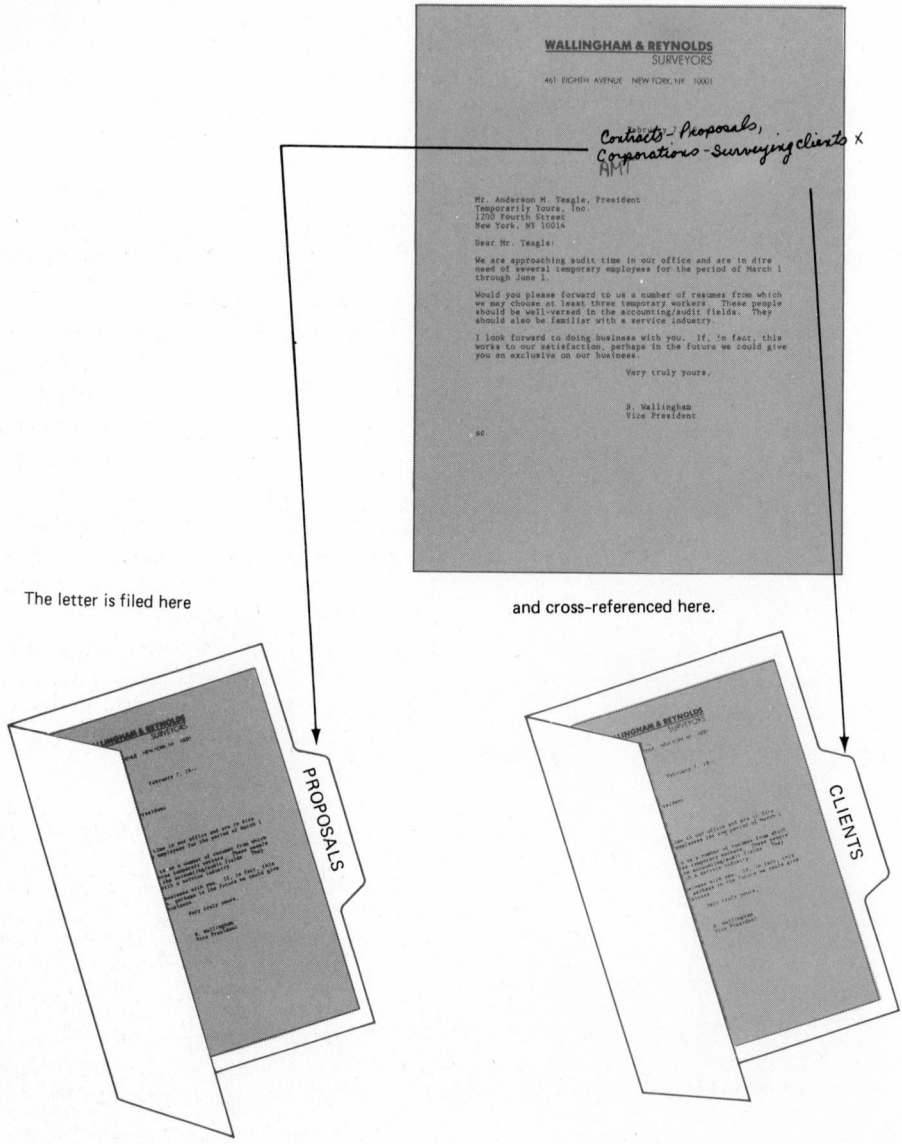

The letter is filed here

and cross-referenced here.

CHRONOLOGICAL FILING

A variation on subject filing is chronological filing: that is, filing items in order by date. This method is often used for follow-up of activities or information. You have already learned that correspondence can be filed chronologically with the most recent on top. Records can also be filed by date in sequence,

COLOR in Filing

Color can be a useful aid to accurate filing as the illustrations on the next four pages show.

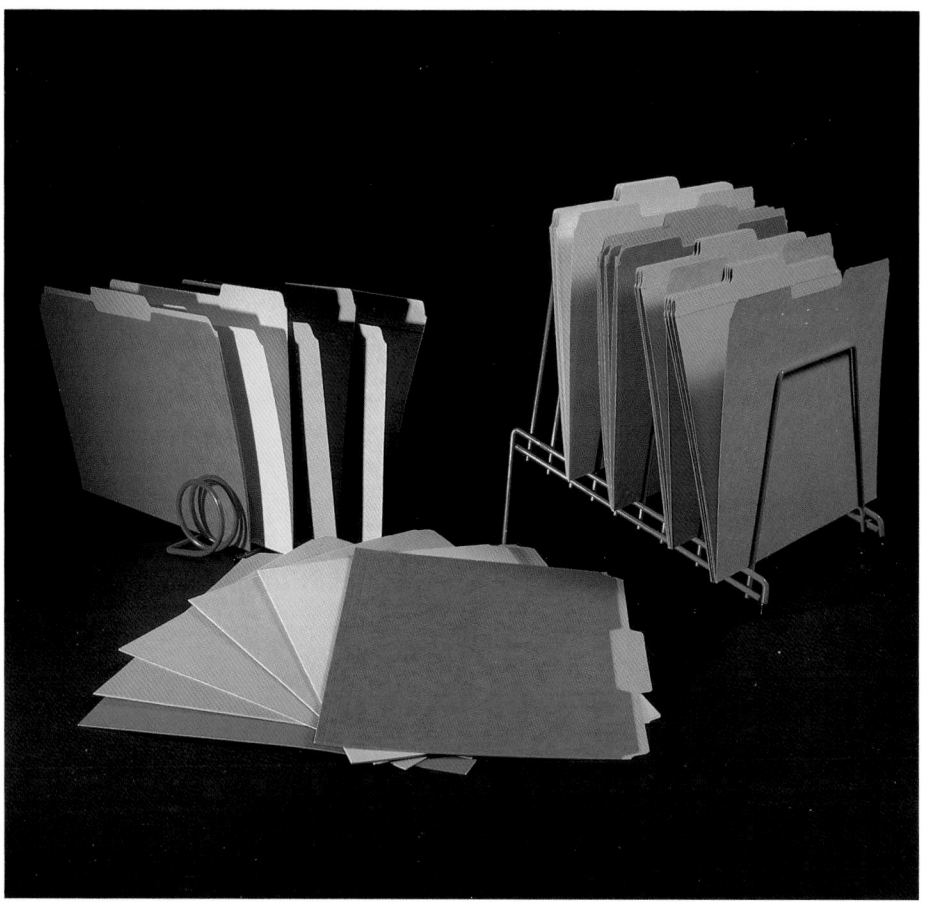

Different colored file folders can make it easy to identify subjects. The distinctive colors also add visual appeal.

Placing color bars on the edges of file folders is another useful way to help sort subjects.

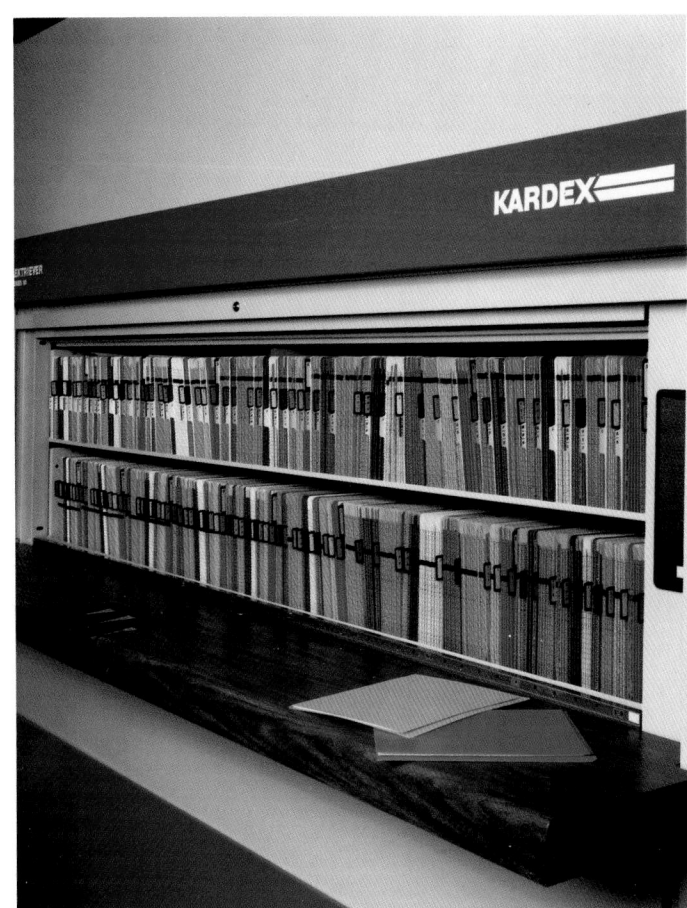

Color-coded folders can also be used in conjunction with an automated filing unit—making it doubly easy to retrieve and return folders.

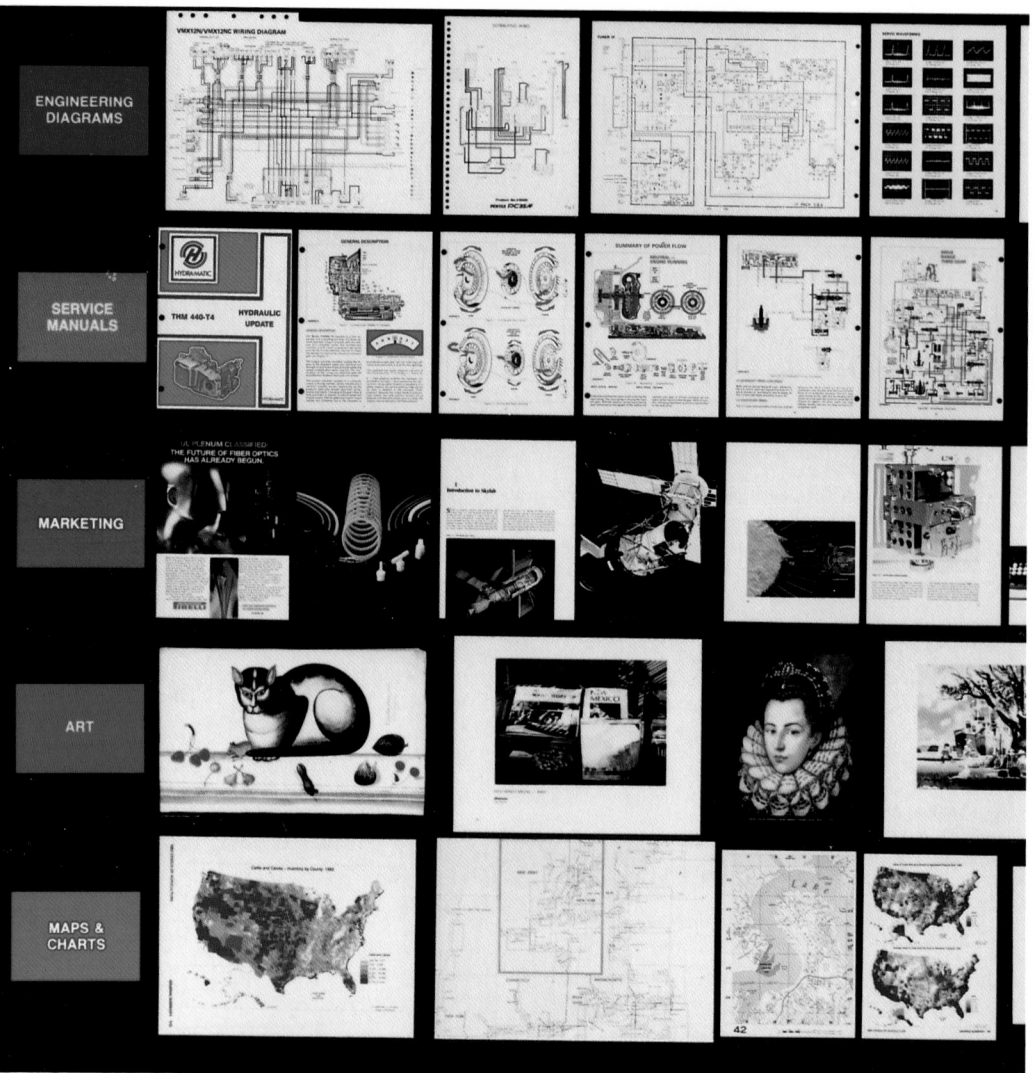

Color microimages make it easy for someone to identify documents, particularly when the documents have detailed or technical information.

grouped by day of the month, month, or year. Chapter 12 deals with chronological filing, which will help you with your day-to-day activities on the job. Job 53 of the *Practice Materials* also deals with chronological filing.

FILING PRACTICE

Complete Job 53 of the *Practice Materials*.

PERSONAL FILES

Each individual has personal records which must be stored and safeguarded. Disasters can happen to homes as well as businesses resulting in loss of financial and personal records, and these records may not be replaceable. Failure to keep good financial records can result in losses through duplicate payments, inability to produce warranties and receipts, and difficulty in proving deductions for income tax returns. Failure to keep personal records may create difficulties when proof of age, education, ownership, or date of purchase is required.

Categories of Personal Records. There are general categories of personal records which can help in the organization and storage of these documents:

1. Financial records:
   a. Medical records
   b. Insurance records
   c. Tax records
   d. Checks and bank statements
   e. Savings account statements
   f. Stock certificates and investment records
   g. Credit card records
   h. Utility bills such as electricity, gas, telephone
   i. Automobile records
   j. Warranties for major appliances and home improvements
2. Personal documents:
   a. Birth certificates
   b. Marriage and divorce papers
   c. Passports
   d. Wills
   e. Military service records
   f. Social security records
3. Ownership documents:
   a. Deeds and leases
   b. Titles and registrations
4. Education documents:
   a. High school transcripts

b. College transcripts

c. Documentation of other education (military, correspondence)

5. Miscellaneous documents:

    a. Personal correspondence

    b. Personal souvenirs and mementos

    c. Photographs

Safeguarding Documents. Often when television reporters cover a catastrophe such as a tornado, the people interviewed say they can replace the house and furniture but such things as personal papers and photographs can never be replaced and are lost forever.

Several ways in which records may be safeguarded are:

1. Organize documents in files and store in a file cabinet, closed cabinet, or sturdy box.
2. Store important documents which cannot be replaced or can be replaced only with time and difficulty in a safe deposit box. The cost is only a few dollars a year for a small box.
3. Give a friend or relative copies of important documents or lists of information such as insurance companies and policy numbers, credit card numbers, and bank account numbers.

It takes time to set up files and organize records. The time spent now in organizing important papers may well be saved later when records need to be located.

Transfer and Disposal. As with office files, home files should be purged periodically of unneeded material. Keeping operating instructions and warranties for small appliances is wise in the event of repair, but if the appliance would be cheaper to replace than to fix, dispose of the paperwork. Tax records need to be kept for a longer period of time than most records. Some records such as copies of last year's utility bills are interesting to keep but only for the purpose of comparison with this year's bills. Such paperwork can be disposed of after a year or two. As with businesses, each household should set up some guidelines about how long to keep documents in the files. Personal files can become just as cluttered as business files.

SELECTING A HOME FILING SYSTEM

Most home filing systems consist of subject files, but home files can be set up according to alphabetic or numeric filing rules as well. Deciding which system to choose is dependent upon an analysis of:

1. Number of records to be filed
2. Categories of records
3. Expansion needs
4. Facilities available for storage

Home Subject Systems. Setting up subject files requires some decisions. For example, INSURANCE may be a guide with folders for AUTO INSURANCE, HOUSE INSURANCE, and HEALTH INSURANCE. Or, you can set up an AUTO category and include AUTO INSURANCE, AUTO REPAIRS, and AUTO WARRANTIES. A HOUSE category might include HOUSE INSURANCE, MORTGAGE INFORMATION, and PROPERTY TAXES.

EXAMPLES OF FILING PERSONAL RECORDS (Subject file)

Example One	
AUTO	**HOUSE**
Insurance	Insurance
Payments	Mortgage/Rent
Repairs	Repairs
Warranties	Utilities

Example Two	
INSURANCE	**REPAIRS**
Auto	Appliances
Health	Auto
House/Apartment	House
UTILITIES	**MONTHLY BILLS**
Electricity	Car Payment
Gas	Credit Cards
Telephone	Insurance
Water	Rent

Other Home Systems. Alphabetic systems are useful when the number of records to be filed is relatively small, the records tend to be easily assigned to a particular name such as DR. WATSON, XYZ INSURANCE COMPANY, and MI APARTMENT COMPLEX, and the records pertain to one individual or organization. Alphabetic systems are ideal for address lists.

A simple alphabetic subject arrangement might be as follows:

Bank Accounts
Car Payments
Credit Cards
Income Tax Information
Insurance
Medical Information
Rent
Social Security
Utilities

Numeric systems are useful when numbers can be easily assigned to material filed. You may decide to file bills by account numbers instead of the name of the company. Numeric systems are useful when you will need to expand the number of files in the future and do not want to reorganize the whole system. Numeric files are also useful if you do not want to identify the contents of the file in the caption. A list of numbers is maintained as the register and an index is maintained to find the number of a file.

AUXILIARY FILE SYSTEMS

In addition to the main personal files, other file systems may be useful. The suggestions given for businesses for filing and keeping records on floppy disks or hard disks apply equally well to households with home computers. A system for organizing the program and data disks will make using the computer much easier and more enjoyable. A record collection may need an index to keep track of the items obtained thus far. Addresses and phone numbers of friends and relatives may be kept in a small card box arranged alphabetically. A chronological or tickler file may be used to keep track of bills, future events, and other dated items. Coupons for grocery store items may be filed by subject categories. Whatever the need, the basic rules of business filing can be applied to applications found in the home.

GENERAL REVIEW

1. What is *subject filing*? (Competency 1)
2. Give at least two examples of business situations in which subject filing is used, listing the advantages of subject filing in each situation. (Competencies 2 and 3)
3. List and describe the parts of a subject correspondence file. (Competency 4)
4. Describe the three kinds of subject filing systems. (Competency 7)
5. What is chronological filing? (Competency 8)
6. Why are files needed for personal use? (Competency 11)
7. What are some personal documents that need to be safeguarded? (Competency 12)
8. How can personal files be safeguarded against destruction? (Competency 13)

CASE PROBLEMS

1. The Supreme Auto Parts Company operates a chain of stores selling parts for all kinds of cars. It uses a subject filing system in which records

of suppliers are filed according to the parts they manufacture. The Purchasing Department has complained of difficulty in locating records when the name of a company, but not the car, is known. What can be done to eliminate this difficulty? (Competencies 2, 3, and 4)

2. The Prometheus Products Company uses a subject filing system. All the work in connection with filing, including the coding, has been performed in the filing department. The following proposal has been placed in the suggestion box for reducing confusion about the subject categories used for storing records: "Because the department receiving an incoming letter is the one most likely to refer to it again after it has been stored, the coding should be done by that department rather than by the filing department." Do you think this suggestion should be adopted? Give your reasons. (Competencies 1, 2, 3, 6)

3. You work in an office which uses subject filing for miscellaneous information. Currently, there are eight drawers of assorted topics neatly arranged. The person who originated the system is no longer there; others in the office are as lost as you are when it comes to trying to locate something. Often you have had to look through two or three drawers to find what you need. You feel there has to be a better way. What is missing? What steps can you take to solve your problem with the files? (Competencies 2, 3, and 4)

4. Leslie has recently begun working for McNally Cards, Incorporated. McNally uses subject filing. Leslie has difficulty locating records she needs to consult. She is hesitant to file any correspondence because she does not fully understand the system. How can she learn the system? (Competencies 2, 3, 6, and 7)

5. John Winters works in a newly opened job placement office. He needs some advice on setting up his files. He has decided that alphabetic filing will be unsuitable because he deals with job titles instead of individual names. He has eliminated numeric filing because he would like to group related information together for easy access. He has made a list of the folder captions he has started to set up. Later on, he thinks he will need to divide the contents of some of these folders. What would you suggest? (Competencies 2, 3)

6. As part of your job for Don Richard Associates, you need to keep files pertaining to office equipment and employee activities. Additionally, you are responsible for supplying information and forms to employees for various benefits and company needs. The person who had your job before you organized an alphabetic subject file with a dictionary arrangement. You feel another arrangement would be easier to use. After reading the folder captions which follow, make a list of the guides you will use and which folders will be placed behind each guide. Then make a relative index to go with your new file arrangement. Make any changes needed in these captions (explanations of contents are given in parentheses).

ANNUAL OFFICE PICNIC
BOWLING TEAM (social activity)
BUSINESS CARDS (recorders)
CALCULATORS (how to operate)
CALCULATORS (repairs)
CHRISTMAS PARTY
COMPANY POLICY AND PROCEDURES HANDOUTS
COPIERS (operating instructions)
COPIERS (repairs)
DUPLICATING EQUIPMENT (operating instructions)
EMPLOYEE HEALTH INSURANCE APPLICATIONS AND CLAIMS FORMS
EMPLOYEE HEALTH INSURANCE CLAIM FORMS
EMPLOYEE HEALTH INSURANCE COVERAGE CHANGE FORMS
EMPLOYEE HEALTH INSURANCE INFORMATION
EMPLOYEE LIFE INSURANCE APPLICATIONS
EMPLOYEE LIFE INSURANCE INFORMATION
EMPLOYEE TRAINING PROGRAM: WORK AND TIME MANAGE-MENT SEMINAR
EQUIPMENT OPERATION INSTRUCTIONS: TYPING EQUIP-MENT
FORMS (ordering information)
HUMAN RELATIONS SEMINAR (for employees)
INCOME TAX WITHHOLDING FORMS
LETTERHEAD AND OTHER STATIONERY SUPPLIES
PERSONNEL INFORMATION BLANKS (to update personnel files)
REPAIRS ON DUPLICATING EQUIPMENT
OFFICE SUPPLIES (small items)
TYPING EQUIPMENT REPAIRS
WP/DP INTEGRATION SEMINAR (for employees) (Competency 9)

7. Survey your personal records and determine which records you need to keep in files at home, which records or information about them needs to be stored at another location, and which filing system would be best for your records. Write a plan for organizing your personal documents and papers into a home filing system. (Competencies 11, 12, 13)

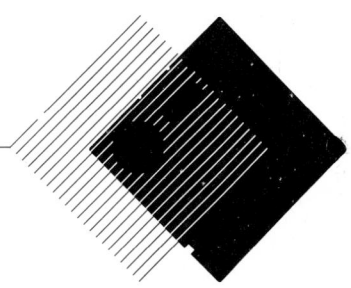

9

GEOGRAPHIC SYSTEMS

COMPETENCIES

When you have completed this chapter, you will be able to:

1. Define geographic filing.
2. Give at least two examples of business situations in which geographic filing is used.
3. List and describe the parts of a geographic correspondence file.
4. File and find cards using a geographic correspondence filing system (See Jobs 47 to 49 in the *Practice Materials*.)
5. Index and code correspondence for filing, prepare cross-references, and file and find correspondence using a geographic filing system. (See Jobs 50 and 51 in the *Practice Materials*.)
6. Select guide and folder captions when given a list of items which are to be filed using a geographic system.

DEFINITION OF GEOGRAPHIC FILING

Geographic filing is an alphabetic arrangement of records first according to location and then according to name or subject.

WHEN GEOGRAPHIC FILING IS USED

When records filed by location serve the organization more efficiently than if they were filed in any other way, geographic filing is used.

Sales organizations, for example, may classify customers by territories or states to provide a mailing list that will speed the sorting of outgoing mail as required by the U.S. Postal Service. Public utilities, which have thousands of customers, may divide the areas they serve into geographic districts with a branch office in each district. National service organizations are organized geographically by state and by division or council within the state; other organizations may be set up by region, state, city, town, village, county, or township. Real estate firms use listings organized by names of the sections of a city.

The telephone book is an example of geographic filing with listings in alphabetic order for the white and blue pages and in alphabetic subject order in the yellow pages. In some areas of the country one or more towns will make up a regional area; in others, each town may be listed separately in the telephone book, with two or more adjoining towns included in the same book. Usually the division depends on whether or not the numbers can be dialed without toll charges to the calling party.

GEOGRAPHIC CARD FILES

In some situations, a card file of information organized by location is useful. For example, a salesperson might keep a card file of all customers in a specific area to notify when a visit is being planned. A utility company might keep a card file of customers arranged by street name. Charitable organizations frequently organize pledge cards and other records by territory to help divide the work load so that a personal follow-up may be made with the greatest efficiency. Geographic cross-reference cards (see page 133) will assist in locating records in geographic card files.

Card files are also necessary to serve as a card index to the main geographic correspondence files.

GEOGRAPHIC CORRESPONDENCE FILES

As mentioned before, geographic filing is used when records need to be grouped by location rather than by name.

Organization of Geographic Correspondence Files. There are two main parts to the geographic correspondence filing system: the main geographic files and the card index. A real estate company, for example, would group leases and the correspondence about its rental properties in a main geographic file; an alphabetic correspondence file by name of tenant would be inefficient because the tenants change. A card index arranged alphabetically according to the name of the tenant, however, is necessary to save time when the address is not known. For those records which do not fit the geographic system, alphabetic or subject files may be set up.

Arrangement of Records in Folders. The three places that a record might be located in a geographic file, beginning with the state miscellaneous folder, are

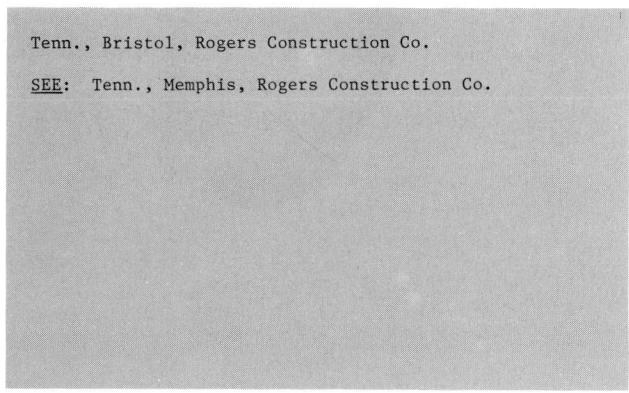

Tenn., Bristol, Rogers Construction Co.

SEE: Tenn., Memphis, Rogers Construction Co.

illustrated on page 134. Within individual folders in a geographic file, records are arranged chronologically, with the record bearing the latest date in front. In town or city miscellaneous folders, records are arranged alphabetically first by the names of the correspondents and then chronologically for each correspondent. In state miscellaneous folders, records are arranged first alphabetically by the name of the town or city, then alphabetically by the name of the correspondent, and finally chronologically for each correspondent.

Steps in Geographic Correspondence Filing. Similar to those in subject correspondence filing, the steps in geographic correspondence filing are described here and illustrated on page 135 in detail.

Inspecting. Correspondence is checked to make sure it has been released for filing just as it is checked in alphabetic or subject correspondence filing.

Indexing and Coding. The name of the correspondent and the location under which the record is to be filed are determined. The location may be circled to make it more distinctive because the name of the organization is also underlined. If cross-referencing under a second location is necessary, it should be done at this time.

Sorting. Records are sorted first by the main geographic divisions and then by the subdivisions.

Storing. The guides of the geographic divisions and subdivisions are used to locate the individual folder. If there is no individual folder, the record is placed in the miscellaneous folder for that division or subdivision. A miscellaneous folder for a state, for example, will hold correspondence for all cities and towns in the state that have fewer than five pieces of correspondence. This

MISCELLANEOUS AND INDIVIDUAL FOLDERS IN A GEOGRAPHIC CORRESPONDENCE FILE

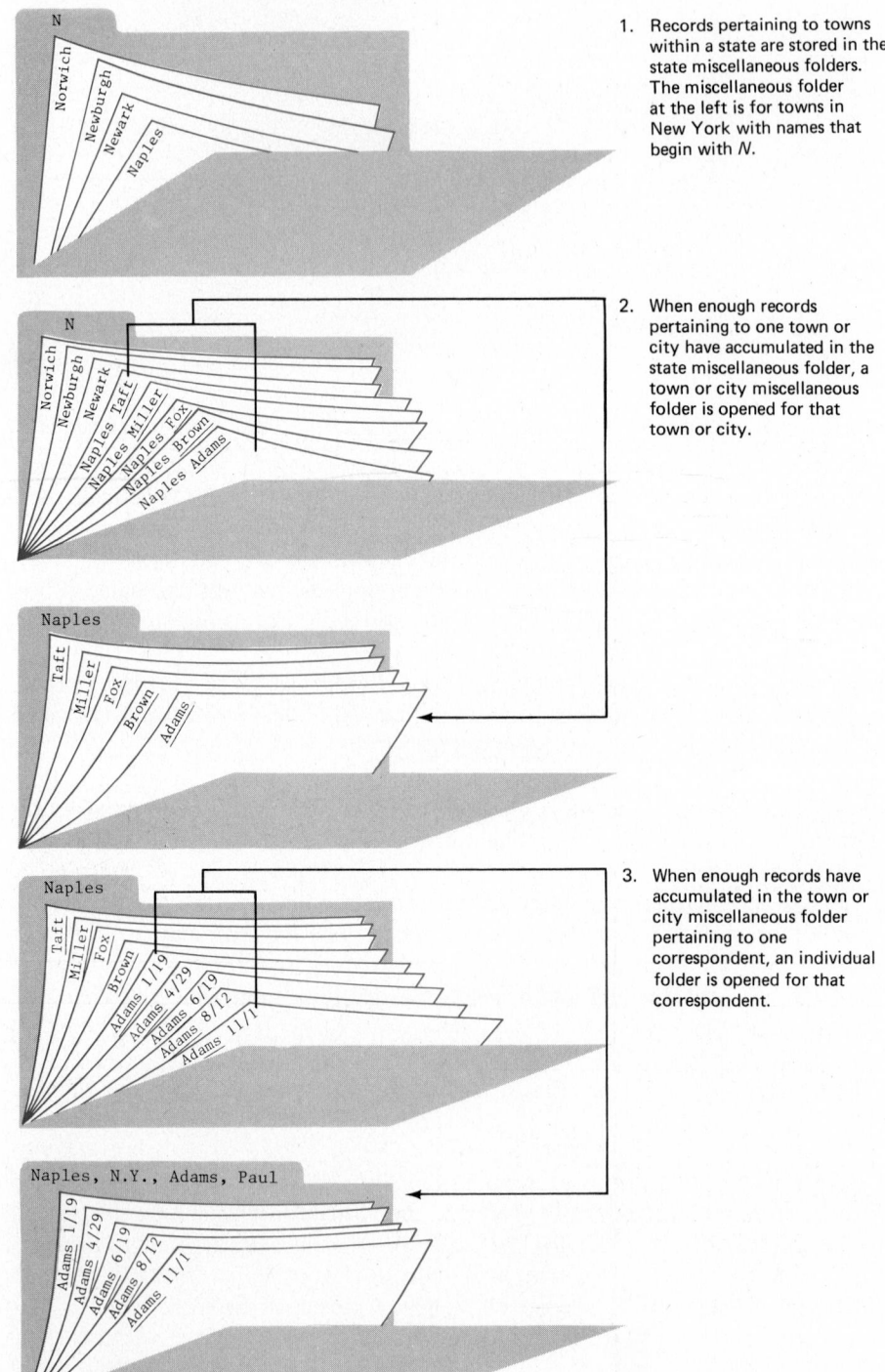

1. Records pertaining to towns within a state are stored in the state miscellaneous folders. The miscellaneous folder at the left is for towns in New York with names that begin with *N*.

2. When enough records pertaining to one town or city have accumulated in the state miscellaneous folder, a town or city miscellaneous folder is opened for that town or city.

3. When enough records have accumulated in the town or city miscellaneous folder pertaining to one correspondent, an individual folder is opened for that correspondent.

STEPS IN GEOGRAPHIC CORRESPONDENCE FILING

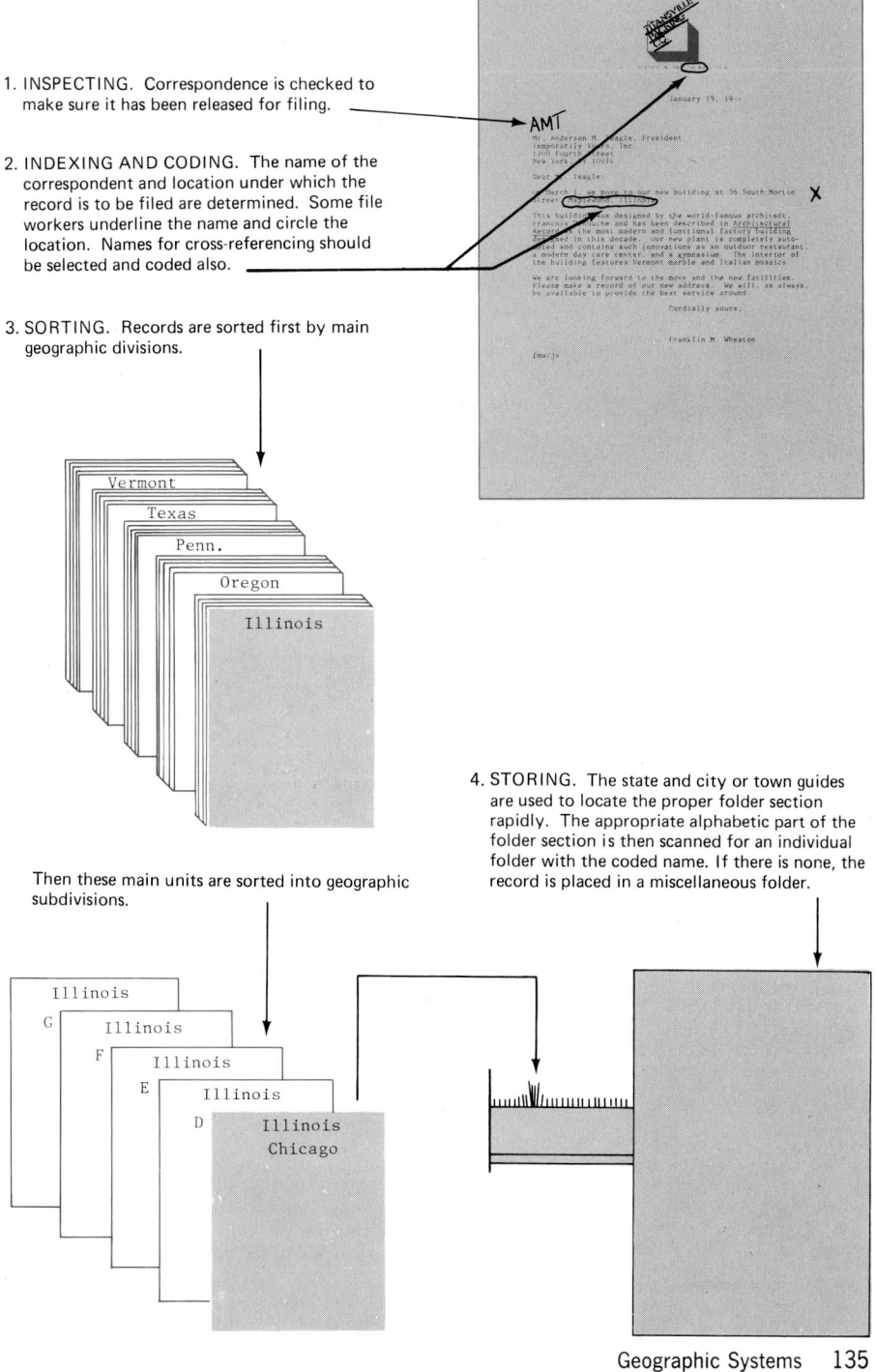

1. INSPECTING. Correspondence is checked to make sure it has been released for filing.

2. INDEXING AND CODING. The name of the correspondent and location under which the record is to be filed are determined. Some file workers underline the name and circle the location. Names for cross-referencing should be selected and coded also.

3. SORTING. Records are sorted first by main geographic divisions.

4. STORING. The state and city or town guides are used to locate the proper folder section rapidly. The appropriate alphabetic part of the folder section is then scanned for an individual folder with the coded name. If there is none, the record is placed in a miscellaneous folder.

Then these main units are sorted into geographic subdivisions.

avoids overloading the files with town or city folders with few papers in them. When five or more records have accumulated for one correspondent in a miscellaneous folder, an individual folder is opened as shown in the illustration on page 134.

Cross-Referencing. The cross-referencing of records in the geographic correspondence filing system is shown below and on page 133. The coding may be done on the correspondence and copies or cross-reference sheets prepared for the other folder or folders. In some cases, the cross-referencing may be done in the card index.

Typical Geographic Files. Let us see how the contents of a typical file drawer, such as the one that is illustrated on page 137, are arranged, (1) looking from front to back and (2) looking at the position of the tabs from left to right.

A GEOGRAPHIC CROSS-REFERENCE SHEET

CROSS-REFERENCE SHEET

Name or Subject

ILLINOIS, MAPLEWOOD
TITANSVILLE PACKING CO.

Date

1/19/19--

Regarding

SEE

Name or Subject

ILLINOIS, CHICAGO
TITANSVILLE PACKING CO.

File cross-reference sheet under name or subject at top of the sheet and by the latest date of papers. Describe matter for identification purposes. The papers, themselves, should be filed under name or subject after "SEE."

Made in U.S.A.

GEOGRAPHIC FILE DRAWER ARRANGEMENT

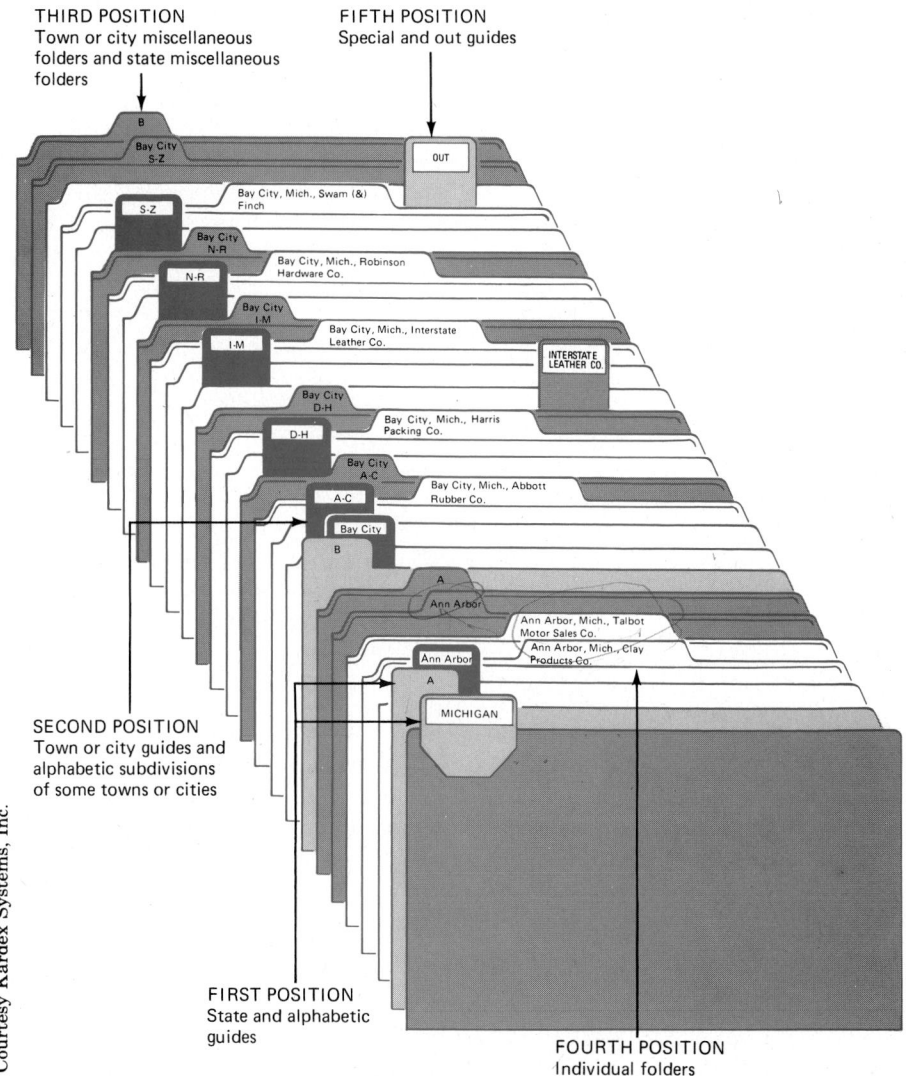

THIRD POSITION
Town or city miscellaneous folders and state miscellaneous folders

FIFTH POSITION
Special and out guides

B

Bay City
S-Z

OUT

S-Z

Bay City, Mich., Swam (&) Finch

Bay City
N-R

N-R

Bay City, Mich., Robinson Hardware Co.

Bay City
I-M

I-M

Bay City, Mich., Interstate Leather Co.

INTERSTATE LEATHER CO.

Bay City
D-H

D-H

Bay City, Mich., Harris Packing Co.

Bay City
A-C

A-C

Bay City, Mich., Abbott Rubber Co.

Bay City

B

A

Ann Arbor

Ann Arbor, Mich., Talbot Motor Sales Co.

Ann Arbor, Mich., Clay Products Co.

Ann Arbor

A

MICHIGAN

SECOND POSITION
Town or city guides and alphabetic subdivisions of some towns or cities

FIRST POSITION
State and alphabetic guides

FOURTH POSITION
Individual folders

A geographic file has guide and folder tabs arranged from left to right. Notice that five city miscellaneous folders, subdivided by alphabetic range, and five individual folders prevent overcrowding of records for Bay City.

1. Looking from front to back:
    a. In the front is a guide covering a major segment of the file. This is called a *state guide,* and its tab has the caption *North Dakota.*
    b. Behind the state guide is an *alphabetic guide,* and its tab has the caption *A.* It covers all cities in North Dakota beginning with *A.*

c. Behind the alphabetic guide is a *town or city guide* for the town of *Abercrombie*.

d. Behind the town guide are *individual folders* for correspondents in Abercrombie.

e. Behind the individual folders is a *town or city miscellaneous folder,* and its tab has the caption *Abercrombie* for correspondents in Abercrombie who do not warrant an individual folder.

f. Behind the town miscellaneous folder is a *state miscellaneous folder* with the caption *A* for towns in North Dakota beginning with *A* that do not warrant a town or city miscellaneous folder. For example, correspondence pertaining to Auburn, North Dakota, would be stored in the *A* state miscellaneous folder.

2. Looking at the position of the tabs from left to right:

First position:	*State Guides* and *alphabetic guides*
Second position:	*Town or city guides*
Third position:	*Town or city miscellaneous folders* and *state miscellaneous folders*
Fourth position:	*Individual folders* (The caption gives the name of the town or city first, the state second, and then the correspondent. The town is listed before the state because the town guide is nearby, making cross-checking easy.)
Fifth position:	*Special guides* and *out guides*

Sometimes, when there is a large volume of correspondence for one town or city, the correspondence in a town or city miscellaneous folder is alphabetically subdivided. In the illustration, for example, BISMARCK has been subdivided so that there are five miscellaneous folders for BISMARCK, each for a different alphabetic group. There is a guide for each of the subdivided folders.

FILING PRACTICE

Complete Jobs 47 through 51 of the *Practice Materials*.

GENERAL REVIEW

1. What is geographic filing? (Competency 1)
2. Give at least two examples of business situations where geographic filing is used. (Competency 2)
3. List and describe the parts of the geographic correspondence file. (Competency 3)

4. List and describe the steps in preparing correspondence to be filed in a geographic system. (Competency 5)
5. How is cross-referencing done in geographic filing systems? (Competency 5)

CASE PROBLEMS

1. DelGado Real Estate Company has two types of miscellaneous folders in its geographic file: (a) town or city and (b) state. One of the file workers, Sandy Dunnington, has suggested that the state miscellaneous folders be eliminated. If you were her file supervisor, would you follow Sandy's suggestion? (Competency 3)
2. Brockhill Furniture Limited operates within the boundaries of Texas. Approximately 85 percent of its business is conducted in the cities of Dallas, Fort Worth, and Houston. The remainder is done in the 25 cities and towns listed below. What primary and secondary guide captions should the company decide upon when it sets up its geographic filing system? (Competency 6)

a. Arlington
b. Barksdale
c. Bedford
d. Conroe
e. Dodge
f. El Camino
g. Fords Corner
h. Gallaway
i. Galveston
j. Highland Park
k. Irving
l. Kellerville
m. La Salle
n. Logan
o. Lynchburg
p. Manchester
q. Montgomery
r. New Salem
s. Oakland
t. Piedmont
u. Quintana
v. Red Hill
w. San Antonio
x. Silver City
y. Wildwood

3. Your employer supervises eight salespeople who work the territories in your state. Records are stored geographically by city. Charles Collins, Rachel Madalinski, and Barbara Johnson have been hired recently to fill three vacancies on the sales staff. You find that they are having difficulty locating some of the folders they need because they are unfamiliar with the area and do not know which customers are in which cities. Some customers have branches in more than one city. How can you help these three individuals? (Competency 3)

10

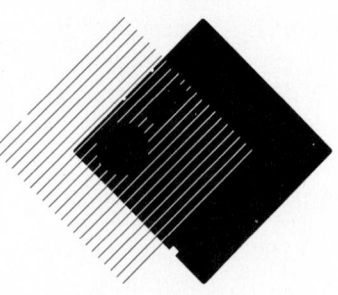

RECORDS AND DATABASE
CONTROL AND RETENTION

COMPETENCIES

When you have completed this chapter, you will be able to:

1. Define the terms *records control, charge systems, electronic files control, records retention, merging files, records transfer and disposal,* and *disaster planning.*
2. Describe the importance of a records control system.
3. List and describe the parts of a charge system.
4. List the information which needs to be included on a requisition form.
5. List four ways to replace a record or folder which has been removed from the file.
6. List steps to take when locating a lost record or folder.
7. Describe why records control is necessary for informal file systems.
8. List two ways to safeguard electronic file material.
9. Describe the importance of restrictions to making changes in electronic file documents.
10. List storage guidelines for safeguarding electronic files.
11. List ways of locating lost files on magnetic media.
12. Describe the differences between hard copy records control and retention and magnetic media records control and retention.
13. Describe why a set period for records retention is difficult to determine.

14. List the three classifications of records and give examples of each classification.
15. Describe why merging files is helpful in the records retention and transfer process.
16. State questions to consider when making records transfer decisions.
17. Name two plans for the transfer of records and describe how each plan works.
18. List the steps in the transfer process.
19. List ways to dispose of records.
20. Describe advantages and disadvantages of using magnetic media and microfilm for transfer and storage purposes.
21. Describe the steps to protect records from disaster.

RECORDS CONTROL

Records control refers to the procedures used to keep track of records after they have been created or received and stored in the files whether the files are manual or electronic. All records should be filed in a timely manner according to a plan developed for the most efficient access and retrieval. If records are not readily available or if they are so hard to get that it is easier to do without them, they are useless for the office worker. Without proper procedures, the business runs the risk of losing valuable time and money attempting to find needed records. The failure to find documents can have serious financial consequences, and in addition it projects a poor image to customers, clients, and others.

Paper Files. Much of the material kept in files is still on hard copy. To illustrate the procedures for handling paper files, the path of a letter after it is received was outlined on page 65. Incoming mail is date- and time-stamped to verify receipt. Correspondence created in the office is ready for filing along with incoming correspondence on which required action has been taken when it is placed in a special folder or out basket for "to be filed" materials.

Large organizations employ people whose job it is to see that materials are filed promptly and their use controlled. Small organizations may have informal procedures. However, all organizations need some procedure to control the use of files and to locate files which have been removed from the storage area. This control of the files is accomplished by means of a charge system.

Electronic Files. Most documents are created using a word processor or word processing program on a microcomputer. These records are generated from rough draft copy, dictation, or by inputting previously printed or typed copy. These documents need to be safeguarded on the magnetic media as this may be the only copy in existence if the office is trying to limit paper files. Some offices store documents on microfilm or magnetic media.

A charge system ensures that all records are accounted for whether they are in the files or in use. The complexity of the system is determined by the needs of the business.

A sales firm, for example, would use a system that makes it possible to locate quickly any information needed on customers. A government installation would need a system that restricts the use of secret information to a designated area so that only those people with a "need to know" would be allowed access.

Failure to develop a charge system, however formal or informal, can result in permanent loss of files or at the very least the need to hunt for necessary files before work can be completed, resulting in loss of valuable employee time.

Parts of a Charge System. A charge system usually consists of the following parts:

1. A requisition form completed by the individual making the request for the record or file folder.
2. A replacement form for the record removed, usually an out card or substitution sheet.
3. A routing slip if a record needs to be used by more than one person.
4. A follow-up system to ensure that the materials are returned to the files.
5. A procedure for locating materials which have become lost.

Requisition. Records may be requested by telephone, by interoffice mail, by messenger, or in person. A requisition form should be completed by the person making the request or by a file worker. The requisition form should include the information listed in the illustration on page 143. Whenever possible the requisition form should be signed by the borrower to establish responsibility for the whereabouts of the record. The borrower's office number, department, and any other information helpful in locating the record should be included on the form.

In a small office where requests are made in person or where the borrower removes the records from the files, the use of a requisition form is not always necessary. Sometimes, the borrower may use a file while in the file area. In these cases, the file clerk might simply put an out card in the file's place until it is returned. Once records leave the proximity of the files, however, more formal requisition procedures should be followed.

Replacement Records. Replacement records, markers to indicate that records have been removed, are useful in three ways:

REQUISITION FORM

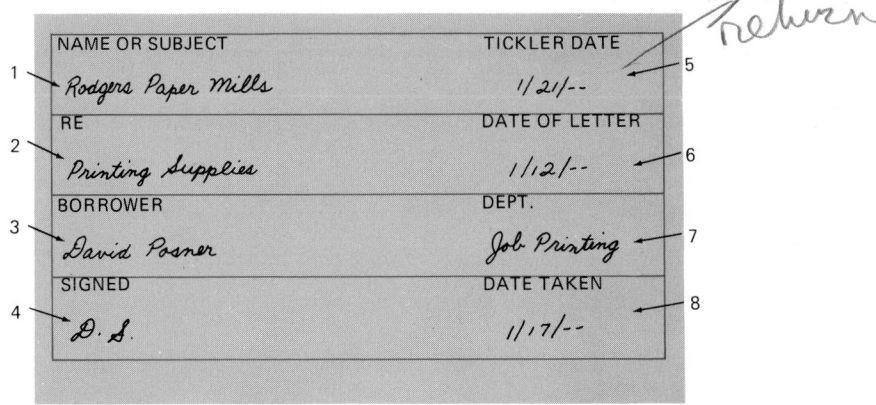

The following information is given on the requisition: (1) the name indexed on the borrowed record, (2) what the record is about or pertains to, (3) the name of the borrower, (4) the name of the person who obtained the record, (5) the date the record is to be returned, (6) the date of the record, (7) the borrower's department, and (8) the date the record was borrowed.

1. They show that records are in use and have not been lost or misfiled.
2. They enable the file worker to follow up the borrowed records to make sure the material is returned to the file.
3. They act as bookmarks to make refiling easy.

Replacement records may be out guides, substitution cards, out folders, or carrier folders.

1. *Out guides*. When an entire folder is removed from the files, an out guide should be placed in the location of the borrowed folder. Out guides are made of the same heavy cardboard as file guides. Two popular types are:

   a. A guide with a pocket at the front for a requisition slip
   b. A cumulative guide on which information about the missing record is written

   Both kinds of out guides have advantages: the pocket type eliminates the need for transferring the information on the requisition slip; the cumulative type provides a history of who has used the records.
   Cumulative guides are usually printed on both sides and are simply turned over when one side is full. These guides are handy in small offices where the employees know each other and can easily obtain a file directly from the user indicated on the guide.
2. *Substitution card*. When an individual paper is removed from a folder, a substitution card should be placed in the folder exactly where the paper was. As with out guides, substitution cards may be either the pocket

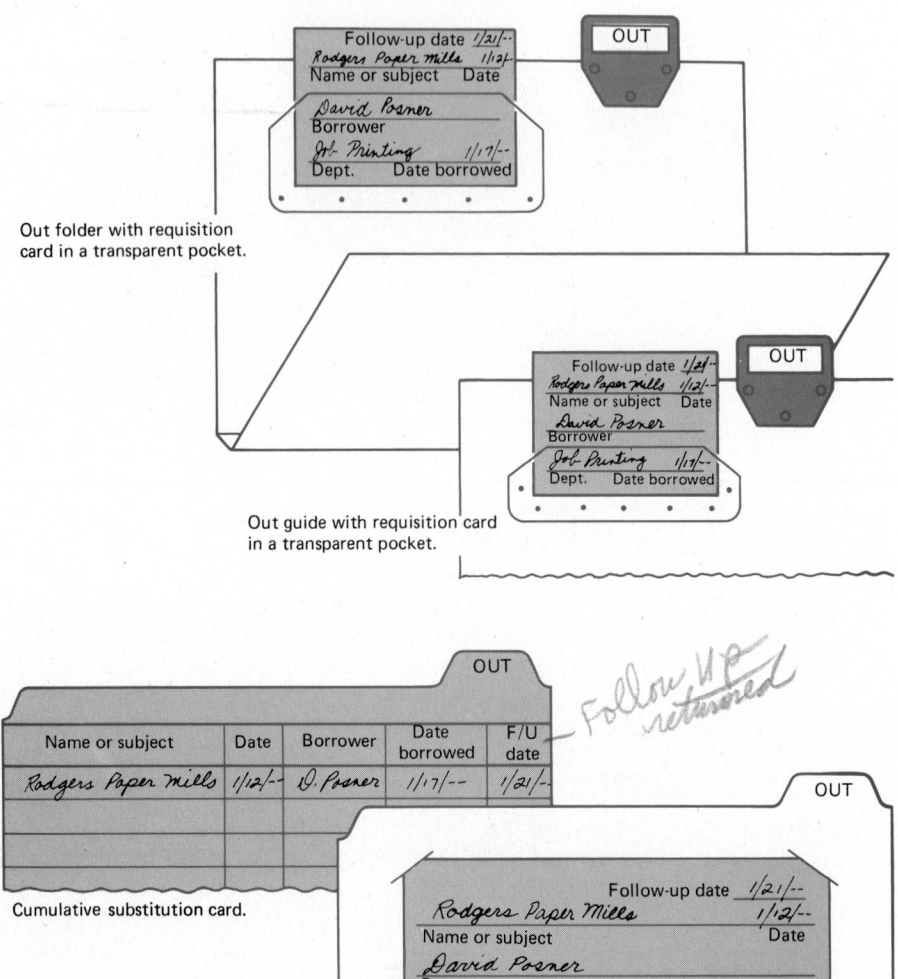

Out folder with requisition card in a transparent pocket.

Out guide with requisition card in a transparent pocket.

Cumulative substitution card.

Substitution card with requisition card attached.

type or the cumulative type. These cards are of a special color and are the same size as the papers in the folders.

3. *Out folders.* Some offices prefer to use out folders instead of out guides. With an out folder, new records that need to be stored can be placed in the temporary folder and transferred to the permanent folder when it is

returned to the files. This eliminates the backlog of unfiled material. The front of an out folder may be like a guide with a pocket or like a cumulative guide.

4. *Carrier folders.* Another method of providing a replacement record is to keep the original folder in the drawer and transfer the contents to a special carrier folder. Carrier folders are made of heavy material that can withstand extensive handling. They are usually a distinctive color which helps to prevent loss and expedites the return of records to the files. A form would be placed in the empty file showing the whereabouts of the records.

Routing Slips. Some records which are requested may need to be used by more than one individual. There are two ways to accomplish this transfer efficiently:

ROUTING SLIP

ROUTING SLIP		
		Date _____
To:	Signed	Date
1. General Manager		
2. Business Manager		
3. Marketing Director		
4.		
5.		
From: _____		
Purpose/Comments:		

Some routing slips have information printed on them to save time in routing.

RECHARGE FORM

```
                    RECHARGE FORM

                                    Date    1/28/--


Name     David Posner            Dept.    Job Printing

Name of person
to whom records
are charged out      David Posner

Record     Rodgers Paper Mills, letter, 1/12/--

Due Date (old)    1/21/--

Date records will be returned    2/4/--
```

The recharge form allows a borrower to establish a new due date. The borrower may be the same person who originally borrowed the record or another person.

1. A routing slip may be attached to the records that are requested and a copy of the routing slip kept with the charge out form. The routing slip will list the names of all the individuals who will be using the records. When finished, the user signs and dates the form. This indicates that the records are ready to be passed to the next person.
2. A recharge form may be completed and forwarded to the file department. This user change is then indicated on the replacement record and the out card in the file.

Follow-up System. The length of time records may be allowed out of the file is determined by the needs of the borrowers, the value of the records, and the need for security. Yet a time limit is necessary because the longer records remain out of the file, the greater the chances for losing or misplacing the records. Records kept past the time limit should be recharged to the user.

At the time a record is requested, a duplicate copy of the requisition form is placed in a follow-up file, called a *tickler file,* under the due date. When the record is returned, the requisition form is pulled and destroyed. A form for records requested prior to the date needed may also be included in the tickler file. On the date the record is needed, a notation should be made that the record was released and which date it should be returned. The file worker

FOLLOW-UP NOTICE

| To | David Posner | Date | 1/21/-- |

From   Central Files

Our records indicate that you have not yet
returned the following material:

Rodgers Paper Mills--letter of 1/12/--.

Please return by   1/28/--
or complete the attached recharge form.

A follow-up notice reminds the borrower that a record is
due and may tell the borrower that an extension of time
to return it will be allowed.

checks the tickler file daily to see if there are any records which have not yet
been returned. After checking the file cabinet to make certain that the records
have not been returned, the file worker sends a notice to the borrower requesting the prompt return of the records or the completion of a recharge
form.

System for Locating a Lost Record and Folder. However careful everyone may
be, records occasionally do get lost or misplaced. Refer to the illustration on
page 149 for a procedure for searching for a lost record. In addition to the eight
steps given in the illustration, check wastebaskets, ask people who borrowed
the record in the recent past, and check whether the record has been sent to
a transfer location outside the main storage area. If the record cannot be
located, then someone familiar with its contents should attempt to reconstruct
it and place that information in the folder.

Similar steps to those suggested for a lost record may be used when attempting to locate a lost folder. Ask others in the office to be on the lookout
for the file. Be cautious that people do not feel they are being accused of
taking and losing the file. Approaching this problem with a cooperative attitude
will enlist the aid of others to assist in the search.

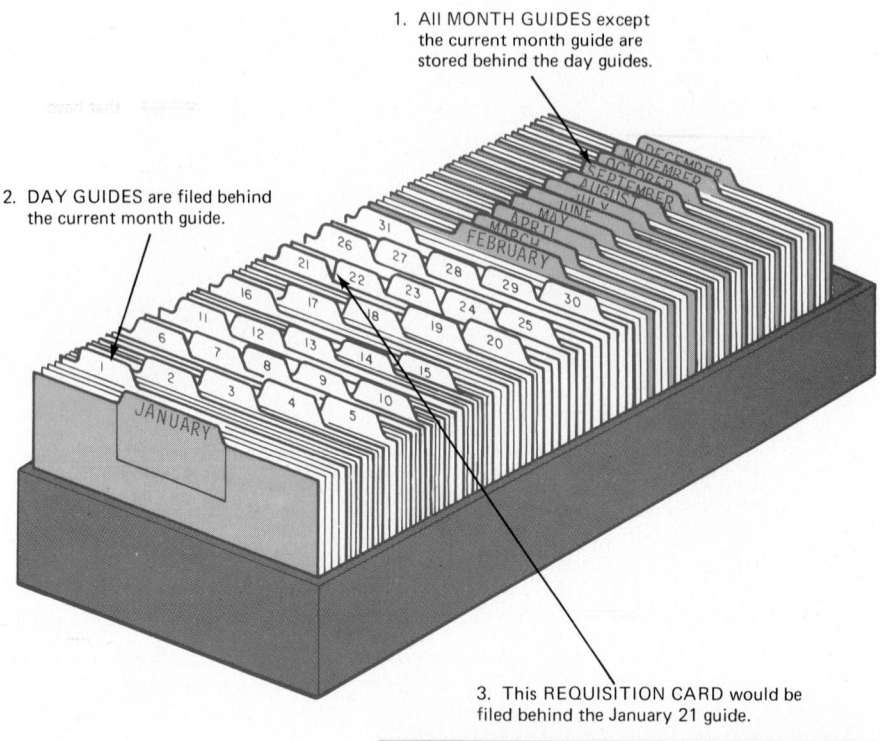

1. All MONTH GUIDES except the current month guide are stored behind the day guides.

2. DAY GUIDES are filed behind the current month guide.

3. This REQUISITION CARD would be filed behind the January 21 guide.

NAME OR SUBJECT	TICKLER DATE
Rodgers Paper Mills	*1/21/--*
RE	DATE OF LETTER
Printing Supplies	*1/12/--*
BORROWER	DEPT.
David Posner	*Job Printing*
SIGNED	DATE TAKEN
D. S.	*1/17/--*

Informal File Systems. Not all offices have the need for a formal charge system. Small offices and files which have limited use may require only a short written notation or oral request from the borrower. Three examples of informal file charge systems are:

1. In and out boxes could be placed on top of the files. A simple form would be filled out by the user indicating the name of the file, when taken, and name of borrower. This form could then be placed in the out

HOW TO CONDUCT AN ORGANIZED SEARCH FOR A LOST RECORD

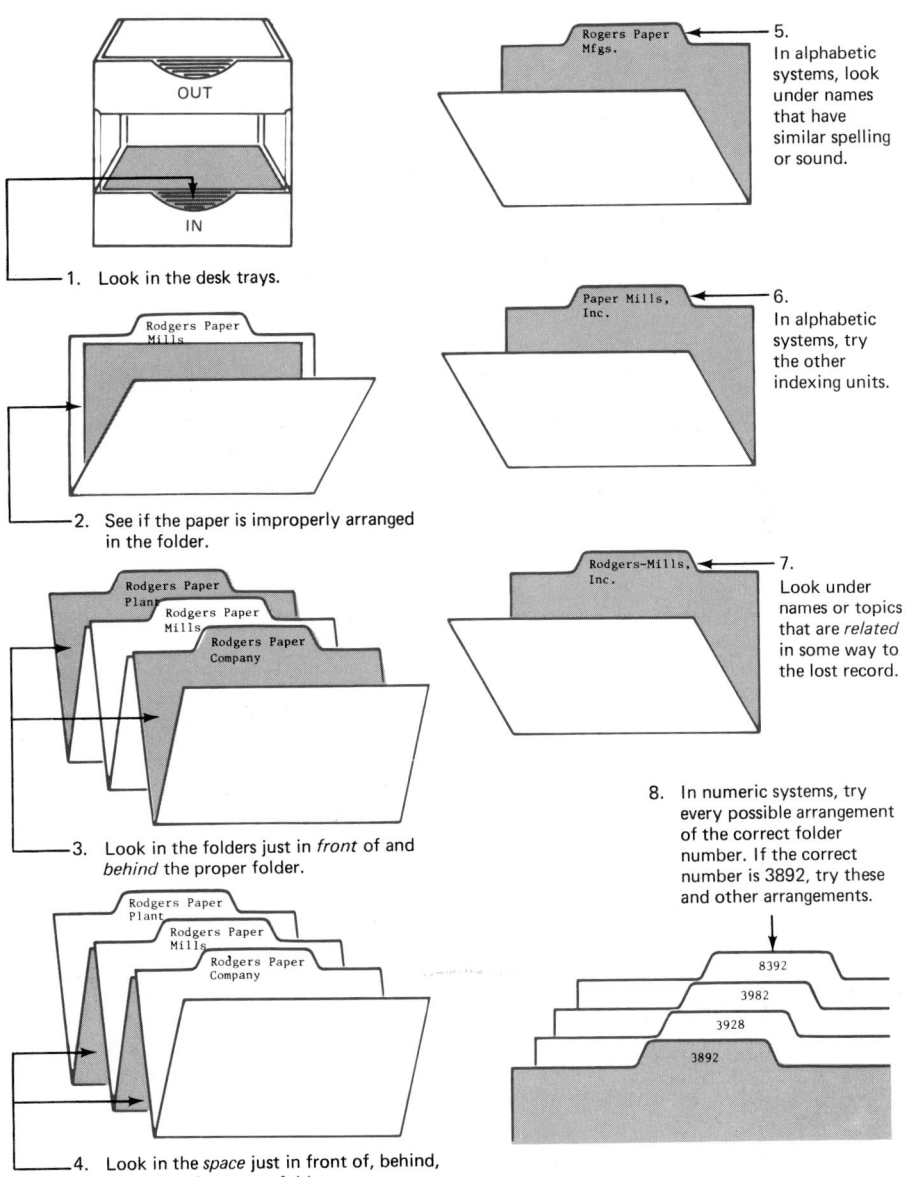

1. Look in the desk trays.

2. See if the paper is improperly arranged in the folder.

3. Look in the folders just in *front* of and *behind* the proper folder.

4. Look in the *space* just in front of, behind, and under the proper folder.

5. In alphabetic systems, look under names that have similar spelling or sound.

6. In alphabetic systems, try the other indexing units.

7. Look under names or topics that are *related* in some way to the lost record.

8. In numeric systems, try every possible arrangement of the correct folder number. If the correct number is 3892, try these and other arrangements.

box. When returned, the file could be placed in the in box or replaced in the files. The out box note could then be discarded.

2. Some files are relatively easy to access but require a skilled person to refile material to prevent misfiling. Libraries with records on microfiche

allow users to remove the fiche from the files, but require the users to place them on top of the file for a professional librarian or file employee to refile.

3. The person who maintains a file used occasionally by others might use a log on which borrowers enter a short description of the record removed, the date, and name or initials of borrower. A check-off space can be used for the returned notation.

Whatever system is developed, procedures should be written and distributed to all users of the files so that no misunderstandings occur. This information should be added to the procedures manual discussed in Chapter 14.

ELECTRONIC FILES CONTROL

Electronic files do not lend themselves to charge and follow-up procedures as easily as hard-copy files. Generally, these materials are used by an individual or a small group of individuals who work closely together. The major concerns of others using electronic files involve safeguarding the material against accidental loss, making changes in documents, and establishing guidelines for storing materials.

Safeguarding Material. If you must loan material that is stored on a disk or allow access through a network to material filed electronically, the following precautions should be taken:

1. Make sure the user knows how to operate the system. An inexperienced user can almost guarantee lost data.
2. Make a copy of the floppy disk or copy from your hard disk onto a floppy disk the necessary documents. This will ensure that no changes will be made to your copies.

Making Changes to Documents. More than one person may work with a document. Those who are involved in making changes and editing documents should be aware of the following:

1. If the user wishes to make changes ask for a copy of the changes—on paper and/or disk. If substantial changes are made, the safest solution is to copy into the system the revised document, noting on the old copy that a new one exists.

   If additions are made to a disk, make sure that these are included on indexes kept of the disk contents.
2. Establish a procedure for granting authority to copy, delete, update, or otherwise use or modify the documents stored. Many times these functions are inherent with the type of work done by an operator; sometimes only the originator or records manager can determine which documents are no longer necessary or which should be used or referenced by others.

Establish Storage Guidelines. Electronic systems, because they are "invisible," make excess storage easy. This results in lack of space for important and vital documents.

1. Establish a procedure for determining before creation those documents which are of short-term value and those documents which require long-term storage. Documents which have no long-term use or application should be deleted in a routine, timely pattern.
2. Indexes of all work stored on electronic media should be kept, preferably in hard copy, to be viewed for completeness and consistency regularly. These indexes can be kept in notebooks or filed on another disk or in another directory. Indexes ensure that file names are assigned in a consistent manner, short-term storage is deleted, and retrieval is efficient.
3. Backup copies should be made of important documents periodically; hard disk or central processing unit systems need to have copies of documents transferred to disks in an archive or backup mode periodically. Some systems allow for backup copies to be made by date, so that the entire set of files does not need to be copied except for a master file. Periodically, especially if substantial changes are made to stored documents, a backup should be made of the whole system.

Locating Lost Files on Magnetic Media. When files are lost on magnetic media, they may well be lost forever. Backup copies play an important role in safeguarding data. The following are some suggestions for verifying that a document is indeed lost:

1. Check directories on other disks or other directory names on the hard disk.
2. Check similar names.
3. If the computer system provides dates for documents, check documents done on or about the same date.
4. If data on a disk has been deleted, attempt to recover it using the undelete feature, if available.
5. Make sure all disks used by the operator have been located.
6. Make sure that no one else has the disk.
7. Look under papers, between draft of other documents, and any place that a paper document could be found. Disks can become mixed in with the paperwork at the workstation.

RECORDS RETENTION

Records retention is the decision to keep records depending on their usefulness, legal requirements, and other factors determined by the business or organization. The length of time that these records must or will be kept in active, inactive, or transfer files before they are destroyed is the *retention period*.

Whether a business keeps or destroys some records is not always a matter of choice. Various requirements for keeping records are mandated by federal, state, and local governments. Most organizations need to keep records for several years for tax purposes.

There also may be historical, archival, or good business reasons for keeping records. For example, a dentist may need to keep records on patients for many years to help with identification or treatment. A business may keep records to determine sales trends over a period of years. New laws on social issues such as equal employment and environmental protection require business firms to keep records that show their compliance with these laws.

When the records retention schedule for a business is being planned, an authority on the subject may be consulted to examine the kinds of records the business has and what legal requirements exist for these records.

Management should set up written guidelines for the retention and disposal of the organization's records according to its particular needs. Whatever calendar is established for keeping records, transferring them to inactive files, storing them on microfilm or magnetic media, or disposing of them, a sound rationale for the decisions should be stated in a procedures manual.

Classifications of Records. Records classified as _vital_ should never be destroyed. These records are usually retained in a vault or a safe for protection from fire, theft, and disasters. Examples of vital records are:

Corporate charter
Correspondence containing information that may be needed for legal reasons
Deeds, mortgages, and bills of sale or contracts for major business transactions
Minute books of meetings—boards of directors and stockholders
Stocks and bonds
Tax returns
Trademark registrations

Records that are classified as _important_ may be kept for about six to seven years. Examples of these records are:

Accounts receivable ledgers
Accounts payable ledgers
Cancelled checks
Creditor invoices
Customer invoices
Inventory records
Payroll records
Purchase orders
Time books

Records classified as _useful_ may be kept for perhaps 1 to 3 years. Examples of these records are:

Bank reconciliations
Employment applications
General correspondence
Insurance policies that have expired
Petty cash vouchers
Receiving records
Stenographers' notebooks

Junk mail - memos - Trade Mag

MERGING FILES

In the process of making decisions about the transfer of records, it may be more efficient to merge certain files. The contents of two or more folders may be combined in one, either using the caption of one of the old folders or creating a new caption to cover the new combination of contents.

Let's say your company has conducted much business with the Jones Company over a period of years. During that time several files were set up for the records. Some of the correspondence contained in these files is routine and of no value after a few months; other records may need to be kept for several years. By first eliminating the routine correspondence, the records of two or more folders may be placed in one with a label indicating the year or years the records cover. This way, you might be able to merge old correspondence in a file labeled "Jones Company, 1980–86" for example.

TRANSFER AND DISPOSAL   Tuesday

Transfer involves making decisions about what records to retain and what records to destroy. Of the records that are retained, decisions must then be made about where to keep them: in present storage locations suitable for frequent use or in transfer storage locations that are out of the way but available for the infrequent occasions when they might be needed. Regular transfer of records is necessary to conserve space, equipment, and labor. The alternative is overcrowded file drawers, time lost in retreiving records, and crowding of office space with file cabinets. Records that are transferred should be reviewed periodically to determine which may be destroyed, so that space will be cleared for newly transferred records. Whether or not records should be transferred depends on answers to the following questions:

1. How valuable are the records? (Are they worth the cost of keeping them?)
2. How often do they need to be used?
3. Where can the records be stored?
4. Is the retention of the records necessary for legal purposes?
5. What company requirements exist for the retention of these records?
6. Should the records be destroyed? If yes, when? If no, what special precautions need to be taken to ensure they will not be lost or destroyed accidentally?

7. Can the records be stored on microfilm and magnetic media to allow for minimum amount of space and rapid access?

PLANS OF TRANSFER

There are several plans for the transfer of records. The one selected will depend on the nature and frequency of reference, the space available, and the filing system in use. In general, transfer plans are either *periodic* or *perpetual*.

Periodic. Periodic transfer is the removal of papers at the end of a definite *filing period* (at the end of each year, for example) from the active files to

PERIODIC PLANS FOR TRANSFERRING RECORDS

A-B ACTIVE	M-N ACTIVE
C-E ACTIVE	O-R ACTIVE
F-H ACTIVE	S-T ACTIVE
I-L ACTIVE	U-Z ACTIVE

With the one-period plan, all file drawers are active.

With the two-period plan and five-drawer files, inactive files often may be contracted to fit the top and the bottom drawers.

A-E INACTIVE	I-Q INACTIVE
A-B ACTIVE	M-N ACTIVE
C-F ACTIVE	O-S ACTIVE
G-L ACTIVE	T-Z ACTIVE
F-H INACTIVE	R-Z INACTIVE

A-E ACTIVE	L-R ACTIVE
F-K ACTIVE	S-Z ACTIVE
A-E INACTIVE	L-R INACTIVE
F-K INACTIVE	S-Z INACTIVE

With the two-period plan and four-drawer files, the upper two rows hold active papers, and the lower two rows hold inactive records.

In this two-period plan, the active files stand beside the inactive.

A-B ACTIVE	A-B INACTIVE	K-L ACTIVE	K-L INACTIVE
C ACTIVE	C INACTIVE	M-N ACTIVE	M-N INACTIVE
D-E ACTIVE	D-E INACTIVE	O-R ACTIVE	O-R INACTIVE
F-G ACTIVE	F-G INACTIVE	S ACTIVE	S INACTIVE
H-J ACTIVE	H-J INACTIVE	T-Z ACTIVE	T-Z INACTIVE

inexpensive transfer files. Periodic transfer can be operated in at least three ways: one period, two period, or maximum-minimum period.

1. *One period plan.* In the one-period plan, only the papers for the current filing period occupy the active files. On certain dates the folders and their contents are moved directly to the transfer files and a new filing period is started. Though this transfer plan is easy to operate, it requires frequent trips to the transfer files to consult records from the previous filing period. If the transfer files are located away from the office, much valuable time may be lost.

2. *Two-period plan.* In the two-period plan, the files are divided to provide space for two filing periods—the present period and the period immediately preceding. Records of the present period are referred to as *active;* those of the previous period are called *inactive.* At the end of each filing period, the following changes take place:

   a. The inactive records are removed to transfer files.
   b. The active records become inactive and are placed in the inactive drawers.
   c. The active drawers are now empty, ready to receive records for the next filing period.

   This plan eliminates the disadvantage of the one-period plan because only the oldest papers have been removed to transfer files, and the current records and the records of the previous period are still readily available. With a two-period plan, the fatigue that comes from working at the files in a stooped or tiptoe position can be reduced by reserving accessible file drawers or shelves for active records.

   An adaptation of the two-period plan to eliminate switching records from active to inactive file drawers at the end of a filing period operates as follows: An active cabinet stands beside an inactive one. At the end of a filing period, the records in the active cabinet automatically become inactive, but they are not moved. Records in the inactive cabinet are transferred, leaving this cabinet empty and ready for new records. Then, simply by interchanging "active" and "inactive" drawer labels, the file worker readies the two cabinets for the next period. Open-shelf files can be set up in a similar way.

3. *Maximum-minimum plan.* In the maximum-minimum period plan, the least recent papers are moved directly from the active files to the transfer files at the end of each filing period. Inactive files are not used. Because the most recent records are kept in the active files, the disadvantage of the one-period plan is overcome. To use this plan, a business must establish maximum and minimum periods of time for keeping records in the active files. A business may want papers up to 6 months old in the files. At specified intervals—every 3 months—for example, the folders would be checked for papers older than 6 months which should be transferred to storage files. The records removed would be between 6 and 9 months old. In another 3 months the process would be repeated. An advantage of this system is that it keeps current papers in the files.

transferred active files

constantly

A disadvantage is that each folder must be checked, a time-consuming process.

Perpetual. Under the perpetual plan, papers are transferred from the active files constantly, or *perpetually*. This plan is generally used when the nature of a business makes it difficult to set definite filing periods. For example, in the type of work done by building contractors, architects, or lawyers, the length of time taken to complete the work varies with each job or case. Transferring records on a periodic basis might result, therefore, in the removal of frequently used records. Under the perpetual transfer plan, whenever a job or case is completed, all records pertaining to it are moved from the active files to the

HOW THE MAXIMUM-MINIMUM TRANSFER PLAN OPERATES

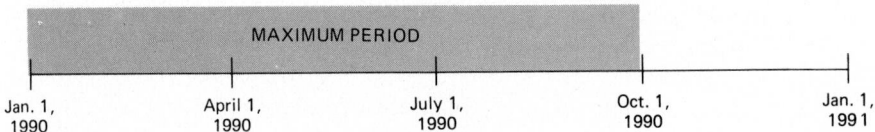

1. On October 1, 1990, files contain records from as early as January 1, 1990, or nine months old (maximum period).

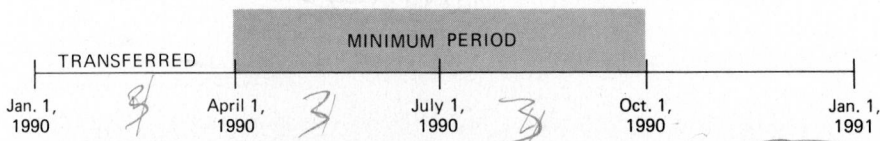

2. On the same day, October 1, 1990, records of the earliest three months are transferred, leaving records of the last six months (minimum period).

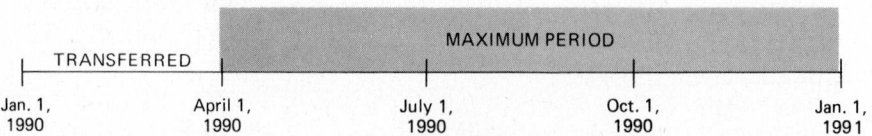

3. Three months later, January 1, 1991, the files have accumulated the records of the past nine months (maximum period).

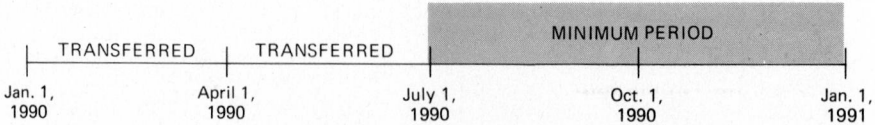

4. On the same day, January 1, 1991, records of the earliest three months are transferred again, leaving records of the last six months (minimum period).

inactive or transfer files. This transfer of completed work is the biggest advantage of the perpetual transfer system since on any given day only records in current use are in the active files.

TRANSFER OPERATION

The transfer operation is a job usually supervised by a records manager if the organization has a centralized filing department. This individual oversees the operation of the files, establishes the transfer and retention procedures, and has the authority to dispose of obsolete records. If the size of the organization does not warrant a records manager position, one individual should be given authority to say what records should be transferred and what records, if any, should be destroyed.

In a business firm with formal transfer procedures, a records inventory would be consulted by the person in charge of the transfer. A *records inventory* is a statement of the kinds and quantity of records and folders in the files. This inventory would have been prepared when the filing system was installed and updated when necessary.

RECORDS INVENTORY AND RETENTION CONTROL CARD

RECORD TITLE Customer Ledgers						
INVENTORY			**RETENTION**			
DEPARTMENT Accounting			APPROVALS			YEARS
RECORD COPY [X]	DUPLICATE COPY ☐		RECOMMENDED (SPECIFY SOURCE) Company policy			
VOLUME			ADMINISTRATIVE BY *Henrietta Smythe* DATE 3/1/90			
INCLUSIVE DATES	LOCATION	QUANTITY	LEGAL COUNSEL BY *Andrew Watson* DATE 3/2/90			
3/16/90–3/31/90	OFFICE	25	EXECUTIVE BY *Patricia Vazonna* DATE 3/5/90			
	STORAGE		FINALIZED SCHEDULE			
REMARKS Ledgers 1000–1025			IN OFFICE 1/25/91	IN STORAGE 1/27/91	DESTROY	
			BY		DATE	
			SPECIAL INSTRUCTIONS			
COUNTED BY		DATE 1/20/91				

RECORDS INVENTORY AND RETENTION CONTROL CARD   🔲🔲 **BANKERS BOX** records storage systems

FORM 1606

Customer ledgers for 3/16/90 to 3/31/90 are counted and recorded on the inventory side of this form. On the retention side, authorization to retain them for five years is given, with authorized signatures. Anyone needing the customer ledgers on 1/25/91 would obtain them from the office; two days later they would be available from the transfer storage location.

The person in charge of transfer would need the following information in order to do an effective job:

1. The space that is available for the transfer of records and the materials which are used for this purpose
2. The record that will be kept of transfer files
3. Whether each department should select records for storage or destruction (under supervision) and box its files or whether this should be done by records specialists
4. Whether each department should provide an inventory of files transferred or whether records specialists should prepare it

Steps in the Transfer Process. A business may use the following steps in preparing for the transfer process:

1. Determine which files are ready to be transferred. This would depend on the transfer plan to be used.
2. Prepare new folders to replace those being transferred.
3. Assemble transfer boxes.
4. Remove the files from the file drawers and place them in the transfer boxes. (Authority should be in writing for any destroyed records.)
5. Inventory carefully the contents of each box to make a list of the contents for future reference and for the records of the storage area.
6. Label each box clearly and completely.

On the day of the transfer, a form is usually signed by the person releasing the files for storage and by the person accepting the records at the storage location.

RECORDS STORAGE INDEX AND DESTRUCTION CONTROL CARD

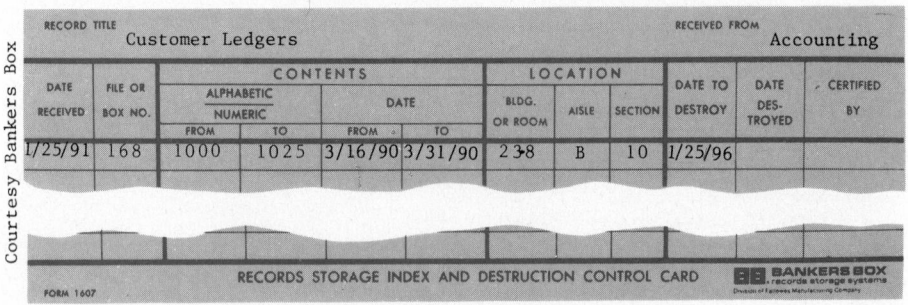

On 1/25/91 the customer ledgers (recorded on the records inventory card on page 157) were received from the accounting department and placed in storage in the transfer storage location entered on the form. This form also authorizes destruction of the records five years later.

Retrieving Records Which Have Been Stored. Provision has to be made for retrieval of records from a transfer storage area. When an office keeps detailed inventories of the files in storage, requested materials can be found quickly and easily. For example, refer to the illustration on page 158. Customer Ledger 1000 is stored in Box 168. A diagram of the storage area would show the exact location of that box.

The contents of files may also be stored on microfilm or microfiche. Uses of microfilm and microfiche are discussed in Chapter 13.

DISPOSAL METHODS

After records have been stored in inactive files for a period of time, they may no longer have any use. These records are then designated for disposal. Some records are destroyed by being fed through a specially designed shredding machine, which cuts them into narrow strips. Other methods of disposal are burning the records, selling them for scrap, or simply throwing them away. The confidential nature and the quantity of papers will usually determine the manner of disposal. Guidelines should be set up by each organization for the most appropriate method of disposal. *Environmental resources*

TRANSFER AND STORAGE OF MAGNETIC MEDIA

Magnetic media may need to be stored for long-term or archival purposes or for the safekeeping of important information.

Advantages of Magnetic Media

1. Takes up very little space
2. Can be transported easily
3. Ideally suited to off-site storage, particularly places which specialize in "vault" storage similar to safe deposit boxes at banks

Disadvantages of Magnetic Media

1. Need to be kept in a controlled climate (regulated heat and humidity).
2. Need to be kept free of air pollutants (smoke, dust).
3. Need to be kept away from magnetic fields.
4. Have unproven durability in storage. It appears that there is no limit on the life of a disk. If this is a concern, however, records can be periodically copied onto a new disk.

5. If the disk is not updated periodically, the equipment that can read it may become obsolete (though this may not happen for some time).
6. Neither the contents nor what program or word processor created the documents can be determined by looking at the disk. This information would be needed to access the data on the media.
7. May not be acceptable for legal uses.

The decision about the storage media for nonpaper records will depend on the needs of the organization. One of the new methods of storage, laser disks, may be an alternative to either magnetic media or microfilm. Some laser disks may lack the capability of being updated but are ideal for storing information which will be used for reference purposes because they are almost indestructible.

DISASTER PLANNING

Along with control and retention of records, a primary concern about the safety of records is protection against disasters such as fire, flood, hurricane, tornado, or earthquake. Businesses depend on files and records for their existence; loss of the records can mean complete failure of the business.

The following steps will provide some general guidelines for protecting records.

1. Store copies of all important and vital documents at an off-site location. This is easy to do with documents that are on microfilm or magnetic media.
2. Keep records protected by sprinkler systems and other safety devices in hazard areas, but make sure that these devices will not themselves result in records destruction. Make sure files are not directly under sprinklers or pipes which may break due to cold.
3. Store records compactly without having them so tight in the drawers or on shelves as to be difficult to use. Loose papers burn or absorb water more quickly than compact papers, which may only be affected at the edges.
4. Make sure all important papers, microfilm records, and magnetic media are filed at the end of each work day so that records are not lost because of careless work habits.
5. Have management mandate that disaster planning is an organization priority and outline procedures and methods of testing those procedures to ensure that adequate preparation has been made in the event of a catastrophe. Review the kinds of records kept by the organization and the critical nature of these records, and develop procedures to best safeguard these materials. Make sure all employees accept disaster planning and record protection as part of their work responsibilities to ensure that carelessness and thoughtlessness do not result in unnecessary loss of records.

CONCLUSION

Whatever the form in which records are kept for use (hard copy, magnetic media, microfilm), some plan must be developed to keep records current and active for easy reference. Categories of records requiring long-term storage must be determined by the business or organization, and a plan for protecting these records yet ensuring efficient access to them must be developed and implemented.

chapter 10
Test Tuesday

1. Define the following terms: *records control, charge systems, electronic files control, records retention, merging files, records transfer and disposal,* and *disaster planning.* (Competency 1)
2. Why is a records control system important? (Competency 2)
3. What are the parts of a charge system? (Competency 3)
4. What information needs to be included on a requisition form? (Competency 4)
5. What is used to replace a record or a folder taken from the files? (Competency 5)   *P9 143*
6. How do you locate a lost record or lost folder? (Competency 6)   *P9147*
7. Why is records control necessary even for informal files? (Competency 7)   *P9-141*
8. How can you safeguard electronic file material? (Competency 8)   *P5150*
9. Why are restrictions necessary for making changes in electronic files? (Competency 9)   *150*
10. What are some guidelines for safeguarding electronic files? (Competency 10)   *150*
11. How can you locate a lost file on magnetic media? (Competency 11) *151*
12. What are the differences between hard copy records control and retention and magnetic media records control and retention? (Competency 12)   *151+153*
13. Why is a set period for records retention difficult to determine? (Competency 13)
14. What are the three examples of classifications of records that are filed? (Competency 14)
15. Why is merging files helpful in the records retention and transfer process? (Competency 15)
16. What questions should be considered when making decisions about the transfer of records? (Competency 16)
17. What are the plans for records transfer and how does each work? (Competency 17)
18. What are the steps in the transfer process? (Competency 18)
19. How is the disposal of records accomplished? (Competency 19)

20. What are the advantages and disadvantages of using magnetic media for transfer and storage purposes? (Competency 20)
21. What steps are necessary to protect records from disaster? (Competency 21)

CASE PROBLEMS

1. You work for a very large organization with centralized files. The person who heads the file department, Mrs. Grayson, will not allow anyone except the user to pick up a file. Your immediate boss travels a great deal and often calls you for information from the files. Mrs. Grayson will not allow you to take the files out of the area, even to check information. Your boss frequently needs the opinion of another person about the contents of the files. You would like to make some changes in the file charge-out procedure. You feel that your boss may be able to write some recommendations for the manager of the file department who may not realize the difficulties caused by the current policy. What suggestions can you give your boss? (Competencies 2, 3)

2. Your employer does not like to throw anything out—ever. As a result, your files are hopelessly overcrowded with correspondence which is as unnecessary now as the day it was filed there. Most of your activities included answering letters from customers who request price lists and brochures about your products. You feel that most of these letters could be disposed of immediately or at least within a very short time since those interested in the products fill out a purchase request. At that time a file is set up for active customers and is kept in the accounting department. In your office there are folders set up for each individual who writes requesting information. What do you suggest? (Competencies 2, 14, 19)

3. One of the operators of a word processor in your office loses documents at least once a day. When she finds documents frequently it is an old version which has been updated. She claims that she follows company policy and procedures for naming files. You feel that she must be doing something wrong. Upon checking her disks, you note that most do not have labels and that she does not keep them in any particular location. What can you suggest to protect her magnetic media? (Competencies 8, 9, 10, 11)

4. A hurricane threat about a year ago and several bad storms have made your colleagues aware of how vulnerable the office is to the elements. Most material is filed on disks, some of which are not even printed out for hard copy files because of the space such paper would require. Very little of the material stored on these disks is of a confidential nature. What suggestions could you make to safeguard these records? (Competencies 12, 20, 21)

5. As a new employee for an architectural firm, Nancy Sweeny is faced with the problem of storing material in the files for easy access. The firm works on about 50 projects simultaneously. Since many of these projects are similar to previous work, the architects frequently refer to completed projects. The architects have put all files in the same cabinets. Space is becoming a problem. Nancy would like to remove some of the older files and place them in an adjoining office which has extra space. Which files should be moved? Which files should remain? What type of transfer system is best suited to this situation? (Competencies 16, 17)

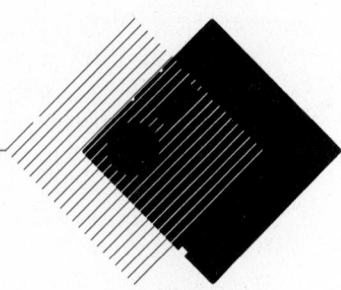

11

RECORDS AND DATABASE EQUIPMENT AND SUPPLIES

COMPETENCIES

When you have completed this chapter, you will be able to:

1. List objectives of equipment and supplies for the records management system.
2. Name sources for obtaining filing equipment and supplies.
3. List and describe kinds of equipment for correspondence files.
4. List and describe equipment for card files.
5. Name and describe types of records which have special equipment needs.
6. Describe guidelines for selecting vertical files.
7. Describe guidelines for selecting other types of files.
8. State the purpose of guides and criteria for selection.
9. State criteria for selecting folders and describe folders used for special purposes.
10. Name accessories that are necessary or helpful in filing.
11. Name equipment or supplies used to store disks and list criteria to use in selection.
12. List questions to ask when selecting cards.
13. Describe why size and properties of paper are important in the selection of business forms.

OBJECTIVES OF EQUIPMENT AND SUPPLIES

The most carefully planned records management system is only as good as all of the components. Selecting the best systems for your needs, following the rules, organizing the paper or electronic system, and planning for records control are all dependent on the equipment and supplies used for the physical storage and protection of the records. Equipment and supplies serve the system in the following ways:

1. *Save time*. Equipment and supplies must be designed so that those who handle records do not go through unnecessary motions. The biggest expense in filing is the cost of the people who do the work; any equipment or procedure that can save time will also save money.
2. *Protect records*. Protection of records can mean keeping them in order to be retrieved easily or it can mean safeguarding records against disaster. The use and importance of the records need to be considered when purchasing equipment.
3. *Conserve space*. Because of the high cost of office construction and increased land values and maintenance expenses, filing equipment should be designed so that it does not take up more space than is absolutely necessary for an efficient system.

SOURCES OF EQUIPMENT AND SUPPLIES

Dozens of manufacturers offer almost every conceivable type, size, price, and design of cabinets, supplies, and special equipment for housing and managing records. Made-to-order equipment is available for unique systems. Office equipment exhibits, catalogs of manufacturers, office management magazines, and showrooms of stationers, business equipment dealers, and office furniture stores are excellent sources of up-to-date information.

New filing products are placed on the market often. Office workers and supervisors who are concerned with records management should keep abreast of new developments. Often the equipment and supplies suggest ways to solve filing problems and maintain efficient filing systems.

For help in selecting equipment and supplies, have a filing catalog handy for reference. Two or more filing equipment companies should be consulted whenever a large purchase is to be made. These companies have the experience and desire to be helpful not only in providing equipment and supplies but also in helping to design a filing system that will bring top efficiency. The quality of this advisory service is an important factor to consider when deciding from what dealer to buy equipment and supplies.

CORRESPONDENCE (PAPER) FILES

Correspondence files are usually made of steel and are available in a variety of types and grades. The major types of correspondence files are vertical, open shelf, lateral, rotary, box and tub.

Vertical Files. Vertical files are cabinets usually with four or five drawers the width of the long dimension of letter or legal folders. In these drawers the folders are placed behind each other about 26 to 30 inches deep. As these files are completely enclosed, they are sturdy and protect the contents. Many have locks and some, called *safes,* have combination locks and are made of special fireproof and protective materials.

Open-Shelf Files. Open-shelf files look like steel bookcases and are flexible in size and arrangement. Folders are placed on the shelves the same way books are placed on a bookcase. These files save up to 50 percent of the space needed to store materials in vertical file cabinets. Open-shelf files often use a color-coded filing system with folder label color "bands" to make locating files easy. Upright supports on the shelves hold the files in place compactly.

A disadvantage of open-shelf files is the lack of protection of the records. Many businesses feel the space-saving and easy-to-use features make open-shelf files preferable to enclosed units, and protection is not a critical factor. Some open-shelf units are available with sliding doors which close around both sides of the shelves to protect the files when not in use. These units can be locked for additional safekeeping.

Some open-shelf file units are installed on a track which allows the file units to be moved together when not in use. This provides protection as well as space savings. The units may be powered for easy movement.

Lateral Files. Lateral files are metal cabinet-type files, about 15 to 18 inches deep, in which the folders are placed in a bookshelf arrangement as with open-shelf files. After a receding door has been raised, the shelf pulls forward on rollers. Lateral files have the space-saving advantage of open-shelf filing and the protection advantage of enclosing the files as in vertical filing. In addition to containing correspondence files, lateral files can be designed to include spaces for reference materials, telephones, dictation and transcription equipment, and supplies so that these items are readily available but do not clutter the work area. Most lateral files are designed to be compatible with other modular furniture used in the office. They are available in many dimensions and are often used as dividers, credenzas, and counters.

Drawer files are a combination of the traditional file drawer turned sideways and the lateral file as part of modular furniture. Some units may be attached to dividers used in a landscaped office. These drawer files usually have built-in holders for hanging or suspended files.

Rotary Files. Rotary files (also called *carousel files*) consist of round shelves attached to a center post by braces. The records to be filed are placed on the shelves as in open-shelf filing. Some shelves have built-in partitions to hold the records in place and upright. Rotary files are particularly useful for housing notebooks or binders because they can form a pie-shaped arrangement. A

It would be easy to find records in this well-organized open-shelf file with clearly marked alphabetic guides. Courtesy The Smead Manufacturing Company.

rotary file is often used when several individuals in a workstation need to use the group of file records; the file can be turned for easy access on all sides.

Box Files. Box files are most commonly used for storage. The boxes are made of low-cost plastic or corrugated fiberboard. They can stand alone or be placed on shelves. Some types have devices which hold the boxes together in a stacked arrangement to form a bank of files. Box files are available in a variety of quality and size choices. Some storage box files have been designed to have the front open as well as the top to make accessing stored records easier.

Tub Files. Tub files are containers which open at the top to expose records suspended in folders or in trays. Many tub files are relatively small and have the advantage of being movable from one workstation to another. Larger tub files are automated and revolve to move the shelves to the worker.

Power File Units. Power file units operate automatically to move a particular shelf of files vertically to a convenient level for the user. The operator merely

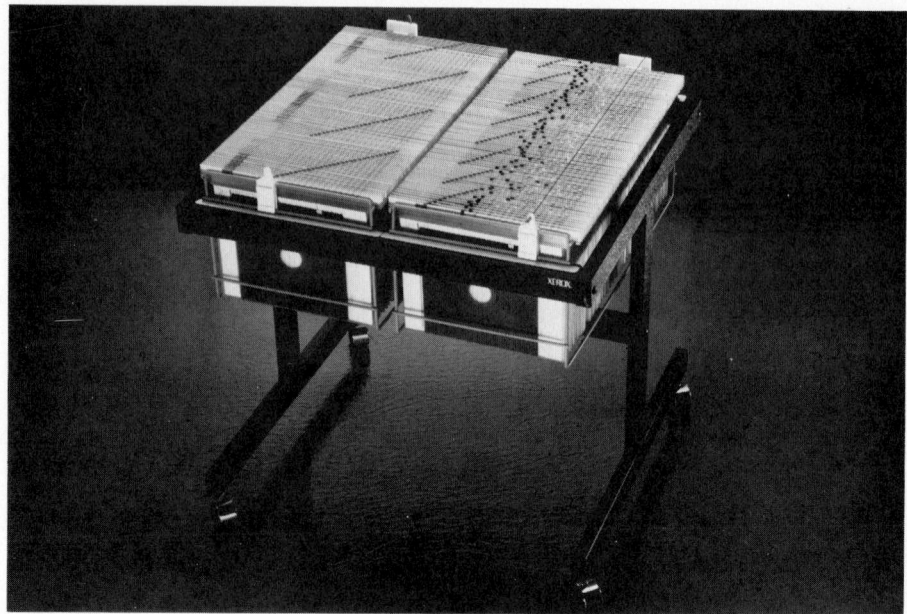

An example of equipment designed for a special purpose is the Rolling T-Cart Storage unit. This transportable unit is to store floppy disks used in word processing and small computer installations. The floppy disk fits into a vinyl pocket with a metal hanger. Colored signals alert the user to different kinds of stored information. Courtesy Xerox Corporation

pushes a button to bring the desired shelf into working position. Within the unit, the files may be arranged as open-shelf files with side-tabbed folders or in small tubs or trays. Because the unit is enclosed, power files can be locked for security. A power file is usually equipped with an electric eye or other safeguard device to scan the shelves for protruding materials which might interfere with the mechanical operation.

Rotating Power Files. Rotating power files move whole sections of shelf files horizontally to the user. Without leaving the desk area, the file worker has access to one or more sections of the files. In this system, tracks are located on the floor and on the ceiling to secure the rollers for the file shelves.

CARD FILES

The same types of files which can hold paper files are used for card files:

Vertical card files are made in a number of sizes. Some companies manufacture compartment inserts which can be used to change vertical file drawers into card files.

Rotary files may be set up for vertical or horizontal motion to facilitate access to cards.

Tub files may be large enough to hold a great many cards, checks, and small forms. Small desktop tub files can be used for reference, for work in progress, and to store materials.

Box files similar to those used for correspondence are available for cards of various sizes. Tickler card files are box files.

Power file units similar to those used for correspondence files are available for systems having a large quantity of cards.

SPECIAL EQUIPMENT

Some records require special filing equipment which is designed to house them compactly. These records include microforms (miniatures of office records), magnetic media (disks and magnetic tapes), X rays, blueprints, computer printouts, and special size forms.

SELECTING VERTICAL FILES

All filing equipment should be judged for quality as well as cost. The guidelines which follow will describe some of the features to look for when buying vertical file cabinets.

Construction. The letter-size file drawer, when full, carries a load of 60 to 70 pounds. Therefore, this drawer should have telescoping slides to furnish support when it is fully extended. The slides should move on ball-bearing or nylon rollers so drawers can be opened and closed with one hand. The inside frame of the cabinet should be rigidly braced. File drawers are not always completely filled, so records within them must be held upright by some device other than the back of the drawer.

Followers. Followers, or compressors, are used to support and compress records. They move forward and backward in the file drawer yet lock in the desired position to hold records. Followers should be strong but not so bulky that they occupy valuable filing space.

So that guides will not accidentally be lifted out of the drawer when folders are removed, there should be some means of anchoring the guides in place. Most file drawers have guide rods that are inserted through holes in one or more projections at the bottom or sides of the guides. This keeps guides in the drawer but permits them to move forward and backward along the rods.

If papers are packed too tightly in file drawers, they will become wrinkled and unsightly, folders and guides will be short-lived, and file workers will have difficulty removing and replacing records. To prevent such difficulties, some filing cabinets provide V-shaped working space. This working space is provided in some models by a drop front that eases the tension on the tops of the records when the drawer is opened and compresses the records when the drawer is closed.

Determining Space Needed. In deciding how many drawers or cabinets are needed, it is necessary to determine the quantity of material to be filed. The chart shown below can then be used to estimate the number of inches (measured from front to back inside the drawer) of filing space that will be needed.

CORRESPONDENCE FILING SPACE REQUIREMENTS

ITEM	AVERAGE FILING SPACE REQUIRED
175 pieces of correspondence	1 inch
25 guides (medium weight)	⅞ inch
100 individual folders (medium weight)	2¼ inches
25 miscellaneous folders (medium weight)	½ inch

By dividing the total number of filing inches by the filing inches in one drawer, the number of file drawers needed will be known. Correspondence files have between 24 and 27 inches of filing space, but about 4 inches should be subtracted for working space. For example, if by using the chart you find that the filed materials will occupy 1000 inches, and there are 24 inches of filing space in each drawer of the cabinets to be purchased, then the number of cabinets that will be needed is figured as follows:

Filing inches in each drawer	24
Minus inches allowed for working space	− 4
Inches of space to be used in each drawer	20
Inches of space all records will use	1,000
Divide by space to be used in each drawer	$1,000 \div 20 = 50$ drawers
	50 drawers $\div$ 4 or 5 =
Number of cabinets needed	13 four-drawer
	or 10 five-drawer

SELECTING OTHER TYPES OF FILES

When selecting open-shelf, lateral, rotary, box, tub, or power file units, the equipment vendor will provide space utilization figures for each unit. If the file units are to be part of the modular office furniture or dividers, the units will be selected partly to fit the decor of the office. However, files should not be selected on looks alone; they should contribute to the efficient storage and retrieval of information. When selecting furniture files, it is a good idea to try out the files in the showroom or another office to make sure that they are suitable for the use intended. Furniture expansion needs should also be considered so that matching equipment can be purchased in the future as needed.

SELECTING SUPPLIES

Supplies needed for filing systems include guides, folders, hanging folders, and file drawer accessories.

Guides. Guides are the key to efficient vertical filing. Without them, records will not stand upright properly in the drawer. Guides also serve as signposts to speed finding and filing.

The number of guides, the tab size and position, and the quality of construction depend on the filing system being used. Guides may be purchased in all standard correspondence drawer sizes as well as for drawers used in special systems, such as bank, hospital, and insurance company files. Guides made of manila stock or index bristol are inexpensive and will serve in transfer files or temporary card files. In active files, however, guides made of pressboard or fiber should be used. A standard 25-point (0.025-inch) thickness of pressboard is durable and rigid enough to support records, yet flexible enough to resist dog-earing or breaking. In some card systems, guides made of plastic or lightweight metal are used.

Guides are produced with the tab or upper-edge projection in various sizes (cuts) and positions so that they can be adapted to any system. The tabs may be simply an extension of the guide with the caption printed or with a blank space for a label. Some tabs of this type are reinforced with transparent plastic. High-quality guides, however, have metal or plastic tabs that are riveted to the body of the guide. Such tabs usually have a slot for the insertion of a caption label under a transparent plastic window. There are a number of other guide features and accessories. Angular tabs are slanted back for good visibility and are especially helpful in lower file drawers. There are even tabs that magnify the guide caption. Separate plastic tabs can be purchased in long strips and cut to the desired size for attachment to guides in any position. These may be used to replace broken tabs or to provide additional captions. Good-quality guides have metal-reinforced guide rod projections. As with filing cabinets, the best-quality guides with the most useful features are usually worth the extra money because they give lasting and efficient service.

Folders. Durable folders that have a minimum of thickness and a smooth surface are needed for active correspondence files. As is true with guides, folders are available in several styles and types of materials. For average use, manila and kraft folders provide good service and can be purchased in several weights; the choice should depend upon the type and extent of handling. Plastic folders have the advantages of reusability and ease of filing. For bulky papers or for very heavy handling, fiber or pressboard folders with cloth expansion

GUIDES AND TABS OF VARYING DESIGN

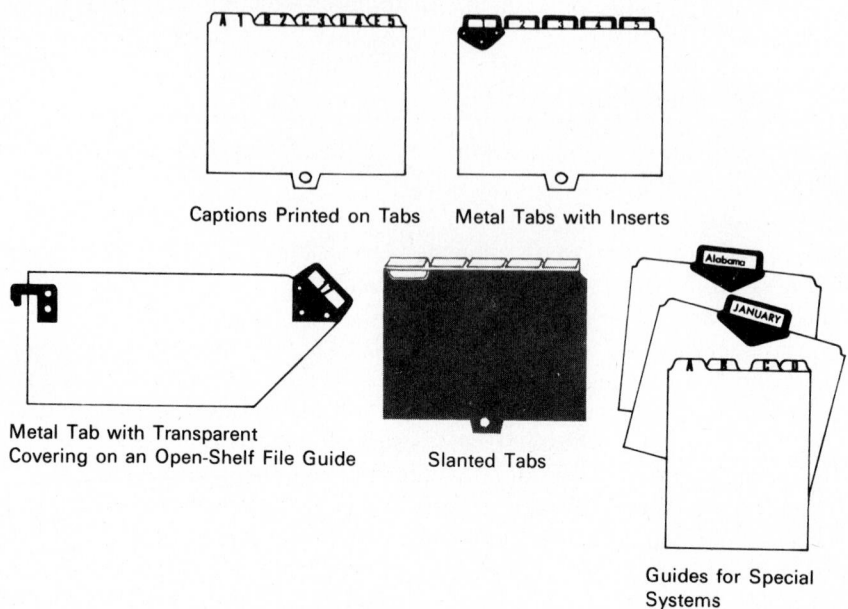

Captions Printed on Tabs   Metal Tabs with Inserts

Metal Tab with Transparent
Covering on an Open-Shelf File Guide   Slanted Tabs

Guides for Special
Systems

hinges at the bottom should be used. For checks and other small business forms, transparent plastic folders may be the most appropriate.

Some folders have a double thickness along the top, which adds to their life span without increasing the bulk of the file drawer. Folders that are scored along the bottom of the front flap can be expanded neatly. As the number of papers increases, a new fold is made along one of the scores. This flattens the bottom and permits all records to stand evenly and squarely on their edges.

Several types of folders are designed for special needs. File pockets, also called envelope folders, are used for materials that are especially bulky or that are frequently taken away from the files. For case histories, medical records, and personnel records, folders that have dividers or compartments within them are frequently used. For follow-up work, folders with adjustable date signals are popular. Other folders that are available have built in paper fasteners to keep records from accidentally sliding out. Folders come in a variety of colors for easy identification.

Folder tabs are obtainable in nearly any cut or position desired. Tabs are generally an extension of the folder itself, but pressboard and fiber folders usually have metal or plastic tabs. For open-shelf files, tabs are on the side of guides and folders instead of the top.

Suspended Folders. Suspended, or hanging, folders are supported from their top edges by a metal frame within the file drawer. They do not rest on the

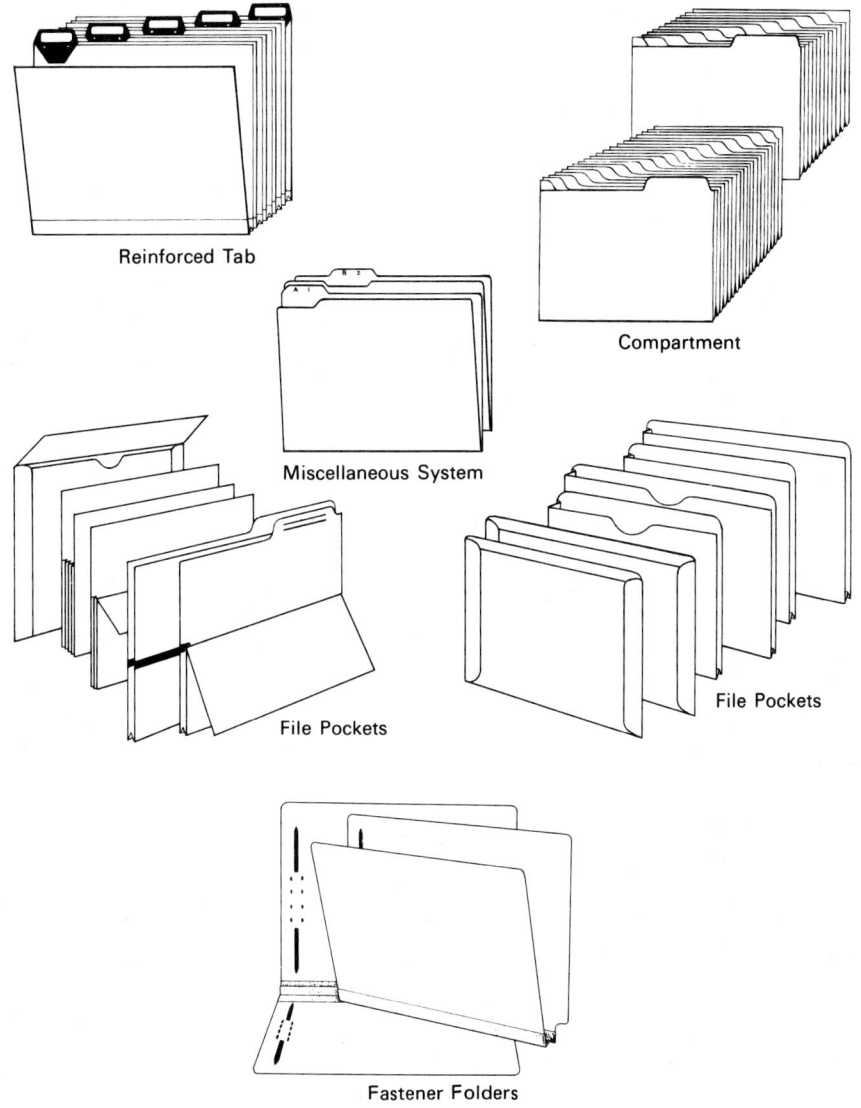

Reinforced Tab

Compartment

Miscellaneous System

File Pockets

File Pockets

Fastener Folders

bottom of the drawer. These folders save space because the follower blocks and guides can be eliminated (attachable tabs on the front of the folders can be used in the place of conventional guides). Suspended folders usually have a neat appearance and permit easy storage and removal of records. Suspended folders save a great deal of space when used to hold papers which have

END TAB FOLDERS

Note: The tab illustrations are approximate size for letter and legal size end tab folders. Finished product may vary slightly from illustrations.

UNDERCUT TABS

END TAB (Front flaps left of tab area). Undercut 1/4'' deep in all tab cuts. Pressboard and classification folders are not undercut. The undercut enlarges tab heading area. Also facilitates label attaching.

STRAIGHT CUT TABS . . . pressboard folders have printed label position lines. All other materials feature embossed label lines.

ONE-THIRD CUT — Undercut 1/4'' deep.
NOTE: Pressboard folders with tabs in bottom position will be 1/2'' up from bottom to allow for gusset tape.

TWO-FIFTHS CUT — Bottom position only. Undercut 1/4'' deep.
NOTE: Classification folders are top position — Not undercut.

ONE-HALF CUT — Undercut 1/4'' deep.
NOTE: Pressboard folders with tabs in bottom position will be 1/2'' up from bottom to allow for gusset tape.

4'' HIGH — 1 1/8'' from bottom of folder to bottom of tab. Undercut 1/4'' deep.

STRAIGHT CUT — 1 1/8'' from bottom of folder to bottom of tab. Undercut 1/4'' deep. With lines on tab for labeling.

CC3 FOLDER with 1/4'' undercut in lower position.

9

9

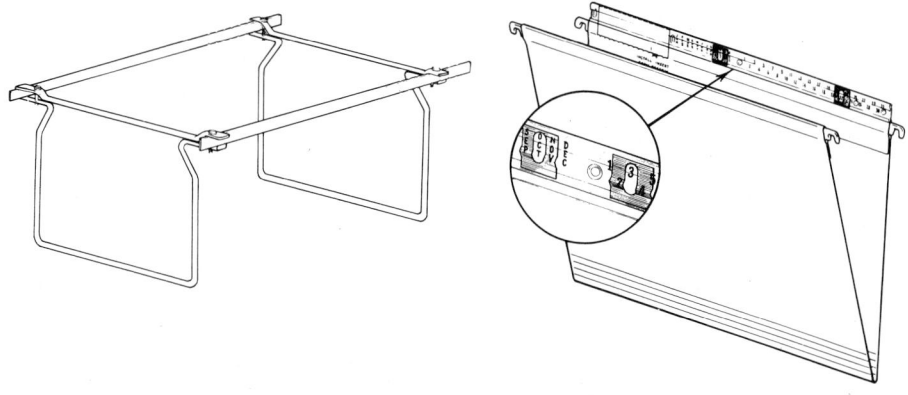

previously been stacked on shelves. They are also ideal for odd-size or bulky items, such as newspapers, computer printouts, maps, or brochures.

File Drawer Accessories. Other accessories which assist in the filing process include labels, signals, forms, and a variety of devices which help the storage process.

Labels. Folder, guide, and drawer labels may be purchased in several styles. One of the most popular is the self-adhesive type, which requires no moistening. Labels can be bought printed or blank, in strips or rolls, with colors or plain.

Signals. Colored signals are useful and can be positioned along the top edges of folders and guides for classification purposes. Signals are also used frequently with visible equipment. They can be fixed or movable and are constructed of paper, plastic, or metal.

Forms. Standard printed forms, such as cross-reference sheets, are often made to order for customers by the filing equipment companies. Some companies will print easy-to-read captions or individual folder tabs from a list of names submitted by the customer.

Other Accessories. Other equipment that will add to filing efficiency includes the following: files stools to make working at lower drawers comfortable, movable shelves to allow workers to use both hands while filing, drawer dividers to separate records conveniently, sorting devices to speed the preliminary arranging of records, and several types of date stamps, trays, and stands.

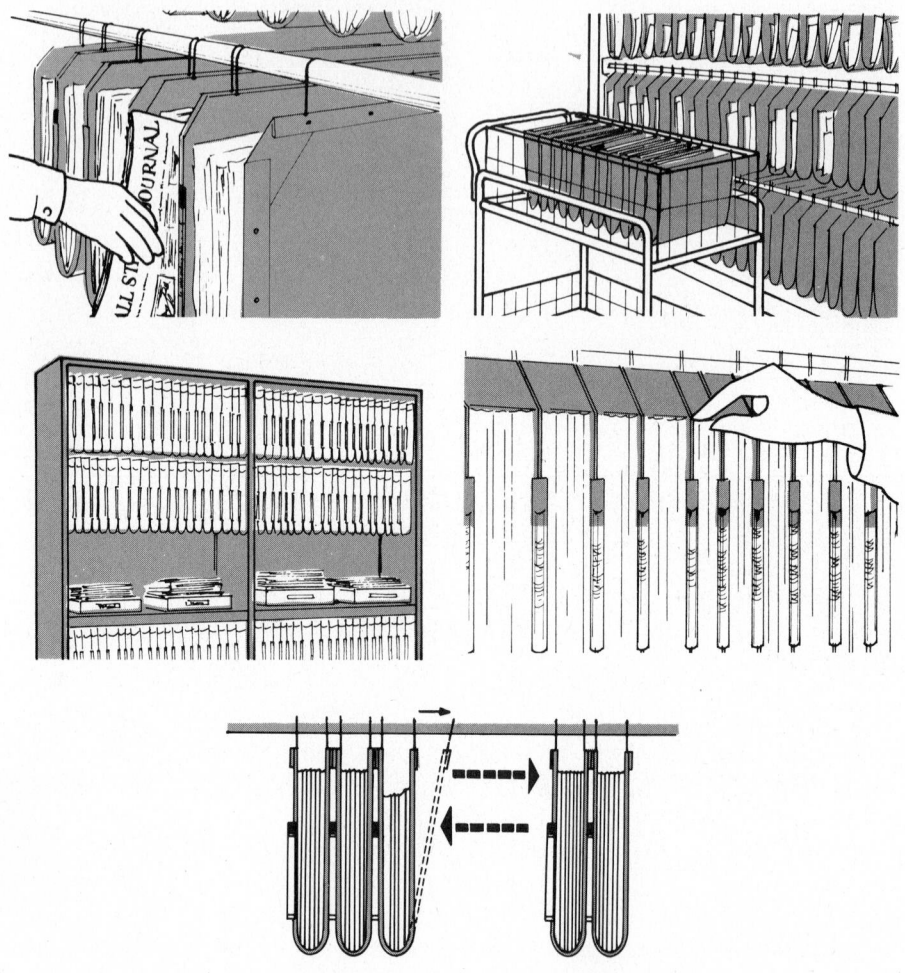

DISK STORAGE

Since many word processors and computers use disks to store records, filing equipment needs to be purchased to hold this medium. There are two basic choices for disk storage:

1. A disk file, with each disk labeled with a code to reference a printed copy
2. A file folder which also contains the hard copy of the records on the disk

The system selected is determined according to:

DISK STORAGE PRODUCTS

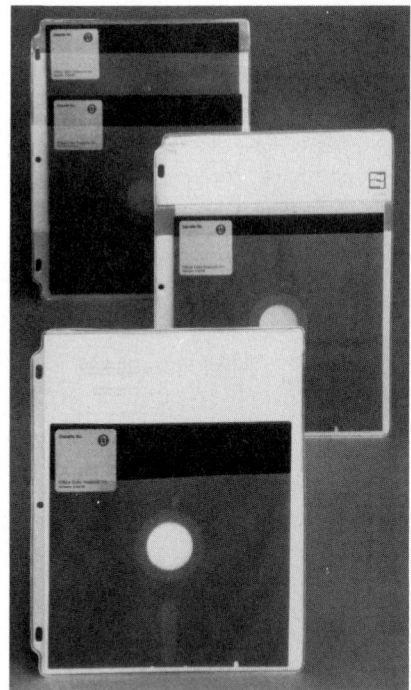

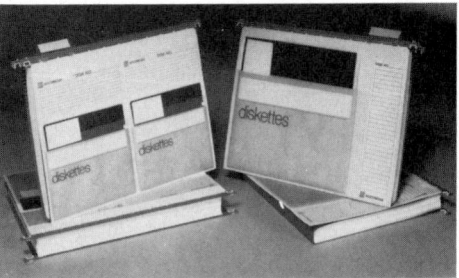

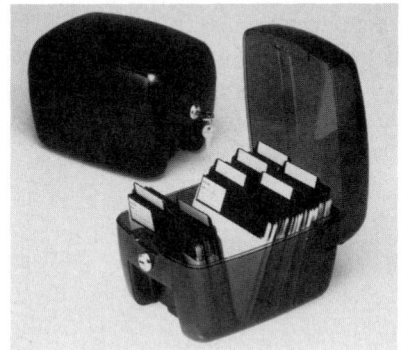

Courtesy of Ring King Visibles.

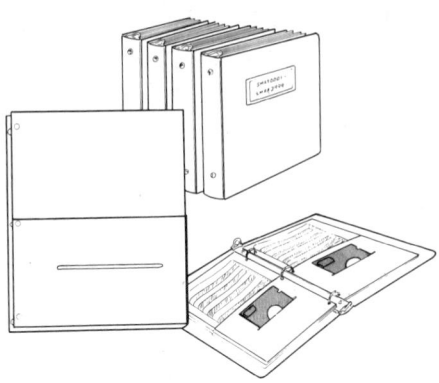

1. The number of documents on the disk
2. The anticipated future use of the document requiring it to remain stored on the disk
3. The potential for destruction of the material on the disk if it is placed in a file drawer

Number of Documents on the Disk. If the document or group of documents is sufficiently large to have a dedicated disk then it may be more convenient to store the disk with the hard copy. It would not make sense to dedicate a disk to a file folder when it contains only one or two letters, but filing the disk with a 100-page report which is revised every 6 months would ensure that the disk did not accidentally get erased. A backup of this disk should be kept in another location.

Anticipated Future Use. A disk that contains documents which are reused periodically, such as the 6-month report described above, would be best stored with the hard copy; however, a disk containing sales data updated weekly using a draft copy of the last report might better be kept in a disk file to save looking for the disk before each revision. When the weekly revision is completed and filed, the previous hard copy can be transferred to an inactive file. Copies of the previous report may be needed for reference by management but should not be kept as a working copy since it no longer reflects the contents of the disk.

Potential for Destruction. Disks are magnetic media subject to the dangers which can instantly remove data. Such dangers include telephones, magnets, dust and smoke, spills, greasy fingers, and any other hazards which interfere with the disk drive heads reading the data encoded on the disk. When in doubt the safest course is to keep the disks in their own file placed in a safe location in the office. One moment's carelessness can result in the destruction of many hours of keyboarding.

The illustrations on page 177 show various ways to store disks. Rotary files, box files, and notebooks with file pockets keep disks organized at the workstation. File folders with attached pockets and notebooks which hold disks along with documents are among the ways to keep magnetic media with the hard copy.

An example of filing equipment designed for a special purpose is the Rolling T-Cart storage unit. This transportable unit is used to store disks used in word processing and small computer installations. The disk fits into a vinyl pocket with a metal hanger. Colored signals alert the user to different kinds of stored information.

SELECTING FILE CARDS

When selecting file cards, the key issue is determining what the card will be used for. The cost of the cards is less important. The cost of the most expensive cards available is a small fraction of the cost of maintaining them as records. Once use has been determined, the characteristics of the cards selected depend on answers to the following questions:

1. Will the card be kept as a permanent or as a temporary record?
2. Will the card be used for posting by hand or machine or only for reference?
3. How frequently will the card be handled? Will the card need a transparent covering for protection?
4. Will the card be used for classifying items by its color?

Permanent or Temporary. A card record that will be kept permanently or that will be handled frequently or be unprotected should, of course, be heavy and of very high quality. Inexpensive, lighter-weight cards may be purchased for temporary, seldom-handled, or protected card records. Various weights of file cards are available—light, medium, heavy, and extra-heavy. Various proportions of sulphite and fiber content determine the durability of the cards. A card with a high fiber content is more durable (and more expensive) than a card with a high sulphite content.

Posted or Reference. For posted card records, the relative smoothness of the surface of a card, known as its *finish,* is important. Several finishes are available, from rough to very smooth and glossy, which are best suited to hand and machine posting, respectively. For reference purposes, cards should be durable enough for the amount of handling expected for the life of the record.

Protection. Card records are sometimes covered with plastic to protect them from soiling, bending, and deteriorating. In many visible files the visible edge of the card, because it is most frequently handled, is protected by a clear plastic strip. In vertical card files, cards that are often referred to are sometimes enclosed entirely in plastic. A device being used in business for permanently enclosing records in clear plastic is the *laminating machine.* A record is fed into the machine, and a plastic coating seals both sides of the record.

Color Classifications. In order to classify certain categories in a card file, such as local and out-of-town customers, cards of various colors are often used—perhaps green cards for local customers and blue cards for out-of-town customers. Not only are several solid colors available, but cards may also be purchased with vertical or horizontal stripes. Items are classified according to the color, width, and position of the colored stripes on the cards.

SELECTING BUSINESS FORMS

When selecting forms to use with the records management system, size and paper quality need to be determined.

Size. Legal-size cabinets cost more and occupy more space than standard letter-size ones. Recently there has been an effort to eliminate legal-size paper so that 8½ × 11 inch paper will become a standard for all files.

A small form can become hidden and difficult to find when filed with larger records. Likewise, a large form can take extra space and slow file searching when it is folded to standard letter-size dimensions. Therefore, a form should usually be designed to have the same dimensions as the other records with which it will be stored. Standard paper-mill sizes should also be considered before deciding on the size of a particular form. This will ensure minimum waste and lowest cost per form. The printer should be consulted for this information. If the form will be stored in special files, the equipment supplier should be consulted for suitable products. The cost of these files may influence the selection of the form.

Paper Quality. The type of paper to be selected is determined by the amount and kind of handling the form will receive. If forms are frequently removed from and reinserted in files, used for posting of additional data, or transported a great deal, they should be able to resist wear and tear. Some of the properties of paper are weight, grade, and grain. When considering weight, the lightest paper that will give satisfactory results should be used. Of course, the heavier weights are more durable. Standard weights recommended for various records are as follows:

RECORD	RECOMMENDED WEIGHT
Legal documents	28-pound
Ledgers	24-pound
Letterheads or forms (single copy)	20-pound
1 to 4 copies of multiple forms	16-pound
5 to 8 copies of multiple forms	13-pound
9 or more copies of multiple forms	Tissue weight (or onionskin)

The grade of paper depends on the ratio of fiber content to sulphite (wood pulp) content. The grade of paper recommended usually depends on the life span of a form:

LIFE OF FORM	GRADE
1 to 5 years	100% sulphite
6 to 12 years	50% sulphite, 50% fiber
Over 12 years	100% fiber

Most paper, like wood, has grain characteristics. The grain should run up and down on a form that is posted by machine and stored vertically so that the form will remain upright and not curl in a vertical tub or tray.

CONCLUSION

Whatever the needs of the business or organization, the most important criteria for selecting equipment and supplies is to increase the efficiency of storing and retrieving files and to ensure the protection of the records.

GENERAL REVIEW

1. What are the objectives of equipment and supplies in the records management system? (Competency 1)
2. Where can you obtain information about filing equipment and supplies? (Competency 2)
3. What equipment is used for storing correspondence? (Competency 3)
4. What equipment is used for card files? Which of these is similar to equipment used for correspondence? Which would not be suitable for correspondence? (Competency 4)
5. What are some records that have special equipment needs? How are these records stored? (Competency 5)
6. What are the guidelines for selecting vertical files? (Competency 6)
7. What are the guidelines for selecting other types of files? (Competency 7)
8. What are the purposes of guides, and what do you need to consider when buying guides? (Competency 8)
9. What are the criteria for selecting folders, and what are some of the special purposes folders may be used for? (Competency 9)
10. What accessories are helpful for the filing process? (Competency 10)
11. What equipment or supplies can be used to store disks? What are some criteria for making your selection? (Competency 11)
12. What questions need to be asked when determining the kind of cards to select for card records? What does laminating do for card records? (Competency 12)
13. What should you consider when selecting business forms? (Competency 13)

CASE PROBLEMS

1. After Josephine Marshall retired, she left her business to her nephew, Marshall Foresight. Marshall has decided to renovate the offices and would like to update the filing equipment. However, he does not know what equipment is available nor what it should do to be effective. He asks your advice. How can you help? (Competencies 1, 2, 3, 4, 6, 7)
2. When you begin working for an office that has vertical files, you find some difficulties with the equipment. The drawers are too crowded and

you cannot pull out folders easily. There are only two or three guides in each drawer, and captions are typed or written directly on the folder tabs. One of your duties is to make suggestions and implement them to make the filing system easier to work with. Describe what you plan to do. (Competencies 1, 6, 9)

3. Carl Porter mentions to his employer, the owner of a travel agency, that there must be a faster and more efficient way of getting folders and other information for people making personal inquiries. The brochures and maps which the agency uses are currently stored on shelves in a back room. Because it is difficult to rearrange them when new ones are added, they currently are in no useful order, making a particular item difficult to find. What would you suggest? (Competencies 3, 5)

4. Your word processing center keeps a copy of all documents which have been prepared there. Frequently you are asked to identify which copy is the current one. Your work involves long documents and correspondence with the same departments many times during the year. A couple of times the disk containing your annual report had a part deleted because other documents were added and space ran out. What can you suggest to the center supervisor to help ensure the safety of your disk and filing of only the current copy. (Competency 11)

5. Janis Jensen is beginning work on a research project which can be handled most efficiently using index cards. She would like an easy way to sort the cards into groups. She also would like some criteria for selecting the best quality card without spending more money than necessary. What suggestions can you give her? (Competency 12)

12

SETTING UP THE
ELECTRONIC WORKSTATION

COMPETENCIES

When you have completed this chapter you will be able to:

1. Define the term *workstation*.
2. List the functions of the electronic workstation.
3. Compare the landscaped office and the traditional office.
4. List supplies commonly kept in and on the desk.
5. List reference materials which help you on the job.
6. List and describe reminder files that you can use.
7. Describe how you set priorities for your work in the office.
8. Describe how the electronic workstation can be used for reminder and follow-up files.

THE WORKSTATION

Offices consist of groups of workstations, the areas where the work is done. A workstation usually consists of a desk, chair, shelves or bookcase, files, typewriter, microcomputer or word processor, telephone, and all the supplies necessary to do whatever the job involves. Parts of the workstation—the files, for example—may be shared by several people. Some workstations are set up so that two or more people share the microcomputer or word processor. Generally speaking, *workstation* means the physical equipment and supplies arranged so that the daily work routine can be performed in an efficient way.

Today, the term workstation can also mean a microcomputer and the tasks it performs. There are five basic functions for this electronic workstation:

1. Word processing to prepare documents
2. Spreadsheet processing to do financial studies
3. Database processing to handle large filing systems
4. Graphics to produce charts and graphs for business reports
5. Electronic mail to transfer documents or data between workstations or computer systems

Microcomputers can also be used for appointment calendars, tickler files, and note pads, among other uses. Lately, microcomputers and specialized software are being used to publish pamphlets, brochures, magazines, and even books. This use, called desktop publishing, cuts down on the time and expense needed to publish by traditional methods. Another sophisticated feature of some microcomputers allows you to enter data by voice instead of keyboard.

While electronic workstations handle quickly and easily many routine functions of the office, paper files are still necessary for many projects and activities which take place as part of the normal office routine.

TYPES OF OFFICE LAYOUTS

There generally are two basic types of office layouts: the traditional, or enclosed, office and the landscaped, or open, office.

The traditional office arrangement has enclosed cubicles or rooms that house workstations for one or more individuals. Office size, location, privacy, view, and furnishings are all status symbols within the organization.

The landscaped office, however, features an open area partitioned by furniture and dividers of various heights for privacy. More employees can fit in the available space than with the traditional office arrangement. Landscaped offices are also usually carpeted and have dividers made of soundproofing materials to absorb the noises of typewriters and printers.

A variation of both the landscaped and the traditional office is the use of cubicles with movable partitions. Many of the newer buildings are shells with large rooms which can be partitioned according to the needs of the organization.

INDIVIDUAL WORK AREAS

Whatever the arrangement of your office, the immediate work area is a reflection of each employee. Individuals should be conscious of the appearance created during the working day and how the desk and surrounding area is left at the end of the day. The following are some questions to determine if the best use is made of the workstation.

1. Is the desk clear of clutter and neatly arranged so that complete attention can be given to the task at hand?
2. Are materials, files, and supplies within easy reach?
3. Are all supplies available and neatly arranged?
4. Are reference materials within easy reach?
5. Is the furniture (desk, chair, files) positioned for comfort and best lighting?
6. Are there drawer files, baskets, or upright desk files to hold work completed or in progress?
7. Is the desk positioned to eliminate distractions from the surrounding office area?
8. Are tickler and other reference files up to date?

When a computer is part of the workstation, the following questions should be asked.

1. Is there enough work area around the computer to allow for the placement of work being done?
2. Is the computer set up properly for greatest comfort in viewing the screen and using the keyboard?
3. Are the reference materials for computer programs within easy reach? Are quick reference materials such as reference cards close at hand? Are templates used on the keyboard to assist with frequently used commands?
4. Are files set up for disks? Are labels and marking pens available for identifying disks?

The diagrams on pages 186 and 187 illustrating arrangements for work and supplies on a desk and electronic workstation may help you to organize your work area.

Desk Supplies. Traditional office desks are constructed to allow for an efficient arrangement of supplies. Everyday paper supplies can be placed in a rack in a drawer (or other closed compartment) of the desk. Most desks have a shallow drawer for supplies which must be kept handy, such as scissors, stapler and staples, paper clips, cellophane tape, rubber stamps and stamp pad, and glue. If new folders and cards need to be set up often for the filing system, these items should also be kept in the desk. Another desk drawer may be convenient to hold vertical files of business forms and records needed for daily reference. Heavy or bulky items that are not convenient to store inside can be kept on the desk or on a nearby shelf.

A telephone should be placed within convenient reach, and telephone information slips or notepaper should be handy for making notes on calls. Other top-of-desk items might include an appointment calendar, a card file, a pencil cup, baskets or trays for incoming and outgoing papers, a time stamp, and

TRADITIONAL WORKSTATION

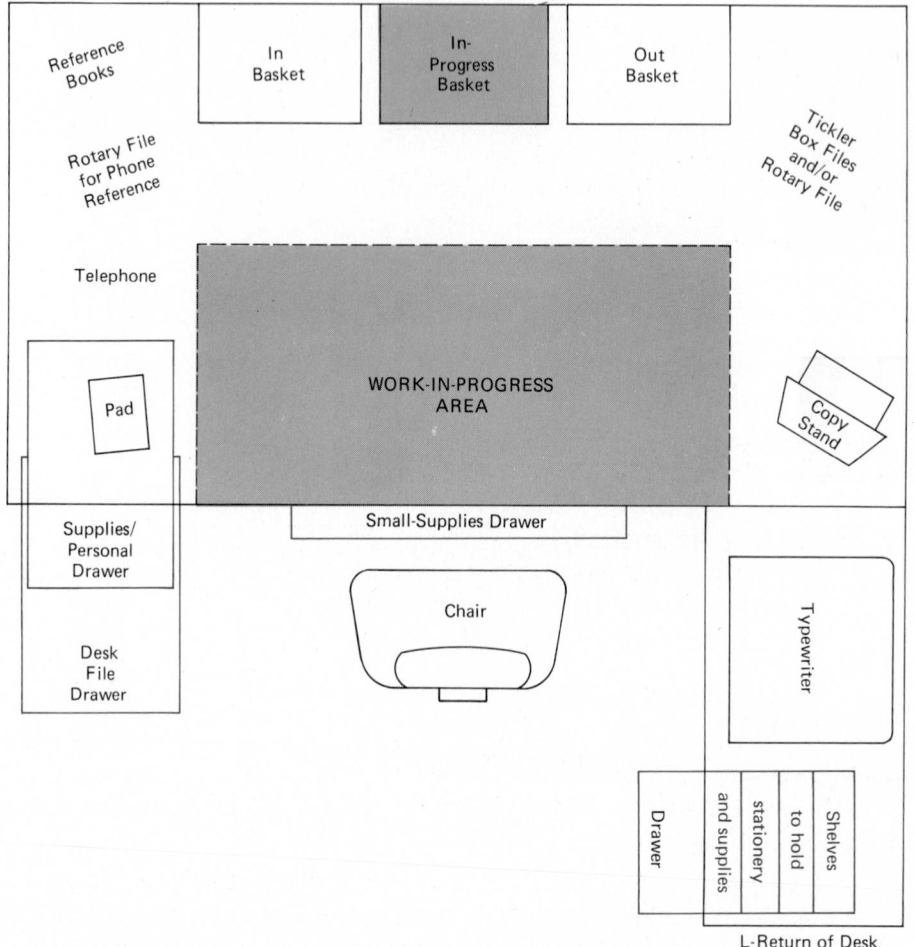

reference materials. The most commonly used reference materials are a telephone book, a company directory, a dictionary, an employee's handbook, and an office procedures manual.

An electronic workstation may not include a traditional desk, but should include some item of furniture with a drawer or two to hold pens, pencils, and small items. Shelves should be available to hold office supplies. The printer should be placed on a flat surface which allows free feeding of the paper. Extra ribbons and other printer supplies should be easily accessible. In some offices, printers are maintained at a central location and used by several computers. Special printers may be set up for envelopes, labels, cards, and special forms. The electronic workstation should include space for laying out work in progress

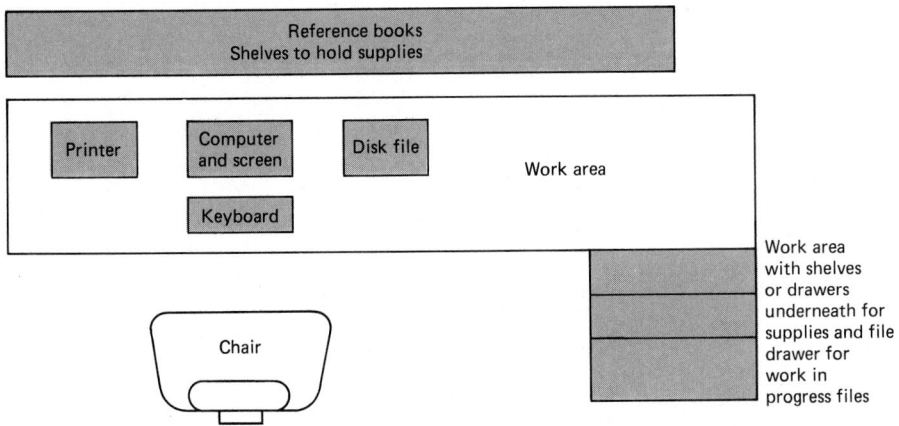

and trays or stand-up file holders for completed work. A disk file should be set up for program and data disks. Reference books for the word processor or computer programs should be close at hand.

REMINDER FILES

Even if electronic files take care of most of the routine work in the office, there are several files which are useful for making sure that the work gets done on time.

1. A *chronological file* holds items in order by date, usually for a 1-month period, with folder or divider captions used to separate days in an accordion file. Items are placed behind the date on which some action must be taken. The file is checked each day and the action is taken, or a decision is made to postpone the action and the item is moved to a new date. Items which would fall on weekends or holidays should be moved to the working day before the holiday or weekend.

2. A *correspondence file* contains model letters and is particularly helpful to the newcomer on the job since it provides a reference to the style, tone, and content of letters which have been written. For example, a word processing operator may be instructed to send a copy of form letter 8 to a customer. This saves dictating the letter or sending a copy to the word processing center.

3. A *follow-up file* may be, but is not necessarily, arranged by date (chronologically). It may also have an alphabetic arrangement. This file contains items which need to be completed or verified at a later date.

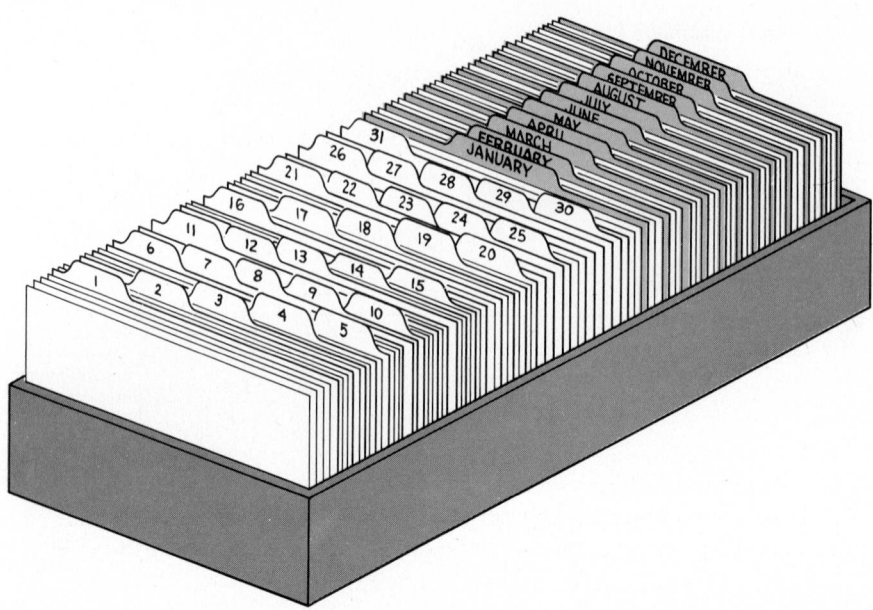

Chronological and tickler files can be set up in a staggered format with days as folder labels. Months can be used for another set of folders. A few days before the beginning of each month, the items in the next month's folder can be placed in the day files which are now empty.

This work may extend over a long period of time or it may be of short duration. Items in it may be either discarded or filed when action has been taken or notice of action has been received. For example, a secretary has contacted the accounting department for figures needed to complete a report. The draft of the document would be placed in the follow-up file until the information has been received and the report finished.

4. A *hold-for-answer file* contains copies of letters requesting information or notes which need a response. These items should be handled as replies are received—either filed, used, or placed in a different reminder folder.

5. A *pending file* contains matters which are not yet finished because of incomplete information, unfinished details, or low priority. The pending file can be used for a combination of work items or for a specific job in progress. For example, a pending file may be maintained of all the jobs which could be done during slack times in the office, ideas for projects for future work, and other assorted jobs.

6. A *reading file* contains a chronological collection of extra copies of correspondence sent out of the office during a specific period of time.

The length of the time varies according to the quantity of correspondence and is usually the amount which conveniently fits in a notebook. This is particularly useful when references are made to recent correspondence or the nature of the correspondence does not lend itself to one specific topic, person, or organization for filing purposes. For example, the confidential secretary of a college president would maintain a reading file of all letters sent out of the office. Since many of these letters deal with more than one topic and consist of several pages, it may not be efficient to file multiple copies.

7. A *suspense file* is similar to a chronological file because it contains folders by date (one for each day of the month), by month, and by year. As items which will come up in the future are noted, the information is placed in the appropriate folder. The difference between the suspense file and the chronological file is that usually suspense file items require some definite action to be taken. For example, a report may be sent to other departments in the company for review before publication, but these review copies *must* be returned by a specific date to meet the publication deadline.

8. A *tickler card file* is used for following up on any items which can conveniently be recorded on small cards. These cards are usually set up by day with dividers for the days of the month and months of the year as in chronological filing, or they may be set up alphabetically. For example, notations about bills to pay, dates to remember, meetings to attend, and preparations to be made for big jobs coming up, as well as employee names and phone numbers, are good candidates for a tickler card file.

9. A *tickler folder file* operates in the same manner as the tickler card file, but the items are too large to be placed on a card. It is particularly useful for items which may serve as reminders or information only and then can be disposed of after use. For example, a manager may receive many notices of meetings to attend. These dates are noted on the calendar, but the notices contain detailed information needed a day or two prior to the meeting. Once the meeting has been attended, the notice can be discarded.

10. A *work in progress file* may contain several projects (or one large project) not yet finished which need periodic attention until completed. For example, all the details for a large report would be kept in this file until the report was written. The report would then be filed where appropriate and notes, drafts, and other working papers would be discarded. Work-in-progress files help to keep the desk clear to work on one task at a time.

All these files are kept in the desk or within easy reach. The tickler card file may be kept on top of the desk or in a small drawer; the folder files may be kept in a desk file drawer or a desktop organizer.

SETTING PRIORITIES

Setting priorities means deciding the order of urgency of jobs to be done. The most important or the most urgent work is assigned top priority and must be done first. Other tasks are then done according to the order of their importance. In the office routine there is work that is urgent, work that is important, work that is routine and work that is done only when extra time is available. Effective workers set goals for work to be accomplished each day and organize their time to meet those goals.

"To Do" List. One of the best ways to keep track of work which needs to be done is to keep a "to do" list. This is a list of all the items that need attention within the next day or so. Items which need attention in the future should be noted on a calendar or filed in one of the follow-up files.

The "to do" list is a way to organize each work day, making sure that the most important items get done while still keeping track of other tasks which are important. As items are completed, they are crossed off the list. The list is reviewed and rewritten periodically throughout the day. At the end of the day, the "to do" list for the next work day is begun including items from the calendar and follow-up files which need to be completed. This allows time to think about the tasks to do and plan ahead.

Desk Trays. To help organize work on the desk, containers are used to hold work which will be brought to you by others and to hold completed work to be picked up by others. These containers are usually metal or plastic trays labeled *in* and *out* baskets. Another tray may also be designated as a *hold* basket for work in progress. Work received during the day may affect the priorities already set and thus require reorganization of the "to do" list.

USING THE ELECTRONIC WORKSTATION TO FOLLOW UP

The electronic workstation has the capability to help follow up activities by using the storage and retrieval capability as an integral part of the daily work. Once the computer or word processor is available for use during most of the day the speed and natural organization required for initial storage make the computer an asset. Many people use computers for reference and recall. Travel agencies and airlines are a good example of businesses which use computers for checking flights available, bookings, reservations, and making seat selections. These tasks would take a great deal of time without the computer, yet with the computer become very routine.

Most reminder files of necessity start out as paper files. The data might then be keyed into a computer file, with updates made by keying any new information.

Files which may be put on the computer include:

1. Chronological reminders for which the original may no longer be needed.

2. Letters that have file names that the computer will accept.
3. Follow-up files, parts of which have been keyed; perhaps drafts sent to others for review.
4. Hold-for-answer files with the mailing list and master copy of the letter on the computer. Notations could be made when information is received. Follow-up letters could be sent to nonrespondents noting or deleting names no longer needed.
5. Pending file items.
6. Reading files could be kept on disk with an index to reference dates of letters and documents brought up on a screen when needed. Some computer programs can access all documents in a directory by key words which would allow instant reference to all documents which contain a certain word or words. For example, the operator could locate all documents which contain the reference to "January 21 stockholders meeting."
7. Suspense file notations could be kept on the computer under each date; information for sending notices could then be merged with the reminder which needs to be sent. By using electronic mail, both retrieval and message delivery can be done entirely by computer.
8. Tickler file notations could be kept in a list under dates on the computer with, perhaps, a document set up for each month or each topic.
9. Work-in-progress can be kept on the computer with the pieces of a large report being worked on in stages kept in separate files.

The variety of filed material which can be kept on an electronic workstation is limited only by the imagination and ingenuity of the user.

CONCLUSION

The workstation is your workspace and includes all the supplies, reference materials, and reminder files you need on a daily basis. Today, most workstations include a computer which need on a daily basis. Today, many workstations include a computer which is is used for daily work activities, the storage of reminder files, and other electronically stored records. Microcomputer programs are limited only by the user's knowledge of the software and the user's ability to adapt and adopt paper documents to magnetic media. Looking for data electronically is usually simpler and easier than searching through manual files.

GENERAL REVIEW

1. What is a workstation? (Competency 1)
2. What are the functions that can be included in the electronic workstation? (Competency 2)

3. What are the differences between the landscaped office and the traditional office? Why has the landscaped office become popular? (Competency 3)
4. What supplies will you need to use? (Competency 4)
5. What reference materials will help you on the job? (Competency 5)
6. What are the different reminder and follow-up file systems that you might use on the job? (Competency 6)
7. How do you set priorities for your work in the office? (Competency 7)
8. How can the electronic workstation be used for reminder and follow-up files? (Competency 8)

CASE PROBLEMS

1. Your office is adding microcomputers to the workstations. Your supervisor has asked you for some ideas about tasks which you think you could do on the computer. Make a list of activities and files which could be part of your electronic workstation. (Competency 2)
2. As administrative assistant for Michael Smith, a real estate agent, you find that you are tired at the end of each day because you cannot keep up with all the details of your job. You feel you could get more done if you were more organized. What advice is given in this chapter to help you? (Competencies 4, 5, 6, 7)
3. You have been working several months for Dr. Alberta Kincaid, a noted author and lecturer. Dr. Kincaid makes commitments months in advance for speaking engagements. You find that the dates for these talks sneak up on you. You constantly have to look through your appointment book and hold basket for materials you need to prepare for her speeches as well as check on the travel arrangements, some of which must be booked months in advance. Of the reminder and follow-up files described in this chapter, which would be the most appropriate for your use? Describe how you will set up your files. (Competencies 6, 7)

13

MICROGRAPHICS AND
ADVANCED SYSTEMS

COMPETENCIES

When you have completed this chapter, you will be able to:

1. List five major developments in specialized systems being used in filing and records management.
2. Define the following terms: *micrographics, microform, microimages, microfilm, microfiche, aperture cards, micropublishing, microrepublishing, microfacsimile, computer-assisted retrieval, computer-output microfilm or microfiche, optical disk,* and *ultrafiche.*
3. List the advantages and disadvantages of microfilm and microfiche.
4. Discuss the uses of optical disks.
5. List the advantages of automated retrieval equipment.
6. List and briefly describe the three formats used for color-coded alphabetic and numeric systems.
7. State why color systems are used and state two differences between these systems and the alphabetic and numeric filing systems outlined previously.
8. List the advantages of using less paper in the office.
9. List some of the traditional items of records management equipment that may not appear in the office of the future.
10. Explain why a knowledge of filing basics is extremely important when working with computers.

Now that you have studied the basic filing systems for alphabetic, numeric, subject, and geographic filing, you know that these systems provide for storing and retrieving records, using standard equipment for filing procedures, including equipment for reproduction of records, storage, and retrieval.

Both micrographics and other specialized systems serve the same functions. However, they are designed and constructed by office equipment manufacturers and are often part of the technological change in the office along with computers and word processing equipment.

Five major developments in the office are discussed in this chapter. These are (1) micrographics, (2) computer-assisted retrieval and computer output microfilm, (3) optical disks, (4) automated retrieval equipment, and (5) color-coded filing systems. Let's look first at micrographics.

MICROGRAPHICS

Micrographics is a term used for the process of reproducing information on microforms. A *microform* is either film or paper which contains microimages. A *microimage* is a reduction of a larger record or document. *Microfilm* is a roll of attached microimages. *Microfiche* is a sheet of film which contains a great many pages in miniature. The sheet is usually 6 × 4 inches and holds from 60 to 100 pages of records, depending on the reduction. An *aperture card* is a card with an opening, or aperture, in which microfilm is mounted. The microfilm image is usually a great reduction of a large document, such as an

MICROFILM CAMERA

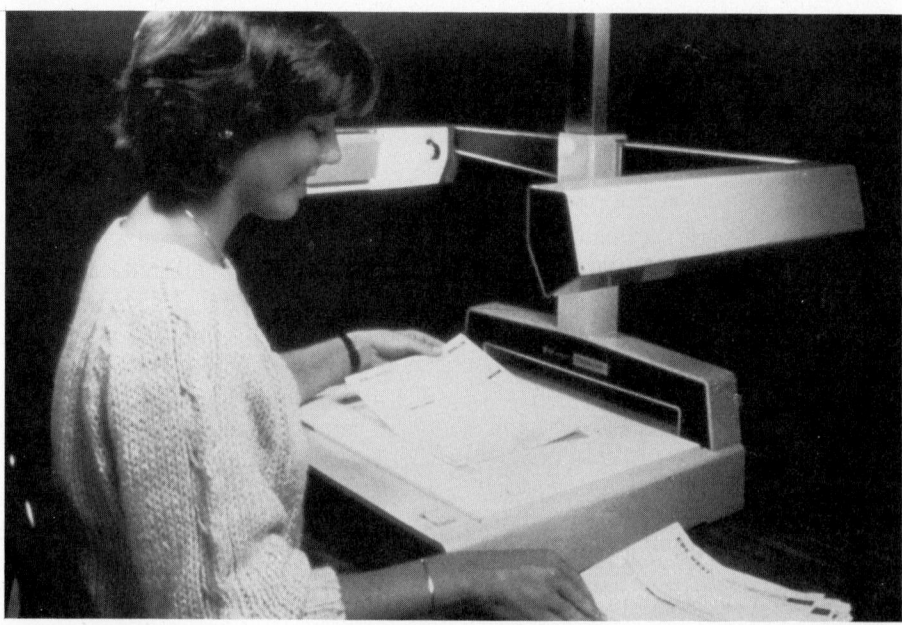

© Bell & Howell Company.

engineering drawing. Identifying data is usually printed on the card.

Ultrafiche is another type of microfiche which is used primarily because of its size. Images are reduced 90 or more times smaller than the original image in a single dimension. For example, ultrafiche is microfiche, say 8½ × 11 inches in size, which contains images of more than 8100 pages of the same size. A 6 × 4 inch sheet of microfiche may contain as many as 72 pages. It is easy to see why ultrafiche reduces the amount of storage space necessary to maintain records.

Advantage of Microfilm. Microfilm is used for storing information and records because:

1. It provides a rapid way to locate information: information is located automatically on a machine called a *reader*. Locating a paper in traditional files takes much longer.
2. Microfilm is small and requires less storage space than paper records in cabinet files. Because of this, an operator can have many rolls of microfilm at the work station.
3. Microfilm readers are usually equipped to print copies of the records being located. Thus the operator can find and print the copy in one operation.
4. Microfilm is neater and cleaner than files, particularly those containing copies of materials.
5. Microfilm stores a series of records on one piece of film; thus it is impossible to misplace an individual record.
6. Microfilm can be used for storing graphic data (pictures and drawings) as well as alphanumeric data.
7. Microfilm results in a permanent tangible record which can be read directly as opposed to computer tapes and word processing media which cannot.
8. Microfilm can be easily transported to be read wherever a reader is available, including at home with a portable reader. Readers are relatively small compared with other types of office equipment.
9. Conversion to microfilm is generally easier than conversion of the same data to computerized files. The hard copy records can be photographed and the film developed either in house or by an outside agency for use within a relatively short period of time. Developing the indexing system is the most complicated part of the implementation of microfilm as a storage medium.
10. Microfilm costs less to mail than paper copies of the same number of pages. This results in a considerable cost savings for business.

Microfilming is used more and more in business for these reasons:

1. The cost of microfilm is decreasing and the equipment is available in a competitive market. As the cost of maintaining traditional filing systems

increases, businesses will consider microforms to reduce space and labor costs.

2. The federal government allows microfilm records to be substituted for original documents; however, the film must not have been spliced. (Some records must be filmed in exact sequence to meet legal requirements. If a record is found to be out of sequence, the entire roll of film must be redone.)

3. New equipment is producing better images, making it easier to read the screens and the copies being produced. (See color insert.)

4. Indexes may be prepared by file workers before or after the microfilming takes place. For some applications, indexes may be automatically prepared by a computer. An accurate index is vital; without it records cannot be located once they have been filmed.

Advantages of Microfiche. Microfiche has many of the same advantages as microfilm. In addition:

1. A sheet of microfiche is easier to use than a roll of film because you can immediately access the item or page you need instead of scanning a whole roll of film. Microfiche is set up with an alphanumeric matrix. Columns and rows are labeled so that if you need an item in Column B, Row 4, for example, you can immediately access that location.

2. Microfiche can be updated by adding pages. Additions, however, may cause pages to be out of sequence, which may destroy the legal value of the film.

MICROFILM READER

© Bell & Howell Company.

3. Images can be deleted by photocopying over the image several times to black it out and make it unreadable. Microfiche can also be duplicated for use by others with some of the images omitted.

Disadvantages of Microfilm and Microfiche. Several disadvantages of using microfilm and microfiche for records storage are:

1. Paper copies from microfilm and microfiche are slow and expensive to produce and are of poor quality compared with other copying methods.
2. Microfilm is difficult to update because a new document cannot be inserted in place of an old one without destroying the integrity of the film by splicing it. Documents can be added to microfiche only in blank spaces; old documents cannot be replaced with new ones.
3. Special equipment is needed to read documents on microfilm and microfiche.
4. It is not possible to write on microfilm and microfiche in order to make notations or highlight information. It may be difficult to write on the copies that are produced.

Offices use micrographics for records storage; microfiche and microfilm readers are set up near the storage area for records. Portable readers enclosed in attaché cases extend the convenience of microforms. Businesses which print large documents that employees must take to other locations often use microforms to reduce the volume.

Other Micro Uses. The value of micrographics extends beyond its use in records management. *Micrographics* applies to production of records for public use. *Micropublishing* is the production of information on microforms. *Microrepublishing* is the reproduction of information, previously in hard-copy form, on microforms.

Microfacsimile is the transmission of data contained on microfiche or aperture cards over telephone lines to produce hard copy at the other end. This is similar to *facsimile,* the transmission of hard copy from one location to another over telephone lines.

COMPUTER-ASSISTED RETRIEVAL (CAR) AND COMPUTER OUTPUT MICROFILM/MICROFICHE (COM)

If you work in an office which has a computer to store and process information, you are likely to hear the term *computer-assisted retrieval (CAR)*. CAR refers to records which are stored within the computer on magnetic tapes or disks. You need the computer to obtain the desired information and produce it for you in readable form.

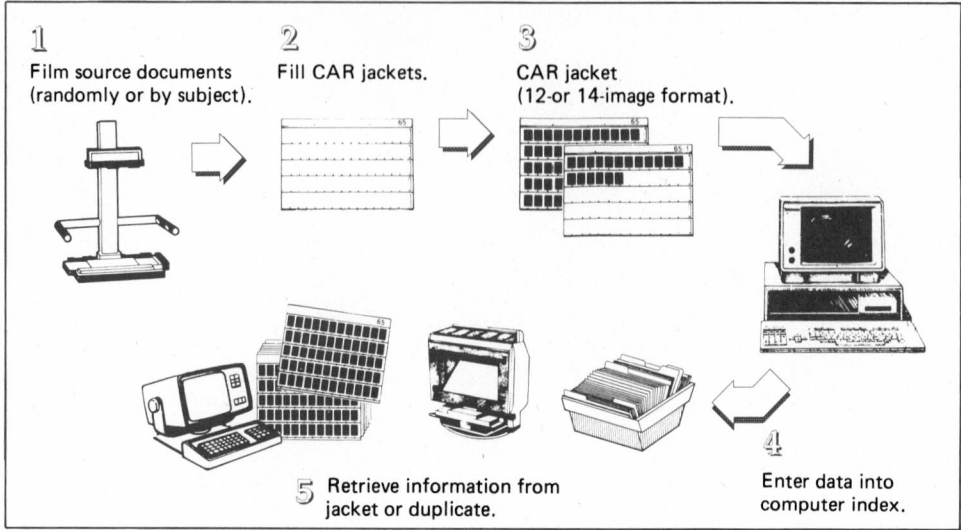

1 Film source documents (randomly or by subject).

2 Fill CAR jackets.

3 CAR jacket (12-or 14-image format).

5 Retrieve information from jacket or duplicate.

4 Enter data into computer index.

The above flowchart illustrates how a CAR jacket system works.

One of the advantages of CAR is that large quantities of information can be stored in a computer and the person requesting information can ask for it under different topics, to check all possibilities. There are storage banks of up-to-date information on topics included in books, articles, and documents. An individual seeking information queries the system to find out what is available about a particular topic. For example, a doctor may seek information about the causes and cures of a rare disease contracted by a patient.

Most computers have the capability to print information in hard copy. *Computer output microfilm* or *computer output microfiche (COM)* allows information to be printed on microforms for use and storage. The computer processes the desired information into a form readable by the microform processing unit, and that unit produces the microform desired by the user.

A recent development is word processing on microfilm (WPOM), which converts information on word processing magnetic media to microfilm for storage and use.

It is predicted that the use of micrographics will continue to increase in the office. The use of microforms to store documents is expected to grow rapidly, especially in those organizations that already have installed complex computer and word processing systems. It is becoming economically feasible to add capabilities to already established equipment and transmit microforms electronically to another location.

Equipment and Storage for Microforms and Magnetic Media. With the rapid growth in the use of microforms and magnetic media used with word processing

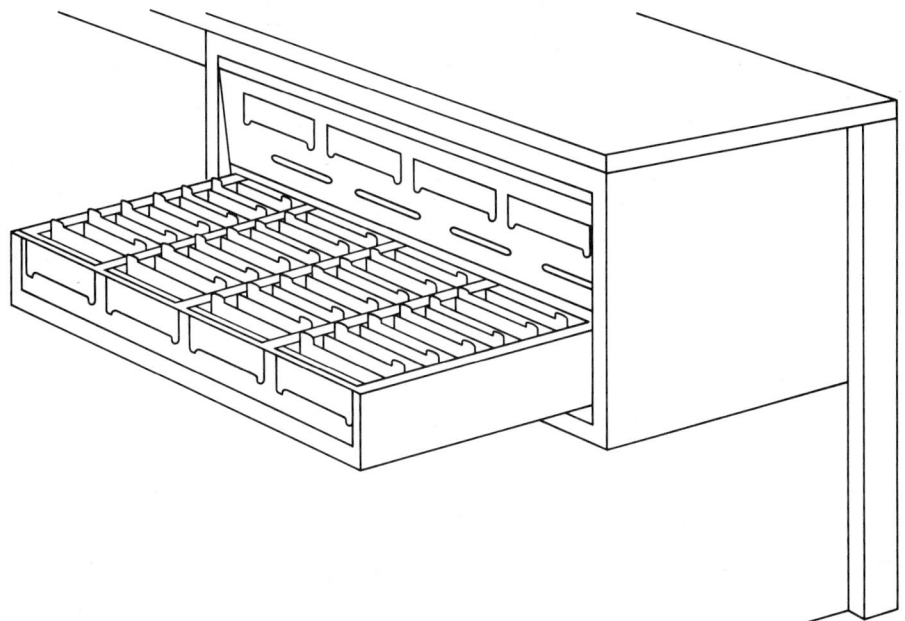

With drawers small enough for microfilm or microfiche, a microform storage system can hold many records.

equipment, office supply manufacturers are developing compact files to use for efficient storage of these items. Such equipment is usually of the drawer or tub type. A cabinet with drawers sized to fit microfilm or microfiche can hold many times the number of records held by a standard vertical correspondence file of similar dimensions.

Because misfiling is a major problem with microforms, only one person should do the actual storage. Microforms are usually coded numerically to make filing and expansion easy. An index is consulted to obtain the number of the desired record. Because microforms are highly organized, the index is often stored on magnetic media or accessed by means of a computer for updating and producing a new copy. One piece of film may be the index for many others.

Optical Disks. The most recent trend in information storage is the optical disk. Government agencies are perhaps the biggest user of this medium. Large government agencies want to reduce storage space and costs, increase document retrieval speed, and route documents reliably and accurately. The optical disk improves the quality of the stored image. Productivity is increased and labor costs are decreased.

© Jules Allen

Police departments use vital information every minute of every day. Paper-work has long been a bane of police work. Because vital information has been misfiled or is difficult and time-consuming to locate, what seems like an endless stream of forms and reports have required too much time. The Anaheim, California, Police Department once used a system consisting of index cards and microfiche files. This system was extremely slow. Each time a detective wanted to retrieve information from the microfiche library, the detective had to go to the records bureau and a clerk would access the microfiche and make a copy while the detective waited.

This system was replaced with a Filenet optical disk system. In order for the police to have more investigation time while increasing efficiency and reducing costs, all daily reports are now scanned into the system. Their digitized images are permanently stored, filed, and indexed on optical disks. Once they have been scanned, the detective has direct access to the information on the screen of an integrated workstation where the detective can easily examine suspect files and compare clues.

Other such offices use similar optical disk systems. Offices for state vital records bureaus, patent and trademark management, military personnel records management, employees pension administration, and commercial credit administration are all maintaining records more efficiently and producing higher quality printed output.

AUTOMATED RETRIEVAL EQUIPMENT

Automated filing units of various levels of sophistication can be purchased. One company manufactures a system for microfiche which, when the index number is keyed in, will search the files and bring the jacket containing one or more microfiches out of the system for the user.

Automated systems have the following advantages:

1. They can be locked for security.
2. They are more convenient and comfortable to use than conventional systems. The operator sits at a workstation, and files are delivered to the operator by a mechanical device.

Using this automated power filing unit, a file worker can access a jacket of microfiche by keyboarding its index number. © Kardex

3. They save space by using vertical space rather than additional floor space.
4. They allow individuals with physical handicaps to work with files.
5. They are more attractive than conventional file cabinets, and fit in with the open office setting.

COLOR-CODED FILING SYSTEMS

The most prevalent specialized systems are the color-coded systems which are designed to prevent misfiling and speed the search for records. There are three basic formats used for color systems: (1) the folder may be a distinctive color, (2) the label may be a distinctive color, or (3) the folder may have one or more bars of color which identify its location in the file. (See color insert.)

Colored folders are used for specific purposes. For example, an office might put all financial records in yellow folders, all contracts in green folders, and all personnel records in blue folders to identify the contents. Some systems use a specific color such as green for the first 1000 folders, blue for the second 1000 folders, and pink for the third 1000 folders to prevent or reduce misfiling.

Colored labels may be used in the same way as colored folders. If your office orders a large quantity of standard folders of one color, different colored labels will allow you to identify different types of records.

Color bar systems are available commercially from several manufacturers. Basically, these systems make use of ''color bands''—combinations of colors on folders of tabs.

Usually, color-coded files are stored on open shelves so that the file worker looking for a particular color group can scan many files at once. When replacing a folder having a red band above a blue band on the tab, scanning the shelves for similar color combinations is faster than looking for the letters of each unit.

In many color systems folders are not filed alphabetically within their group; instead, they are placed at the front of the group because 80 percent of the filing activity is usually concentrated in 20 percent of the records. Thus the chances are 8 out of 10 that the search for a file will be limited to the front 20 percent of the color section. A color system can be used for straight numeric, middle digit, or terminal digit as well as for alphabetic filing systems.

TOTAL OFFICE AUTOMATION (LESS-PAPER OFFICES)

Over two million pages of records are produced every minute in the United States. There was a time when records managers thought the future held a ''paperless'' office. But the fact that one office worker produces 4000 new documents a year and computers produce more than 350 billion pages a year have made the paperless office merely a dream.

We can, however, strive for an office with less paper. Many organizations change correspondence and other business records into electronic or micrographic media in order to carry on everyday business activities. The collection, compilation, computation, and distribution of information can be handled by the use of large-scale computer networks. With the employment of sophisticated text-editing software, users can have at their fingertips, via a small computer, access to all the files and other information pertaining to the company's business. Most text-editing systems require authority (such as terminal identification and passwords) to limit access to those who have authority to make changes.

Advantages of a "Less-Paper" System. The source documents for business information, although originally paper, become the electronic storage media in the computer. The advantages of a system such as this include:

1. Reduced cost through less consumption of paper
2. Immediate access to information
3. Elimination of the problems of misfiling and lost records
4. Improved security of records because they are protected through authority routines required to gain access to the information
5. Significantly reduced physical storage space
6. Easy interchange of necessary information between distant points

Office Environment and System Design. With office automation that eliminates a large number of paper records, many items can be totally removed from the office scene. Such items as the tickler file, calculator, personal file, card file, personal telephone directory, spelling dictionary, clock, and personal calendar or diary which are routinely found on the typical desk can be eliminated.

The electronic typewriter will still be necessary in many automated offices. It is also significant to note that *keyboarding skills are of extreme importance in such an office environment*. It is through keyboarding that information is collected, compiled, computed, and distributed. The pencil and pencil sharpener will not be as necessary as they once were. With personal computers in many executive suites, even the executive will need keyboarding skills.

One good example of the elimination of paper in an office system is the airline ticket desk. You can call a travel agent or an airline and acquire reservations for a flight. Your reservation is recorded by the personnel in the travel agency or the airline office. No paper is generated until you arrive at the ticket desk at the airport. At that time, the agent in charge accesses the computer by using keyboarding skills to locate your reservation and tells the computer to print your ticket.

Because these systems are designed by humans, system architecture is developed through processes we understand and know. Hence, an understanding of manual filing and data management systems is extremely valuable as it allows the user to know what the computer is doing with the information it maintains. The system handles data the way you manage a manual system. Needless to say, the system works at an extremely high rate of speed, making it much more efficient. Yet anyone who works in an office needs to know the basics of filing—that is, indexing rules, procedures, and basic elements of manual filing systems—in order to be able to understand and fully utilize the computer as a tool.

Mobility. In the past, workers have been confined to an office because it was necessary to have paper files readily available for use. Once offices commit to the use of less paper, access to the workstation is limited only to the availability of a telephone. The use of portable terminals enables the worker to feed and retrieve information from the system while at home, at field sites, in customers' offices, and in hotels thousands of miles away, or with a mobile telephone while driving to and from work.

Electronic Mail. One of the more common means of office communications that has not been automated is the postal system—the *mail.* An office using less paper may find that an alternative to the postal system, *electronic mail,* is the key to more efficient communication. Electronic mail allows a person to type a message at one computer or terminal and then send that message to someone at another terminal or computer which is either in the same building or in a different city miles away. The message is stored until the reader chooses to read it.

Computers linked to telephone lines allow documents to be transmitted at high rates of speed as simply and easily as making a phone call. This electronic mail creates many opportunities for companies to reduce costs.

What Will Tomorrow's Office Look Like? The decor of the office of the future will change somewhat to allow a less-structured and more relaxed, thought-provoking atmosphere. There will be fewer filing cabinets; much of the firm's records will be maintained in other ways. Desks will be built to accommodate computer terminals. Managerial and administrative workers will have terminals available to them.

From Voice to Written Word. In the future, as these systems become more sophisticated, data management and manipulation—both input and output—will be accomplished through the human voice. Many computers using voice technology are on the drawing board and in various other stages of development today.

For example, the worker will be able to pick up a phone and talk to the computer directly in plain English. The machine and the worker will be able to converse about what the worker desires and requires, and the worker will direct the computer to provide for those needs.

Laser Thumbprint Scanner and Voice Analyzers. Among other innovations to aid in the creation of an office and a society with less paper are such devices as the laser thumbprint scanner and voice analyzers which substitute for handwritten signatures which can be easily forged.) These also can be used as a key to provide access to computer information.

Job Advancement. Job advancement will be determined by the employee's knowledge of basics. In order to advance in the automated office, it is imperative that you know the basics. Otherwise, you will only be able to do tomorrow what you have done today. Many people believe that it is possible to avoid learning these basics—that they can "let the computer do it." But you will only advance with a solid background of fundamentals that will allow you to fully utilize all the tools available to you.

CONCLUSION

Micrographics and advanced systems, such as computer-assisted retrieval and optical disks, have automated the filing process. This automation has led to the decline in the use of paper for storing records. Manual filing systems have been enhanced by the use of color to make filing and retrieval of records more efficient. A knowledge of the basic concepts of filing and records management is necessary to effectively use the tools of office automation.

GENERAL REVIEW

The questions which follow will help you to reinforce your learning of the competencies in this chapter.

1. List and briefly describe the five major developments in specialized systems being used in filing and records management. (Competency 1)
2. Define the following terms (Competency 2):

micrographics	microrepublishing
microform	microfacsimile
microimage	CAR
microfilm	COM
microfiche	optical disk
aperature card	ultrafiche
micropublishing	

3. What is the difference between microfilm and microfiche? What are the advantages and disadvantages of each? (Competency 3)
4. Discuss the uses of optical disks. (Competency 4)
5. List five advantages of automated filing systems. (Competency 5)
6. List and briefly describe the three formats used for color-coded alphabetic and numeric systems. (Competency 6)
7. Why are color systems used? State two differences between these systems and the alphabetic and numeric filing systems you learned previously in this book. (Competency 7)

8. List six advantages of using less paper in the office. (Competency 8)
9. List some of the traditional items of records management equipment that may not appear in the office of the future. (Competency 9.)
10. Explain why a knowledge of filing basics is extremely important when working with computers. (Competency 10)

CASE PROBLEMS

1. Your employer, Barbara Manley, has become concerned regarding security in the records management department of your company. She's also concerned about space within that department. However, any changes that are made must accommodate one of the records management employees, Irving Richards, who uses a wheelchair. What advice can you give Ms. Manley regarding this situation? (Competencies 1, 5)
2. A friend, George Campbell, works in the local police department. He is concerned about the quality of the records on file there. He is also interested in reducing storage space and costs. Most significant, though, is the delay in retrieving documents and routing them to the proper people. He feels it would be more efficient if the detectives were able to access the files themselves. Can you offer any advice to help George and his department? (Competencies 1, 2, 4)
3. You had lunch with two individuals who work in an office down the hall from you. They were complaining about the amount of paper in their office. They have been reading about offices with less paper. Can you offer any words of wisdom to these two people based on what you have learned in this chapter? (Competencies 1, 8, 9, 10)

14

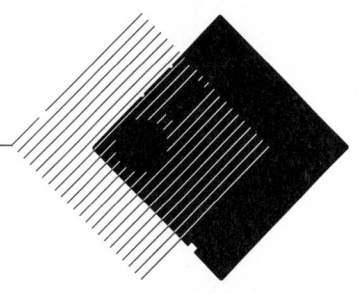

RECORDS SYSTEM ANALYSIS
AND DESIGN

COMPETENCIES

When you have completed this chapter, you will be able to:

1. Define the terms *centralized* and *decentralized* and describe how these arrangements affect where the files are kept.
2. List questions which should be asked to analyze the needs of a business or organization.
3. List the steps to be followed when setting up a file system.
4. Describe how to make changes in an existing file system.
5. List the parts of a procedures manual and state why a procedures manual is important.
6. Describe how color and numbers may be used for specific filing purposes.
7. Define *activity ratio* and *accuracy ratio,* and state how each is used to evaluate a records system.
8. List questions that should be asked when evaluating equipment.
9. List questions that should be asked when evaluating supplies.
10. List questions that should be asked when evaluating the filing system in a small organization.
11. State why forms are useful and why forms analysis is necessary.
12. Describe how to evaluate existing forms.
13. List and describe considerations for designing forms.

CREATING AND EVALUATING RECORDS SYSTEMS

The previous chapters in this text have introduced the tools and procedures required for the management of manual and electronic records systems. This chapter outlines the process necessary to set up a new records system as well as to evaluate an existing system to improve its efficiency. Criteria for evaluating and designing forms are also discussed.

CENTRALIZED AND DECENTRALIZED FILES

The two basic arrangements of files are *centralized* and *decentralized*. Centralized files are those records in one location under the supervision of one person or one department. Decentralized files are located in the various departments where they are used. Variations of both arrangements are possible. A business may establish one set of procedures that applies to all files in various locations. The procedures are centralized—or under one control—but the actual files are decentralized. Another variation is to store in a central location the files that are needed by all or most of the departments in the business and to store in decentralized locations those files which pertain only to one or two departments. In most businesses a few files are always decentralized because they are needed for the daily work routine at individual workstations.

Today many computer systems make centralized data accessible to all departments within the organization. Whether a business or organization can use a centralized computer system for records will depend upon:

1. The information in the files. The biggest problem in sharing files is the "need to know" and confidentiality aspects of the materials contained therein. The possibility of uncontrolled access to the files needs to be addressed when the system is implemented.
2. The types of computers and their ability to "talk" with each other; the compatibility of the software packages used by the organization.

ANALYZING THE NEEDS OF THE BUSINESS

Before creating a records management system, you must take a long, hard look at the nature of the business and the objectives and paperwork which are involved in running that business. You need to get answers to the following questions:

1. What is the nature of the business or organization; what does the business do?
2. How is the business organized and where will the files be located?
3. What is the format of the records to be kept?
4. What retention schedules apply to the business?

Nature of the Business. The main purpose of any filing system is *retrieval*. Information is stored because it will be used again in the future; it is of no use if it cannot be located quickly. The records created by the business will naturally fall into alphabetic, numeric, subject, or geographic categories. Some businesses may have more than one records system. One type of system will store most of the files and other systems will serve auxiliary filing purposes.

Occasionally a business will have two or more sets of files which need to be organized by different systems. Legal offices, for example, may use numeric files for confidential records; subject files for forms for various types of cases; alphabetic files for names and addresses of clients; and chronological files for billing statements.

Organization of the Business and Location of the Files. Files need to be set up to fit the organizational structure of the business. Employees generally want files to be stored within easy reach, but space limitations and the organization of the business may dictate a different location. Some organizations prefer the centralized system to keep records under strict control; others for space and convenience prefer decentralized locations for the records.

The space that is available, the personnel who need to consult the records, the work flow from one department to another, the number of records, the equipment needed to store them, and the availability of computer databases are factors which enter into the decision about whether files should be centralized or decentralized.

Format of the Records. What do the records look like? Standard business letters are filed in cabinets or shelves that hold 8½- × 11-inch paper in standard size folders. However, records which are kept on card forms of a different size should be housed in equipment designed for them. In addition, the information and how it is requested will determine whether the alphabetic, numeric, subject, or geographic system is chosen for the main files. There may be more than one filing system in use, but the first determination is what system will best enhance efficient retrieval.

Retention Schedule. The retention schedule which applies to the business will also affect the records system selected. It particularly affects the long-term storage of records. If most of the records need to be stored for a long period of time, putting them on microfilm may be done in the early stages of the storage process. Paper files should be kept for only a short time. Space needed for active records and facilities needed for inactive records are a major consideration in selecting equipment and designing storage areas. If most of the files are active for a long period of time, much space and large numbers of file cabinets or shelves will be necessary to house the records.

SETTING UP A FILE SYSTEM

A large business or organization is likely to employ a records manager to handle its records systems. However, in a small business or organization an office worker may be asked to set up a file system. This happens when a new business is created and the procedures for storing the records have not yet been developed. The first office support person hired may be the one charged with the task of developing the filing system.

The following steps will help in the analysis, selection, and implementation of the system:

1. Analyze the needs of the office.
   a. What is the type of business?
   b. What kinds of records will the business have?
   c. What filing systems are used by other offices that handle the same types of paperwork or electronic media?
   d. What is the expected volume of records, making allowance for future expansion and proper distribution in the files?
   e. What factors need to be considered for flexibility as the business grows?
2. Select a system based on the answers to the questions. Consult an office supplier or vendors of commercial systems to see what is available and to make sure that a source of supplies and equipment for the system selected is readily available.
3. Plan the auxiliary systems needed, such as subject files for miscellaneous materials and follow-up files for work in progress.
4. Implement the system.
5. Evaluate the system.
6. Based upon the evaluation, make necessary revisions.
7. Write a procedures manual to document the records management system.

REVISING AND UPDATING AN EXISTING SYSTEM

As a business grows and changes, the filing system and records management functions of the office may need to be reviewed and refined. Before any changes are made, the present system should be carefully reviewed.

Major Revisions. If the business needs to make major revisions in the filing system, a procedure should be followed similar to that of setting up an entirely new system. Since changing an existing system may be very expensive, careful thought and planning must go into the decision to make the change. There will be not only costs for the new equipment and supplies but also labor costs for the time employees must spend making the conversion. Extensive changes in a system may also cause a disruption in the use of the files.

Analysis of Problems. Analysis of what is wrong with the existing system may disclose that with a few modifications the system can function more efficiently.

For example, a simple situation such as file drawers being too crowded may create problems in storage and retrieval. Before deciding that more equipment is the solution, files should be checked for unnecessary papers. Purging the files could be the solution to the problem. What materials are making the file drawers crowded? Do the files contain papers which could be transferred or destroyed? Are all the drawers crowded or only a few? Would moving some files result in more even distribution? Should the transfer plan be changed to remove more inactive files or papers sooner? Would checking files to remove nonessential paperwork as the files are being used improve the situation? Would converting to open-shelf files provide more filing space in a smaller area?

Input From Users. When changes need to be made to an existing filing system, the people who use the files should be consulted for problems they encounter and for possible solutions to those problems. The input of others will accomplish two things:

1. They may have good ideas and solutions based on practical experience.
2. Soliciting opinions will secure the users' cooperation as the changes are made.

Trial Run. When more than a small change is made in any existing system, it should be done in parts. Make the revisions in a small part of the system and see if there is an improvement. This will also determine:

1. How much time is involved in making the revision
2. Other changes that may need to be made
3. If the change works—the system is better than it was before

After the trial run has been completed, the decision to convert all the files can be made.

Planning for Electronic Files. If revisions are made to paper files, these revisions should also include the possibility that the files may eventually be transferred to an electronic system. As part of the update, a new key field may need to be added to ensure that each record is unique. For example, a doctors' office may decide that some files will be computerized—the billing function, for example. As new patients are seen and old ones return, each patient's social security number could be added to the information already contained in the file. The social security number is a unique identifier that can be used to facilitate health insurance claims.

PROCEDURES MANUAL

The procedures manual is an important part of the records system creation and revision. It will permit consistency in the application of the procedures used to maintain the files. The procedures manual should describe the records management system and include all pertinent information to enable others to use the system efficiently. It should contain, but may not be limited to, the following information:

1. A brief but basic description of the system and how it works: alphabetic, subject, numeric, geographic, or a combination. The cross-referencing procedures should also be included.
2. Practical information such as location of supplies, how to set up a new folder, and where to purchase new supplies. One sure way to cause chaos in the office is to leave materials unfiled because no one knows how to get them into the system.
3. An explanation of the charge-out and follow-up system. Forms used and how long materials may be kept out should be documented with sample copies. Some suggestions for locating lost files may also be included.
4. The routine for storing records should be described, including whose responsibility it is, how often it should be done, and what steps should be followed for collecting and efficient handling of materials to be filed.
5. A retention plan, including the people responsible for determining how long documents are retained. The procedures for transfer and disposal of records should be included.
6. The auxiliary systems needed to keep other records in the office. These include the follow-up file systems discussed in Chapter 12; any other systems used in addition to the main filing system; and registers, indexes, and files on computer disks.

The procedures manual should provide guidelines for those who work with the system. When the answer to a question is not found in the procedures manual, it should be added. The manual does not have to be written in great detail; however, it should be understandable to others in the office and be complete enough so a new employee could operate the system.

COLOR AND NUMBERS

Commercial color and number systems were discussed in Chapter 13. It may not always be necessary to purchase a commercial system for a small group of files. The follow-up files may be in color or may be numbered to make them distinctive from the customer or client files. In some offices, the work filed falls into a few distinct categories. Using a different colored folder for each category results in immediate identification. The same idea can be used in an office where office support personnel handle work for several different individuals and work must be kept separate. A lawyer's office might use different colored folders for different types of cases.

Numbers make record identification easy. The order in which numbers are used may be modified for better distribution in the files. For example, using the last digit of a telephone number as the first indexing unit and then using the alphabetic letters result in better distribution in the file than using the letters of the alphabet alone. Social security numbers, which are assigned by region, may have similar beginning digits. Using the last four digits provides a better distribution of records.

EVALUATING RECORDS SYSTEMS

Efficient records management requires periodic checkups on filing systems, procedures, office forms, and methods used by employees. Can records be obtained promptly and economically? Are office forms designed to provide information readily and accurately? Is the present equipment serving the system efficiently? Questions such as these must be considered periodically. A large firm with centralized files may keep a record of the filing activity in the organization through daily, weekly, or monthly volume reports. These reports show the total number of records filed, the number of records requested from the files, and the number found and not found. The evaluation is made either by comparing present performance with past performance or by determining the *activity ratio* or the *accuracy ratio*. This information is useful in evaluating the effectiveness of the filing system.

Activity Ratio. The activity ratio, or percentage of filed records requested, lets the file worker or supervisor know whether too many records are being kept in the active files. The formula for the ratio is:

$$\frac{\text{Request for records}}{\text{Number of records in active files}} = \text{Activity ratio}$$

If 20,000 records are in the files and 5,000 are requested from them during a filing period, the activity ratio for that period is:

$$\frac{5,000}{20,000} = 25\% \text{ activity ratio}$$

If the activity ratio is higher than 20 percent, it is more than likely that the files do not contain too many unnecessary records. If the ratio is between 10 and 20 percent, some of the records in the active files probably should be transferred. An activity ratio below 10 percent means that many records in the active files should be transferred to storage.

Accuracy Ratio. The accuracy ratio, or percentage of requested records found, is a good indication of the efficiency of both the filing system and employee work routines. The formula is as follows:

$$\frac{\text{Records found}}{\text{Records requested}} = \text{Accuracy ratio}$$

If 3000 records are requested and 2940 are found during a filing period, the accuracy ratio for that period is:

$$\frac{2940}{3000} \ = \ 98\% \text{ accuracy ratio}$$

If the accuracy ratio is higher than 99.5 percent, filing can be considered very efficient. A ratio under 97 percent is an indication that attention should be given to one or more of the following: indexing and coding, cross-referencing, storing procedures, charge-out and follow-up procedures, and checking on unnecessary retention of records in employees' desks. Ideally, the accuracy ratio should be 100 percent. And when records cannot be located using electronic files, they may be lost forever.

EVALUATING FILING EQUIPMENT AND SUPPLIES

Evaluation of filing efficiency must also include a systematic study of file equipment and supplies. Have the right tools been selected to do the job? Since the biggest expenses are the salaries of the employees who work with the files, any changes or modifications in the equipment and supplies that will save workers' time will save money for the business.

Evaluating Equipment. The evaluation of filing equipment requires careful thought and consideration.

1. Is the equipment in good condition? If not, what repairs need to be made? Would the cost of new equipment be offset by an increase in worker performance?
2. Is the equipment arranged for efficient use? Does the layout need to be rearranged to increase worker performance? Is there enough aisle space?
3. Can files be located more conveniently and serve double duty, that is, as counters, credenzas, or dividers in a landscaped office?
4. Would a change in equipment, particularly from file drawers to open-shelf filing, allow more efficient use of space and easier access?
5. Is proper storage equipment used for various types of records? Cards, magnetic tapes, cassettes, floppy disks, computer printouts, and blueprints have special storage requirements. Are the facilities available being used properly, or does new equipment need to be provided?

Evaluating Supplies. The kinds of supplies used should be surveyed and analyzed periodically to ascertain whether or not they are doing their job.

1. Are the proper number of guides being used in each file drawer or on each shelf? The number of file guides in each drawer—usually between 20 and 40 (or about 1 guide to every 20 folders)—will provide proper

distribution of records, make reference to the files easy, and furnish support for the folders.

2. Are the supplies durable enough for the job? Are the least expensive supplies being used for items which are stored only for short periods?
3. Would laminating or some other means of protecting a record save redoing the original?
4. Are the supplies that are being used readily available from vendors? Can quantities needed be planned enough in advance to obtain discounts or take advantage of special offers?
5. Are the out guides and carrier folders or other supplies used for transporting or replacing records the right size, type, and durability?
6. Would it be more efficient to make copies of some items rather than remove the original and then have to return it to the file?
7. Can any of the supplies be sold for recycling after they are no longer usable or needed?

EVALUATING THE FILING SYSTEM OF A SMALL ORGANIZATION

Large organizations usually employ records managers or hire outside consultants to evaluate their filing systems, but small organizations often do not take the time to do a thorough evaluation of equipment and supplies. However, evaluation is important whatever the size of the organization. A group of individuals in the office may form a committee to study the files and supplies and make suggestions and recommendations for improvements. The questions which follow may be helpful:

1. Has the proper filing system been selected for the records generated by the organization? Should changes be made in the main filing system?
2. Should auxiliary systems be used to facilitate the storage and retrieval of records?
3. Are the records given the required protection against disasters such as fire, theft, and water damage?
4. Are records filed daily or more often if necessary?
5. Are important records being "filed" in desk drawers or trays?
6. Are only necessary materials being filed?
7. Are there many instances of misfiled or lost records?
8. Are there new developments in equipment or supplies that will improve operations?
9. Are file cabinets or shelves uncrowded?
10. Are records distributed evenly throughout the filing equipment?
11. Is there an adequate number of guides for each drawer?
12. Is an individual folder prepared as necessary?
13. Is the number of papers in any standard folder limited to a maximum of 100?

14. When papers need fastening within a folder, are staples rather than paper clips used? Should folders equipped with fasteners be used?
15. Do the file drawers, guides, and folders bear descriptive labels and captions?
16. Are standard indexing rules used?
17. Is there adequate cross-referencing? Is the cross-referencing procedure documented?
18. Are the records properly coded?
19. Are the records sorted before storing to facilitate the procedure?
20. Is there a charge-out and follow-up system, and is it used properly by all employees?
21. Is there a plan for transfer and disposal?
22. Is there a procedures manual that describes the filing systems of the business?
23. Should some records be converted to electronic storage?
24. Has a plan been developed for adding electronic storage in the future?
25. Has adequate provision been made in setting up the files to allow for expansion?
26. Are forms being developed and evaluated periodically to improve the work flow and filing process?

The answers to these questions may reveal ways to improve records management. A good time to review them is prior to each filing period (just before transfer time). With such periodic evaluation, files are likely to remain in efficient working condition and keep pace with changes in the office paperwork. Even in the one-employee office, frequent attention to such a list can mean the difference between a neat, businesslike atmosphere and a desk full of disorganized papers.

FORMS ANALYSIS

Since printed forms are the most efficient carriers of business data, they are the record most frequently used in offices. Writing a letter to order supplies, for example, is not nearly as efficient as using a printed form. It takes more time to compose and key a letter; it is harder for the departments that need to process the information or for the vendor to locate the essential information in a letter; it is not as convenient to circulate a letter as it is a printed form with multiple copies labeled for routing. A letter also is likely to omit essential information or to provide unnecessary information and thereby cause delay or error in completing the order. Properly designed forms "prompt" the user to complete *all* required information.

If a form is not well designed, however, it may not serve its purpose. For this reason, forms analysis is an important function; it should be carried out at regular intervals to see whether the office forms that are being used are doing their job.

Forms analysis includes

1. The evaluation of existing forms
2. The revision of existing forms
3. The purchase of new forms

Evaluating Existing Forms. Forms should be evaluated to determine how they relate to other forms and how they affect the work flow of the office. When repetitive information is required—such as date, invoice number, name and address—and when these facts must be organized for fast processing, forms are extremely useful. Records managers do not recommend using a form unless there is a definite need because it is expensive to purchase or to design and print a form. A business form is not needed and should be eliminated if:

1. The information it calls for is not used.
2. Another source for the information is available.
3. The cost of the form (largely the labor cost of filing it) exceeds its value.

When forms are being evaluated, this question should be asked for each item: How will this information be used?

The question of whether or not multiple copies are needed should also be investigated. Multiple-copy carbon packs or packs with chemically treated paper are expensive. If they are not needed or do not serve their intended purpose, they should be eliminated. Besides the cost of the multiple-copy form itself, unneeded extra copies result in:

1. Loss of employee time in handling, reading, and filing copies
2. Waste of valuable filing space

Revising Existing Forms. Forms analysis may suggest ways to improve the design of the office forms in use, such as combining several forms into one, eliminating one or more copies, adding copies, splitting one form into two or more new ones, or eliminating certain forms. The analysis may also reveal the need for additional forms to improve the work flow in the office.

Purchasing New Forms. Standard forms are available at office supply stores. Telephone message pads, purchase requisitions, invoices, receipts, statements, journals, ledgers, and other accounting forms are available. Purchasing forms through office supply stores or standard printers' forms is less costly for a business than designing and creating its own forms, but the forms analyst or office worker should be careful that the standard forms meet the needs of the office. If standard forms are unacceptable, then a form should be designed.

FORMS DESIGN

When plans for the design of a new form or redesign of an existing form are made, the important part a form plays in the functioning of the firm becomes clear. The following paragraphs explain some of the considerations that enter into the design. Construction of the form has to do with its physical characteristics—routing or mailing, multiple copies, size, layout, readability, spacing, and sequence of items.

Routing and Mailing. The designer of a form must take into consideration how it will be routed and dispatched to and from other departments or businesses. If the use of the form is restricted to the office, the routing information may be placed on the form itself, thereby eliminating routing slips or transmittal memorandums. Forms that are mailed to other organizations should be designed to speed the addressing, collating, folding, and inserting steps that the form must go through. For example, if window envelopes are to be used, the form should be designed so that the address can be seen through the window without unusual folding of the form. Since it is often necessary to encourage the return of forms, they can be designed to be self-mailers. The form can be printed on double postcards or on heavy paper that can be folded in thirds, fastened, and mailed without an envelope.

Multiple Copies. If the form should have multiple copies for processing information by different departments, how the multiple copies will be made must be decided. Should the form have carbon inserts or be on chemically treated paper to carry the impression? Papers of different colors may be used to signal which copies go where, or an identifying label may be printed at the bottom of the form. The correct number of copies should be determined—too many is wasteful; too few causes duplication of effort to get the required number. The method of completion should also be considered. How many copies can a person complete clearly using a ball-point pen? How many copies can be completed clearly using a typewriter? How many copies can be fed through a computer printer? If the number needed exceeds the fill-in process, a single clear original should be created and the required number made using a copier.

Size. As discussed in Chapter 11, forms requiring storage in other than standard-size filing cabinets can prove to be inefficient because of the extra cost of the equipment and extra time involved in the filing process.

Layout. The layout of the information on the form requires decisions on the wording of the printed guide words and phrases for readability, spacing to be allowed for information to be filled in, and the arrangement of the items on the form.

Readability. Readability is important because the purpose of a form is to provide accurate, readily accessible information that can be used to make correct business decisions. The people filling in the form must understand it before they can give the desired information. Techniques that improve readability of a form include the following:

ROUTING MULTIPLE COPIES

In some large organizations, records are prepared in multiple copies so that different departments may have their own copies. Notice that the same record is stored in three different ways, according to how it will be requested.

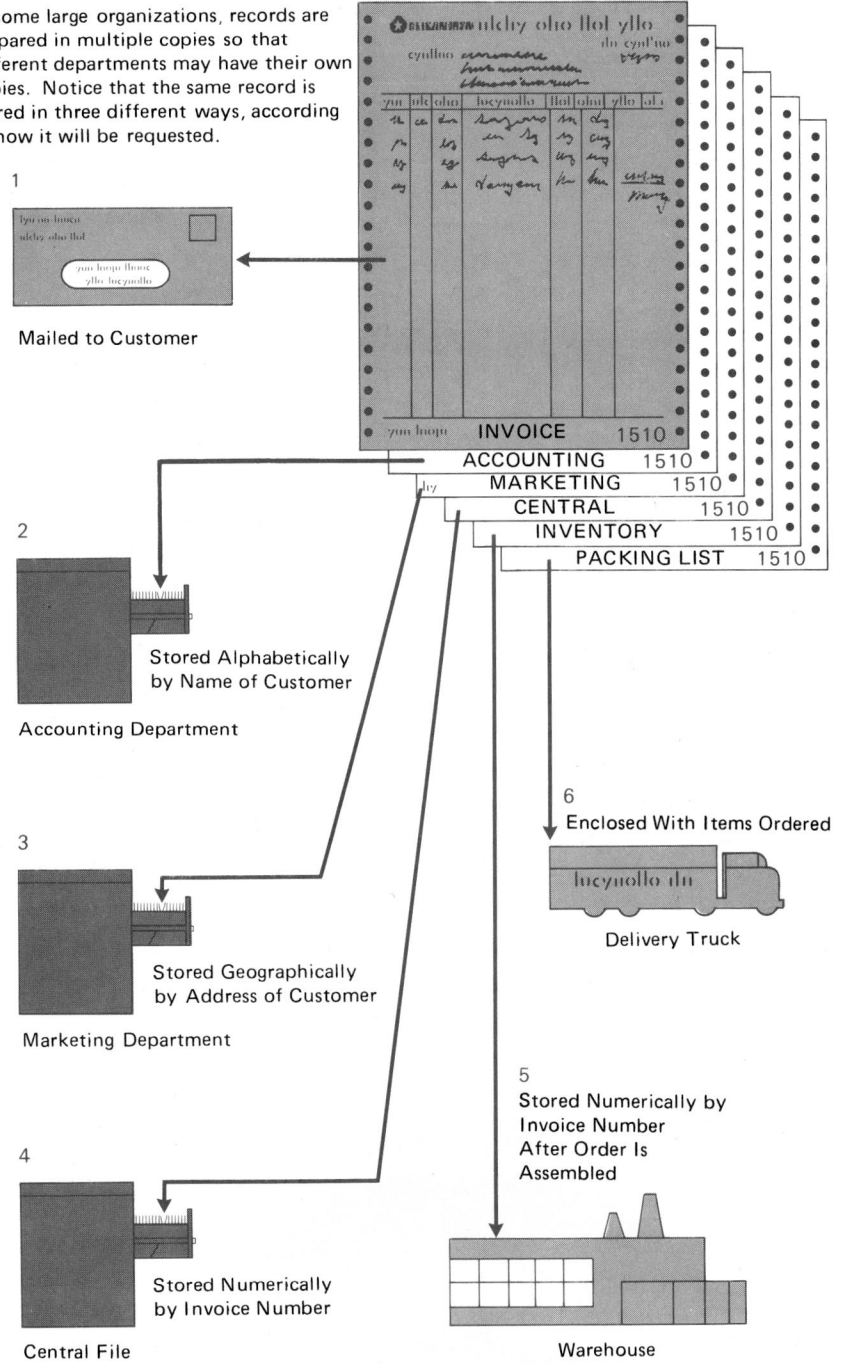

1

Mailed to Customer

2

Stored Alphabetically by Name of Customer

Accounting Department

3

Stored Geographically by Address of Customer

Marketing Department

4

Stored Numerically by Invoice Number

Central File

6

Enclosed With Items Ordered

Delivery Truck

5

Stored Numerically by Invoice Number After Order Is Assembled

Warehouse

1. *Titles* should be short and should indicate the purpose of the form. The word *form, sheet,* or *record* in a title is usually unnecessary. Compare these titles:

Example A: Inventory Card Record for Files
Example B: Factory Supplies Inventory

In Example A, four words are unnecessary: *Card, Record, for* and *Files.* Furthermore, the title omits important information about the kind of inventory record it is.

2. *Captions* (or questions) should be adapted to the background of the user of the form, and they should make responses easy—leaving no doubt as to what information is wanted. Compare these:

Example A
What is your name and address?
What is your age?
How tall are you?
How much do you weigh?
What color are your eyes?

Example B

PRINT FULL NAME	FIRST	MIDDLE	LAST

PRINT STREET
ADDRESS OR
R. F. D. NO.

PRINT CITY
AND STATE

MONTH BORN	YEAR BORN	HEIGHT FT. IN.	WEIGHT	COLOR OF EYES

In Example B each item is blocked off for ease of reading and correct placement of data, and there is no doubt about what information should be given. Before a form is printed, readability should be tested by having potential users fill in sample copies.

3. Most forms require accompanying instructions. When they are brief, such as "Print full name" in the example above, they may be on the form itself. When they are lengthy or complex, instructions should be printed on the back of the form or in a separate manual that includes a filled-in sample illustration of the form.

Spacing. Forms filled in by hand should have writing spaces at least ¼ inch high for desk work and ⅓ inch high for field work, such as surveying or delivering. Horizontal space should be adequate for the information to be written in neatly. For the design or improvement of forms to be typewritten or completed by computer, the standard settings for typewriters or printers must be considered. For example on a typewriter, there are 6 vertical spaces per inch; there are 12 horizontal spaces per inch on elite-type machines and 10 on pica-type machines. It is usually more efficient if the tabulator rather than the space bar can be used for moving from one item to another. When using a computer, the capabilities of the printer and software package should be considered.

There are three basic spacing designs for forms that require handwritten or typewritten fill-ins.

1. Caption on or under the line of writing:

Ship via _____

_____

Ship via

2. Box design:

Ship via

3. Column arrangement:

			Ship via			

Each has advantages and disadvantages. When captions are on the line of writing, the typist filling in the form must space through the printed words to reach the next typing position. Captions below the line are satisfactory for forms filled in by hand, but below-the-line captions are hidden on a typewriter. The box design, with captions printed in small type in the upper portion of the box, saves space and eliminates excessive typewriter spacing or adjustment. It also ensures correct placement of data. Column design facilitates the use of the typewriter tabulator. This design is especially useful when many numbers, such as prices of goods, are to be entered.

Sequence of Items. The sequence of items on a form should be determined by traditional reading habits, relation of the form to other forms, and frequency of use. People are accustomed to reading left to right, top to bottom. They are also used to seeing related items in a standard order, such as an address given first by house number, then by street, city, state, and ZIP code. For fast processing of data, all items that are on related forms should be in the same sequence on all those forms. Items that are filled in on all the forms should be first; any that are not always filled in are placed at the right; those filled in on only a few of the forms should be at the bottom.

Boxes (sometimes called *ballot boxes*) are used when a question may be answered yes or no or when a selection of answers can be listed. Contrast the following.

Example A

| List the sports you are qualified to coach: |

Example B

Check the sports you are qualified to coach:

☐ football   ☐ baseball   ☐ soccer   ☐ other _____

☐ basketball   ☐ track   ☐ tennis   ☐ other _____

Sequence of items is important also for efficient filing. For example, an application form used at one time by a very large organization had the filing data—the applicant's name—in the center of the form. The forms were stored in vertical files. Employees had to remove each form completely from the file and read the name, and this process had to be continued until the right application was reached. It took 9 minutes, on the average, to find an application and only 5 minutes to process it. If the name had been on the upper edge of the form, instead of in the middle of the form, the correct application form could have been located in a fraction of a minute.

As a general rule, filing data on forms should be at the top when forms are filed vertically, at the visible edge when forms are filed in visible equipment, and at the side opposite the point of fastening when forms are bound. In making decisions as to placement of filing data, the following must be considered: in what type of equipment will the form be stored—standard file cabinet,

RECEIVING REPORT		London Corporation *Subsidiary of frozen produce company* WELLSBORO, PENNSYLVANIA 16901			R	12010

This form combines several basic spacing designs, including captions (guide words) above the line of writing, boxes for checking responses, and a column arrangement to separate like information.

open shelves, visible files, or other? Will the form be filed in folders? Will the form be fastened to other forms or papers or to the folder?

When designing forms to be used with electronic file systems, the order in which information will be input must be considered. If the data entry operator must look in several different places on the form for the key data, the input process will be much slower.

CONCLUSION

Any records system will be created according to a basic arrangement of centralized or decentralized files. Once the system is in operation it should be evaluated periodically to determine whether it is as efficient as possible or whether improvements can be made. The equipment and supplies used should also be evaluated to determine if they are performing as expected. Forms should be designed and evaluated to make sure they contribute to the work flow of the office. The ultimate test of any records management system is the degree to which the system promotes the overall objectives of the organization.

GENERAL REVIEW

1. What is meant by centralized and decentralized files? How does the arrangement affect where the files are kept? (Competency 1)

2. What questions should be asked to analyze the needs of a business or organization? (Competency 2)
3. What are the steps to follow when setting up a filing system? (Competency 3)
4. How are changes made in an existing filing system? (Competency 4)
5. What are the parts of a procedures manual? Why is a procedures manual necessary? (Competency 5)
6. What purposes can the use of colors and numbers serve in filing systems? (Competency 6)
7. What is the activity ratio? The accuracy ratio? How are these two ratios used to evaluate the records system? (Competency 7)
8. What questions should be asked when evaluating equipment? (Competency 8)
9. What questions should be asked when evaluating supplies? (Competency 9)
10. What questions should be asked when evaluating the filing system in a small organization? (Competency 10)
11. Why are forms useful in an office? Why should forms be analyzed periodically? (Competency 11)
12. How are existing forms evaluated? (Competency 12)
13. What factors should be considered when designing forms? (Competency 13)

CASE PROBLEMS

1. You work in an office that has decentralized files. You find that you need to go to other departments when you need information about customers, such as credit information from the billing department and data on frequently purchased items from the purchasing department. Would centralized files help your situation? What impact would centralized files have on the other departments? Would a computer filing system help? (Competencies 1 and 2)
2. Your friend complains that documents are lost more than they are found in the office. The business is a video sales and rental store where records include the following: customers' membership applications, invoices from vendors for movies to be sold, invoices from the central supply office for movies to be rented, and invoices for blank tapes and a few other supplies offered for sale. Customers' applications are filed by last name, and all invoices are filed together by number. Your friend thinks that the three types of invoices should be kept in separate files since the forms are of different sizes and the numbers are located in different places on the forms. It takes a long time to find a specific document because the records are hard to scan for needed information. In addition, despite the fact the store has been in operation for 5 years, no records

have been destroyed or transferred to inactive files. What specific suggestions can you make to help? (Competencies 4, 5, 6, 10)

3. Your friend Joyce Mason has several complaints about the filing system in her office. The drawers are too crowded, and there does not seem to be enough space to install more cabinets. Her employer will consider purchasing new equipment, but Joyce is not sure that will solve the problem. Much of the material currently being filed is printed on forms. Joyce thinks some of these forms duplicate information. What advice can you give Joyce? (Competency 12)

4. You decide to evaluate how well you did in filing and finding items today. (a) You looked for 150 items and found 142 of them. What is your accuracy ratio? Is this sufficiently high? What questions should you ask yourself to improve your ratio? (b) Suppose on another day 150 records were requested and you were able to find 148. What is your ratio on that day? Is this ratio acceptable? What ratio should you aim for? Does this ratio evaluate you as an employee? (c) Suppose you have 10,000 records on file and you use 150 different records each day. What is your activity ratio for 30 working days? Are any unnecessary records being kept on file? Should you be keeping more records than you are? (d) Suppose during this same 30-day filing period you had only 900 requests for records. What would be your activity ratio, and what would it indicate? (Competency 7)

5. Design a form for a Swanson's Department Store to find out the following information: name, address, telephone number, social security number, age, date of purchases from Swanson's Department Store, type of purchase (cash/credit), department the item was purchased from.

   Design the first line to show telephone number as the key field; then design the form to show last name as the key field; could the form be designed so that either could be used for the key field? (Competency 13)

GLOSSARY

abbreviation A shortened form of a word. In indexing, abbreviations are alphabetized as they are written.

accuracy ratio The percentage of requested records found during a filing period.

acronym A word that has been constructed from initials or parts of other words, such as ARMA (Association of Records Managers and Administrators).

active file A file container reserved for records that are used frequently. Also, those files currently in use in a database.

activity ratio The percentage of filed records requested during a filing period.

address file A card file containing frequently used names and addresses—usually kept in a box or on a rotary wheel.

alphabetic filing Any system in which the captions are names of people, organizations, or letters of the alphabet.

alphabetic subject filing A filing system in which topical headings and divisions are alphabetized.

alphabetize To arrange in sequence according to the letters of the alphabet.

aperture cards Cards with a piece of microfilm mounted in an aperture to reduce part of a document, usually something quite large.

archival storage Records that must be kept for a long time but will seldom be used, such as backup copies of working programs for computers.

archives The historical records kept by an organization.

ARMA Association of Records Managers and Administrators, Inc.

ASCII American Standard Code for Information Interchange, a standard code for representing characters used in most microcomputers, computer terminals, and printers.

auxiliary guide See *Secondary guide*.

backshifting Shifting the location of records to allow for expansion at the beginning of a file.

backups Copies of disks containing data files and programs which are kept in case the original is damaged or lost.

box files Low-cost steel or corrugated fiberboard files used for storage.

business forms Papers or cards used in offices to record or process information of a repetitive nature in an efficient way.

cabinet A container with one or more drawers or shelves for housing filed records.

caption A name, letter, or number used to identify records for filing.

CAR See *computer-assisted retrieval.*

card filing Processing and storing business information on cards. There are two kinds of card files—vertical and visible.

card index A list that identifies assigned numbers in a numeric correspondence filing system.

carousel files See *Rotary files.*

carrier folder A folder, usually of a distinctive color and made of a strong material, that is used to transport records.

case Refers to whether a letter of the alphabet is capitalized (uppercase) or written in small letters (lowercase).

case sensitivity Because ASCII codes are different for uppercase letters and lowercase letters, the computer is aware of the difference between them.

centralized control A plan of organization in which one person or department is responsible for all records management in the organization, whether files are centralized or decentralized.

centralized files Files in which all records except highly specialized departmental ones are stored together.

character On a keyboard, a character is a letter, number, or symbol. In computer storage, a blank space also counts as a character.

charge method A procedure used to account for records that have been removed from the files.

charging out The procedure used to request and account for records removed from the files.

chronological In sequence according to date. When records are filed chronologically, the latest date is usually in front.

coding The process of marking correspondence with the caption under which it will be stored.

color-coded filing system A specialized filing system that uses color to help prevent misfiling and speed searching for records.

COM See *computer output microfilm/microfiche.*

combination subject file A method used when the volume of correspondence to be grouped by subject is small in comparison with records to be filed under name of a person or organization. Subject captions are combined with name captions in one file.

commercial system A set of ready-made guides and folders.

computer assisted retrieval (CAR) A method of obtaining records stored within the computer or on magnetic tapes or disks.

computer outputk microfilm/microfiche (COM) Processing of information from magnetic media to microfilm or microfiche.

consecutive numeric system The most commonly used numeric system. In this system, numbers are used consecutively, or in order. For example, 101 precedes 102, which precedes 103.

correspondence Any written communication that has not been designed to be placed in a card or forms file, such as letters, telegrams, orders, invoices, bills, checks, reports, and miscellaneous papers that are on sheets of paper and not on cards.

correspondence book or **correspondence file** A set of model letters frequently used.

cross-reference A notation in a file or an index showing that the record being sought is stored elsewhere; or the filing of a duplicate of an original record in other locations where it might be sought.

cut The size of the tab on the back flap of a folder, usually expressed in a fraction. *One-half cut,* for example means that the tab takes up one-half of the back flap of a folder.

database An orderly, usually very large, body of information which allows the processing, accessing, and retrieval of information.

database management Storing data in an organized fashion and rapidly manipulating and retrieving information from those data. There are four features of database management: (1) entering (2) storing, (3) manipulating, and (4) retrieving information within the system.

data processing A computer system for producing, using, and maintaining information.

date stamp A notation on an incoming piece of correspondence to indicate the date and, often, the hour of receipt. Also called *time stamp*.

decentralized files Files in which records of one department are stored separately from records of other departments.

decimal-numeric system A subject numeric filing system used when headings are subdivided more than twice.

desk trays Containers for incoming and outgoing correspondence kept on desks.

desk-drawer file A large file drawer contained in a desk.

dictionary arrangement Organization of a subject file with headings that do not have divisions or subdivisions.

direct A filing system that permits the location of records without reference to an index.

directory A list of the documents stored on the computer disk by filename.

disaster planning A security system to safeguard data against accidental loss, hackers, deliberate sabotage, or disasters such as fire and flood. Accidental loss of information in a computer can also result from a power failure. Backup systems are usually maintained off the premises in case of such disasters.

disposing, disposition Destroying or eliminating records that are no longer needed. Paper records may simply be thrown away. Confidential records may be shredded. Computers generally have the capability of erasing records that are no longer needed.

double (or closed) captions Captions that indicate not only where the section of the file starts but also where it ends.

duplex-numeric system A type of subject numeric filing system used when there are more than ten main headings or more than nine divisions or subdivisions under the same heading.

electronic database system A computer filing system.

encyclopedic arrangement Organization of a subject file with main headings, divisions, and subdivisions.

entering data Keying or otherwise inputting information into a computer.

equipment The cabinets, furniture, computers, and miscellaneous devices used in handling and storing records.

essential records All those records needed to carry on a business.

expansion Any increase in the amount of equipment and supplies to make possible the storing of more records.

extension With microcomputers, each filename has two parts: the name and the extension. The extension is usually limited to three characters and separated from the name by a period.

facsimile The transmission of information over telephone lines in which a hard copy at the transmitting location is duplicated at the receiving location.

field A group of characters (letters, numbers, special characters, or spaces) that make up an item of information, usually in a computer database.

file A collection of records which are stored either manually or on computer. Also a container for storing records.

file cards Cardboard slips that are used in both vertical and visible files.

filename A caption in an electronic filing system. It usually consists of two parts: the name and the extension.

filing The process of classifying, arranging, and storing records so that they can be obtained quickly when needed.

filing period The span of time during which records remain in the active files.

filing system A plan for the use of equipment, supplies, and procedures to store and retrieve records.

flowchart A diagram of an operation, from its beginning to its end, so that all of its steps can be analyzed and evaluated.

folder A manila or fiber container that holds correspondence in files.

followers (or compressors) Movable supports that expand or contract the usable space within a file drawer.

follow-up A system of checking on borrowed records to effect their return to the files.

follow-up file A file that calls attention to either (1) charged-out records or (2) an office job that requires action on a certain date. It is usually arranged chronologically.

follow-up folder A folder with dates along the top edge that can be clearly marked with a signal indicating when the records within the folder require action.

forms analysis A study of whether a form is needed and what static information it should contain, in what sequence and design.

Freedom of Information Act A law that allows people to have access to information kept on file about themselves.

geographic filing An arrangement of records alphabetically by location.

given name An individual's first name.

guide A sheet of heavy cardboard with a tab and caption, used to guide the eye to the desired section in a file container. A guide also serves as a support for the records.

guide rod A metal rod in most file drawers that is placed through the guide rod extension in the bottom of the guides to hold them in place within the file drawer.

guide rod extension A projection at the bottom center of a guide that contains a metal-reinforced hole in the middle through which a guide rod is placed within the file drawer.

hard copy Material which is in paper and print form instead of in film or magnetic media.

"hold for answer" file (HFA file) Another name for a tickler or follow-up file. Sometimes called *hold for action file*.

hyphenated name An individual or firm name that consists of words or letters connected by a hyphen. Both a hyphenated personal name and a hyphenated company name are considered as one unit for indexing.

inactive records Records not subject to frequent use that are stored in less accessible and less costly equipment than active records.

incoming paper correspondence Any written communication coming into a firm or organization, such as letters, telegrams, orders, invoices, bills, checks, reports, and miscellaneous papers.

index card record A card, such as an address file card, that is used primarily as a reference to other information.

indexing Deciding under which name to file a record and the proper form and order of the units in that name.

indirect A type of filing system that usually requires reference to an index before records can be found.

individual folder A folder that contains records concerning only one correspondent or subject.

inspecting Checking correspondence for a release mark before storing.

integrated package A software package that is used for several applications, such as word processing, database, and spreadsheet.

internal paper correspondence Any written communication used within a firm or organization, such as memorandums, purchase requisitions, purchase orders, reports, and other miscellaneous papers.

label A sticker that is attached to the tab of a guide, folder, or computer disk on which the caption appears.

laminating Permanently enclosing a record in clear plastic.

landscaped office See *Open office.*

lateral file A file cabinet in which records are stored perpendicular to the opening of the file.

letterhead Stationery with a printed heading.

logbook A notebook containing records of important business transactions. A logbook may be used to record incoming and outgoing mail, telephone calls, and other business transactions.

magnetic media Means of storing information for computers and other electronic equipment. It is usually in the form of disks, cards, tapes, or drums.

main numeric file The primary file in a system using numbers. This file contains individual folders that are placed behind the appropriate guide. Inside these folders, records are maintained in chronological order with the most recent record in front.

manila Medium-weight pressboard used for file folders.

maximum-minimum transfer A plan for periodically transferring records from active to transfer files. A maximum and a minimum period of time are set for storing records in active files.

merging Combining the contents of two or more files into one, either using the caption or filename of one of the old files folders or creating a new caption or filename to cover the new combination of contents.

microfacsimile Transmission of data on microfiche or aperture cards over telephone lines to produce hard copy at the other end.

microfiche Miniature filmed records in card form.

microfilm A film roll of microimages.

microfilming The photographing of records at greatly reduced size on filmstrips, cards, or rolls. The film can be maintained in a small fraction of the space required for the original records.

microform Either film or paper which contains microimages.

micrographics Reproduction of information on microforms.

microimage A reduction of a record or document.

micropublishing Production of information on microforms for public use, either for sale or for free distribution.

microrepublishing Reproducing of information previously in hard copy for public use.

middle-digit filing A numeric arrangement of records according to the middle, rather than the first, digits.

miscellaneous alphabetic file The part of a numeric file used for those correspondents for whom sufficient records have not accumulated to merit a number being assigned to them.

miscellaneous folder A folder that contains records for correspondents or subjects not active enough to warrant individual folders.

misfile To store a record in the wrong location.

numeric correspondence file A filing system organized in three parts: a main numeric file, a miscellaneous alphabetic file, and a card index in which the names of correspondents or subjects are arranged alphabetically.

numeric filing The filing of correspondence or cards according to numbers.

numeric subject file A basic kind of subject file that includes several systems that use numbers for captions in place of words.

one-period transfer A plan in which the active files contain records for the current filing period only. At predetermined intervals all the records are transferred.

open office The landscaped office arrangement in which several employees occupy a large room divided by furniture or partitions to form work groups or to allow various configurations of equipment.

open-shelf filing A method of filing

in which shelves, rather than filing cabinets with drawers, are used to house records.

optical disk A storage media that is read by laser and can contain massive amounts of information.

out folder A folder used to store correspondence while the regular folder is out of the files. It indicates that the regular folder has been borrowed and gives the name of the borrower.

out guide A guide used to indicate that an entire folder has been removed from the files.

outgoing paper correspondence Any written communication, such as letters, telegrams, orders, invoices, checks, reports, and miscellaneous papers that are sent out of the organization or firm to others.

pending file A file containing matters which are not yet completed and upon which some action must be taken.

periodic transfer The removal of records at predetermined intervals from the current active files to the inactive or transfer files.

perpetual transfer The transfer of records from current to inactive files on the basis of activity rather than predetermined filing periods.

position The location, counting from left to right, of the tab on a guide or folder.

posted card records Card files that are used to record new information on a continuous basis.

power file units Files which bring

the desired shelf to the user automatically.

prefix   A word element, such as *Mc,* at the beginning of a word or name. A prefix is indexed as part of the word or name.

primary guide   The main guide for a section of filed records.

Privacy Act   A law that allows individuals to designate who may see records and information kept on file about themselves.

reader   A machine used to view microfilms or microfiche.

reading file   A chronological record of outgoing correspondence made by placing a copy of each piece of correspondence in a loose-leaf notebook with the most current document first.

recharge form   A slip used to charge out records when they are passed from one person to another without being returned to the files.

records   All information that is kept by an organization, whether it is in the form of correspondence, cards, magnetic media, or microforms.

records control   Procedure used to keep track of records after they have been created or received and stored in the files.

records inventory   A statement of the kinds of material and folders in the files, the quantity of those records, and their location.

records management   Planning, organizing, and controlling the creation, protection, use, storage, and disposition of records.

records manager   An individual who oversees the operation of the records system, including the active files and the charge system, and who establishes the transfer and retention procedures and has the authority to destroy records.

register   A list of correspondents and the numbers assigned to them in a numeric correspondence file.

relative index   An alphabetic list of all the headings and subheadings in a subject file.

release mark   A notation showing that a record has received the required attention and is ready for filing.

requisition slip   A form used to request records from the files.

retention period   A period of time during which records are kept in either active or transfer files before they are destroyed.

retrieval   Finding—the major goal of any filing system.

root directory   The main listing of contents of a computer disk file.

rotary files   Round shelves attached to a center pole, which can be turned for easy access; also desktop files on a wheel.

routing form   A slip attached to charged-out records indicating the sequence in which they are to be delivered to several individuals in an organization before being returned to the files.

scores   Creases along the front flap of a folder that allow for expansion.

secondary guide   A guide that subdivides the section of a file controlled by a primary guide.

security center An underground or isolated storage place for very valuable records.

signals Plastic, metal, or paper devices that are used to guide the eye to pertinent information, usually in card and visible files.

simple numeric A type of subject numeric filing system that uses only nine divisions or subdivisions under the same heading.

single caption A caption that indicates only where the section of the file starts. Only one letter or one combination of letters appears.

sorting Arranging records in sequence after they have been coded to facilitate storing.

special guide See *Secondary guide*.

staggered arrangement Placement of guide or folder tabs in successive positions from left to right.

static information All the printed information on a form before it is filled out.

storing The placing of records in a file container.

subdirectory Divisions of a root directory or other subdirectory of a computer disk file.

subject filing The alphabetic arrangement of records by names of topics or things.

substitution card A card used to replace records removed from a file folder. This card indicates the name of the borrower.

surname The last name of an individual.

suspended folders Folders supported from their top edges by a metal frame within the file drawer. Also called *hanging folders*.

suspense file A follow-up or tickler file used for items which need action in the future.

system A series of related steps followed in accomplishing a major office activity.

tab The projection above the body of a guide or folder on which the caption appears.

template A scale-size cutout or stencil of equipment, used in planning layouts. Also a piece of plastic that fits over the function keys on the computer keyboard to label the function of each key.

terminal-digit filing A numeric arrangement of records according to the last, rather than the first, digits.

tickler file A follow-up file, usually organized by date.

time stamp See *date stamp*.

title A word indicating rank, office, or privilege. The last indexing unit when needed to distinguish between two or more identical names. Titles are indexed as written.

"to do" list List of items which need attention within the next day or so.

topical filing See *subject filing*.

traditional office The enclosed office space occupied by one or more individuals.

transfer Removal of records from the active files to inactive files.

transfer file or box A container that houses transferred records. This container is usually constructed of inexpensive materials.

transpose To rearrange the normal order of a name; for example, *Leslie Patton* transposed is *Patton, Leslie.*

tub files Containers which open at the top to expose records suspended in folders or in trays.

two-period transfer A plan in which the active files provide space for current records and records from the last filing period. At transfer time, only the oldest records are removed.

ultrafiche A type of microfiche which is used primarily because of its size; images are reduced to 90 or more times smaller than the original image.

unit Each part of a name used in indexing.

update To add, delete, or change information in computer files to reflect current information.

variable information Data filled in on a form. Also known as *fill-ins* or *fill-in information.*

vertical filing The storage of records on edge.

visible filing Storage of cards in specially designed equipment so that the information near the edges of the cards can be seen easily.

word processing log A record book kept in the word processing department in which a notation is made of all incoming work. Logs are also kept for information that is recorded on magnetic media for computers and dedicated word processing devices.

workstation An employee's equipment and materials (desk, chair, file, etc.) in an office.

work-in-progress file Contains one or more projects which have not yet been completed and which may require periodic attention.

Index

Abbreviations, indexing of:
  business names, 29–30
  personal names, 19–20
Accuracy ratio, 213–214
Active records, 155
Activity ratio, 213
Addresses, indexing of, 35–36
Alphabetic filing, 56
  captions in, 3
  for home filing, 127
  in numeric filing, 3, 104, 106, 109–110
  organization in, 61–63
  in telephone directory, 2–3
Alphabetical order, 13
Alphabetizing, 13–14
  with computers, 46
  nothing comes before something rule, 14
  unit-by-unit, 14–15
  (*See also* Indexing rules)
American Standard Code for Information
    Interchange (ASCII), 45–46
Aperture card, 194–195
Arabic numerals, indexing of, 31
Archival storage, 6–7
ARMA (Association of Records
    Managers and Administrators, Inc.),
    11, 15
ASCII (American Standard Code
    for Information Interchange), 45–46
Association of Records Managers
    and Administrators, Inc. (ARMA),
    11, 15
Automated retrieval equipment, 201–202
Auxiliary file systems, 128

Backup disk, 5, 94
Ballot boxes, 222
Bank account filing, 2–3
Blueprints, 6
Bookmark method, 71
Box files, 168–170
Business, analysis of needs,
    208–210
  business organization, 209
  files location, 209
  nature of business, 209
  records format, 209
  retention schedule, 209
Business forms, 71, 77–80, 175
  action records, 78, 80
  analysis of, 216–217
  box design, 221
  boxes, 222, 223
  captions on, 220, 221, 223
  column arrangement, 221, 222

Business forms (*Cont.*):
  design of, 217–223
  for electronic file system, 223
  evaluation of, 217
  fill-in information, 78
  information processing, 78
  information recorded on, 77–78
  input source, 78, 79
  intermediate record, 79
  layout of, 218
  magnetic ink character recognition
    (MICR), 78
  mailing of, 218
  multiple copies, 218, 219
  output, 78–80
  paper quality, 180
  printed guide words, 77–78
  purchase of, 217
  readability of, 218, 220
  revision of, 217
  routing of, 218
  selection of, 179–180
  sequence of items, 222–223
  size of, 179–180, 218
  source document, 78
  source record, 78
  spacing on, 221
  static information, 77
  titles on, 220
  variable information, 78
Business names, indexing of, 28–29
  with abbreviations, 29–30
  on computer, 48–51
  cross-referencing, 37–38
  with numbers, 31–32, 50–51
  with punctuation, 30–31
  with symbols, 32–33
Business records (*see* Records)

Captions, 3, 175
  in alphabetic filing, 3
  on business forms, 220, 221, 223
  for cross-referencing, 21, 37, 68
  double, 58
  on file drawer labels, 57
  on file folders, 3, 58
  in geographic filing, 3
  on guides, 57–58
  labels for, 59–60
  in numeric filing, 3
  single, 57–58
  staggered arrangement, 61
  in subject filing, 3, 114
  typing of, 60, 61
CAR (computer-assisted retrieval), 197–198

Guides (*Cont.*):
    tabs, 57, 171
    town/city, 137
    (*See also* Labels)

Hanging drawer folders, 172, 175
Hard copy, 85, 94–95
Hard disks, 5
    crashing of, 94
    disk directories, 91–93
Hold-for-answer file, 188, 191
Home filing system, 126–128
    alphabetic, 127
    numeric, 128
    subject, 127
Hyphenated names, indexing of:
    business names, 30
    personal names, 18–19
Hyphenated numbers, indexing of, 31

Important records, 4–5, 152
Inactive records, 155
Index, relative, 114–115
Index card records, 71, 72
Indexed form, 46–48
Indexing, 14
    of correspondence, 66–68, 107, 122, 133
Indexing order on captions, 60
Indexing rules:
    abbreviations in personal names, 19–20
    addresses, 35–36
    alphabetic, 15–16
    for business names, 28–29
        abbreviations in, 29–30
        on database, 48–51
        hyphenated, 30
        numbers in, 31–32, 50–51
        punctuation in, 30–31
        symbols in, 32–33
        variations for businesses,
            38–39
    for government names, 33–35, 51
        federal, 33–34
        foreign, 34–35
        local, 34
        state, 34
    hyphenated numbers, 31
    need for, 15
    personal names, 16
        on database, 49–50
        hyphenated, 18–19
        prefixes in, 17–18
        suffixes in, 20–21, 49–50
        titles in, 20–21, 49–50
    seniority terms, 20, 49–50
    subjects on database, 51–52
    for "the," 28, 48, 52
    (*See also* Database indexing)
Information, errors in, 7
Input, 4

Inspection of correspondence files, 66, 107,
    122, 133
Inventory records, 72, 75, 79

Key, 14
Keyboarding skills, 203

Labels, 175
    for captions, 59–60
    colored, 59, 60, 93, 202
    for disks, 93
    for file drawers, 57
    file folder preparation, 60
    for file folders, 58
    (*See also* Guides)
Landscaped office layout, 184
Laser disks, 160
Laser thumbprint scanner, 204–205
Lateral files, 166, 170
Legal documents, 6
Letter, path of, 63, 65, 66
Letterhead form, 48
Lost records, 2
    electronic, 151
    paper, 147–149
Lowercase, 14, 45, 46

Magnetic ink character recognition (MICR),
    78
Magnetic media:
    advantages of, 159
    disadvantages of, 159
    equipment for, 198–199
    storage of, 159–160, 198–199
    transfer of, 159–160
Main numeric file, 104, 105
Manager, Records Analysis, 10
Manual filing system, 3
Manual records management, 2–3, 56–80
    business forms, 77–78
    card files, 72–76
    card records, 71–72
    correspondence classifying, 56
    file drawers set-up, 56–60
    file folder organization, 61–63
    filing process, 66–71
    guides organization, 61–63
    letter path, 63, 65, 66
    records storage organization, 56
Medical records, 2
Method, 3
MICR (magnetic ink character recognition),
    78
Microcomputers, 2, 184, 185
Microfacsimile, 197
Microfiche, 194
    advantages of, 196–197
    disadvantages of, 197
Microfilm, 194
    advantages of, 195